A TAPESTRY OF FAITHS

The Common Threads Between Christianity
& World Religions

WINFRIED CORDUAN

InterVarsity Press
Downers Grove, Illinois

InterVarsity Press
P.O. Box 1400, Downers Grove, IL 60515-1426
World Wide Web: www.ivpress.com
E-mail: mail@ivpress.com

Cover illustration: Roberta Polfus

ISBN 0-8308-2692-0

Printed in the United States of America ∞

Library of Congress Cataloging-in-Publication Data

Corduan, Winfried.
  A tapestry of faiths: the common threads between Christianity & world
religions / Winfried Corduan.
     p. cm.
Includes bibliographical references and index.
  ISBN 0-8308-2692-0 (pbk.: alk paper)
  1. Apologetics. 2. Christianity and other religions. I. Title.
  BT1230 .C67 2002
  261.2—dc21

                                                                                      2002007427

P	17	16	15	14	13	12	11	10	9	8	7	6	5	4	3	2	1
Y	15	14	13	12	11	10	09	08	07	06	05	04	03	02			

To my mentors, with gratitude

DON HUDSON
manager of The Lamplighter bookstore

NORMAN L. GEISLER
M.A. thesis chair

NIELS C. NIELSEN JR.
Ph.D. dissertation chair

E. HERBERT NYGREN
first department chair

CONTENTS

PREFACE

What is the relationship between Christianity and other religions? In this book I hope to show that this is really a multifaceted question deserving multilayered answers. Among evangelicals, this discussion has almost exclusively focused on the question of whether salvation is possible apart from a direct response to the Christian gospel.[1] For the last fifteen years in particular, there has been a flurry of writings from evangelicals on the issue of inclusivism vs. exclusivism vs. pluralism; in fact, most of the writings zero in on this debate and sustain themselves there. This is a good topic to discuss, but it can also create the impression that this is all that evangelicals can say about other religions, as though all our conversations may consist of nothing but the assessment of whether the adherents of non-Christian religions are saved. I do not mean to belittle the issue—in fact I cannot think of a more important one in this context—but I still would maintain that by not concerning ourselves with other matters, we are truncating the potential conversations that could ultimately lead to some fruitful bridge building.

Thus, this is a book about many topics. This is not a book about books about Christianity and world religions; it is a book about Christianity and world religions. There are many books surveying the theories and secondary literature, and many of them do an excellent job (though obviously I have my favorites and my not-so-favorites). Even though I will not be able to avoid interacting with the theoretical side of the topic and, consequently, will need to refer to that literature, the secondary literature is not the target of this book.

---

[1] A notable exception is provided by Gerald R. McDermott, *Can Evangelicals Learn from World Religions?* (Downers Grove, Ill.: InterVarsity Press, 2000).

In this book I intend to correlate Christianity with other religions in the world, and to do so I am going to look at various content areas. These will include the matters of revelation, ethics, Scripture, salvation, messiahs and others. Given my Christian orientation, each issue raised will be appraised from the Christian point of view, and thus the issue of salvation outside of Christianity will come up in due time, but not as the only issue in the book.

I would like to thank Andy LePeau and Jim Hoover, editors at InterVarsity Press, for their patience in working with me. Among my many friends and colleagues at Taylor University, I particulary want to thank Steve Bedi for his unflagging encouragement and belief in me. June, my wife and partner in all, continues to be the source of never-ending motivation. Nick and Seth, now grown, persist in being an encouragement to me, in both words and deeds. I want to thank June in particular for editing and proofreading this manuscript. I also appreciate the very helpful comments and suggestions I received from Douglas Groothuis and William G. Travis. You would think that with all of this help I could have written a better book; the faults are entirely my own.

I am dedicating this book to four men who were instrumental in helping me become a student, a scholar and an academician. Owing them more than these few words, I hope to be worthy of the effort that they put into my life. I trust that they are not entirely displeased with the product that they helped create.

---- | 1 | ----

ASKING THE RIGHT QUESTIONS

What is the relationship between Christianity and other religions? At the beginning of the answer to this question, there stands one nonnegotiable fact, namely, the utter preeminence of Jesus Christ. In Colossians 1:15-20 we read that he

> is the image of the invisible God, the firstborn over all creation. For by him all things were created: things in heaven and on earth, visible and invisible, whether thrones or powers or rulers or authorities; all things were created by him and for him. He is before all things, and in him all things hold together. And he is the head of the body, the church; he is the beginning and the firstborn from among the dead, so that in everything he might have the supremacy. For God was pleased to have all his fullness dwell in him, and through him to reconcile to himself all things, whether things on earth or things in heaven, by making peace through his blood, shed on the cross.

Jesus Christ is depicted as Creator, Sustainer, Sovereign Ruler, Redeemer, Reconciler, the fullness of God—in a word, supreme in all things. Thus, in a real and serious sense, insofar as Christianity is the religion that expresses the preeminence of Christ, Christianity alone is true and worthwhile. This book could be over before it ever really gets started.

And yet, the question of the relationship between Christianity and other religions is one that comprises a number of different dimensions. In much of the current discussion of this topic, the dimension that many Christians focus on has to do with salvation, a dimension that gives rise to the two primary options among disputants: exclusivism and inclusivism—the one option holding that only Christianity provides salvation, the other one believing that there is salvation outside of Christianity. However, this is only one of many legitimate issues that one needs to consider in order to arrive at a truly well-rounded picture of the relationship between Christianity and the many other religions of the world.

The book of Acts records two speeches made by the apostle Paul to pagan Gentile audiences. In Acts 14:15-17 Paul reproves those who were starting to venerate him as a god:

> Men, why are you doing this? We too are only men, human like you. We are bringing you good news, telling you to turn from these worthless things to the living God, who made heaven and earth and sea and everything in them. In the past, he let all nations go their own way. Yet he has not left himself without testimony: He has shown kindness by giving you rain from heaven and crops in their seasons; he provides you with plenty of food and fills your hearts with joy.

In Acts 17:22-31 he declares:

> Men of Athens! I see that in every way you are very religious. For as I walked around and looked carefully at your objects of worship, I even found an altar with this inscription: TO AN UNKNOWN GOD. Now what you worship as something unknown I am going to proclaim to you.
>
> The God who made the world and everything in it is the Lord of heaven and earth, and does not live in temples built by hands. And he is not served by human hands, as if he needed anything, because he himself gives all men life and breath and everything else. From one man he made every nation of men, that they should inhabit the whole earth; and he determined the times set for them and the exact places where they should live. God did this so that men would seek him and perhaps reach out for him and find him, though he is not far from each of us. "For in him we live and move and have our being." As some of your own poets have said, "We are his offspring."
>
> Therefore, since we are God's offspring, we should not think that the divine being is like gold or silver or stone—an image made by man's design and skill. In the past God overlooked such ignorance, but now he commands all people everywhere to repent. For he has set a day when he will judge the world with justice by the man he has appointed. He has given proof of this to all men by raising him from the dead.

In each of these two speeches there are certain common elements:

1. Paul's speeches are evangelistic in purpose; he is attempting to persuade his audience to embrace belief in the one true God.
2. The speeches are cast in the framework of good news. Paul is presenting his message as the fulfillment of something for which his audience has been longing.

3. In both these speeches Paul makes reference to certain items according to which his audience should have some basic awareness of the reality of God. He pays particular attention to the way in which God has manifested himself in creation.

4. The speeches contrast the living God with the idols of the surrounding culture, and in both cases Paul leaves no doubt that idolatry should be seen as false religion.

Thus, Paul is addressing his audiences on several different levels. He is asserting certain truths, while not denying that his audience has access to some truths already. He is disparaging idolatry as false, but he also assumes that his audience does know some truths concerning the reality of God. He presents them with a doctrine that to some extent is seen as the fulfillment of something that they already believe. Paul's speech is both confrontational and conciliatory; Paul is denying error but also building bridges to truth.

We can take our cue from these speeches when attempting to answer the question of how Christianity is related to other religions. There is no single dimension in which this relationship manifests itself, but there are many dimensions that make this relationship a very complex one. Consequently, in order to come to an accurate answer concerning the relationship, one must ask more than one question. There are many dimensions giving rise to many issues, and the answer to one question does not necessarily determine all the other answers to all the other questions.

Here are some of the dimensions that make up this relationship.

1. The soteriological dimension. As mentioned already, for many Christians this issue of salvation is the most important issue, and I will have much to say about it in the course of this book. For the Christian, this question begins with the assumption that Jesus Christ has provided a way of salvation for those who believe in him and then asks whether this way of salvation also extends to anyone who does not believe in Christ, and, if so, to whom? Particularly for evangelical Christians for whom salvation is the very core of what it means to be a Christian, this issue cannot be overemphasized. Nevertheless, there are other dimensions, and some of them may have a serious impact on the soteriological one. Furthermore, even among Christians who hold to an exclusive understanding of salvation, there are differences in the details of how they construe their views.[1]

---

[1]John Sanders, *No Other Name: An Investigation into the Destiny of the Unevangelized* (Grand Rapids, Mich.: Eerdmans, 1992), provides a clear and helpful taxonomy of the various views, though I do find some room for disagreement with his classification. See below.

2. *The content dimension.* Anyone taking a close look at non-Christian religions will find that there are various beliefs that Christianity shares with those religions. An understanding of the relationship between Christianity and those religions needs to take such similarities into account along with the differences. And an acceptance of those similarities must of necessity raise questions about the uniqueness of Christian truth claims. A part of this book will be given over to elaborating on some of the similarities and differences between Christianity and other religions.

3. *The revelatory dimension.* On what basis do people the world over claim to have truth? Within the world of religions, a frequent claim is that truth has been grounded in revelation. Christians certainly make that claim for their beliefs, and they appeal to the Bible as God's written revelation. But do other religions also have revelations? If there is truth in other religions, must that truth have been revealed to them by God? Many other religions also have scriptures, which they too claim to be revealed in some way. We need to deal with the question of to what extent, and on what levels, revelation is present in other contexts.

4. *The apologetic dimension.* An investigation into the relationship between Christianity and other religions needs to take into account the question of truth. Inevitably, such a discussion must function on several levels: *(a)* the legitimacy of even making truth claims in the face of contemporary religious pluralism; *(b)* the search for an adequate methodology; and *(c)* the application of the methodology to various religions and specific religious beliefs.

5. *The moral dimension.* Although the purpose of religion is not just to underpin a moral system, and although not all religions support the same moral directives, it is nevertheless just as true that most religions do include a moral system and that there are many areas of resemblance. The analysis of the relationship between Christianity and other religions needs to take this dimension into account and to develop a theory that accommodates both similarities and differences.

6. *The communication dimension.* For the Christian, the theological task is never completely done until it includes the task of proclamation. Just as Paul in the speeches referred to above did not simply make assertions but also intended to communicate the gospel to his audience, so the Christian today must also find ways of communicating the unique truths of Christianity. And so the analysis of similarities and differences is not merely a doctrinal concern but also paves the way for proclaiming the truth of

Christianity to the world. At this point theory must issue in praxis. But the praxis must be based on appropriate theory.

This book will address these dimensions to varying degrees. The question of Christian exclusiveness will never be far from the subject matter, but will not actually be addressed until some of the other dimensions have received attention, partially because only then can the question receive a fair answer, but also partially in order to emphasize the point that there is much to be said aside from this concern, as important as it is.

A VERY BRIEF HISTORY OF RELIGION

It is impossible to enter into a discussion of the relationship of Christianity to the world's religions without having some idea of what those religions believe and practice. The discussion in this book is not intended to replace a survey of the world's religions that gives detailed information on their histories, beliefs, developments and practices.[2] Nevertheless, in order to give the reader who does not have any background in the history of religions a fundamental grid for understanding what follows, I will now present a very brief summary of the development and patterns of world religions. This description cannot do more at this point than simply present some extremely general categories.

1. Traditional/tribal religions in contrast to enscripturated religions. A constantly decreasing part of the world's population lives in so-called traditional cultures. Their religions tend to be very closely tied to their local cultures. Categorized under many different labels (basic, primal, primitive, indigenous, traditional, tribal, etc.), they tend to be animistic and ritualistic in nature, recognizing nature spirits and ancestor spirits as well as

---

[2]There are many good books that survey the world's religions. Those that are textbooks designed for classroom use go into new editions every few years, so for many of them there will be updated editions available by the time the reader looks at this bibliography: Winfried Corduan, *Neighboring Faiths: A Christian Introduction to World Religions* (Downers Grove, Ill.: InterVarsity Press, 1998); Lewis M. Hopfe, *Religions of the World*, 6th ed. (New York: Macmillan, 1994); James F. Lewis and William G. Travis, *Religious Traditions of the World* (Grand Rapids, Mich.: Zondervan, 1991); Warren Matthews, *World Religions*, 2nd ed. (Minneapolis: West, 1994); Niels C. Nielsen, *Religions of the World*, 3rd ed. (New York: St. Martin's, 1993); S. A. Nigosian, *World Faiths*, 2nd ed. (New York: St. Martin's, 1994); David S. Noss and John B. Noss, *A History of the World's Religions*, 9th ed. (New York: Macmillan, 1994). See also various reference works: Keith Crim, ed., *The Perennial Dictionary of World Religions* (San Francisco: Harper & Row, 1981); Mircea Eliade, ed., *The Encyclopedia of Religion*, 16 vols. (New York: Macmillan, 1987); James Hastings, ed., *Encyclopedia of Religion and Ethics*, 13 vols. (New York: Scribner's, 1908-1926); Irving Hexham, *Concise Dictionary of Religion* (Downers Grove, Ill.: InterVarsity Press, 1993).

(frequently) a high god in the sky. These kinds of religions are totally integrated into the rest of the culture so that they cannot be extracted in order to be transferred to other cultures, and they do not base themselves on sets of writings. The only way to identify a specific religion under this heading is to refer to the specific tribal group that practices it. By contrast, the larger religions of the world usually include Scriptures, and, even though they cannot help but identify with a specific culture, they can and do adapt themselves to different cultures if they spread beyond their area of origin.

2. Western traditions in contrast to Eastern traditions. It has become customary to divide the large enscripturated traditions into two overarching categories, frequently called "Western" and "Eastern." There is no particular need to make an absolute distinction, but it is a handy way of pointing out important broadly applicable distinctions between two major areas of religious development.

The Western traditions encompass the largely monotheistic religions of Judaism, Zoroastrianism, Christianity, Islam and Baha'i. Out of these five religions, four are definitely a part of the same line of development in that Christianity began as a part of Judaism, Islam contains important doctrines of Judaism and Christianity, and Baha'i began as an outgrowth of Islam. The historical relationship of Zoroastrianism to these religions is controversial. Many scholars claim that Zoroastrianism profoundly influenced Judaism,[3] while many others reject this claim.[4] Conceptually, these religions have the following in common:[5]

- a strong monotheistic emphasis. Even though there are certain important distinctions among these religions in their conceptualization of God, they all affirm that there is only one God and that this is a God who has personhood.

- a strong ethical emphasis. The Western traditions make much of the importance of moral standards that human beings are obligated to follow.

- a positive approach to history. Each of these religions sees human history as a vehicle for the unfolding of divine revelation and action. Specific historical individuals are bearers of religious truth, and as history continues to move along, God continues his work in the

---

[3]Mary Boyce, *A History of Zoroastrianism,* 2 vols. (Leiden; Cologne: Brill, 1982).
[4]See my compilation of the evidence in "The Date of Zoroaster: Some Apologetic Considerations," *Presbyterion* 23 (Spring 1997): 25-42.
[5]Most of these themes are the least specifically concretized in Baha'i and perhaps most pointedly insisted upon without complications in Islam.

world, leading up to a final culmination. To what extent historical development is essential to the content of religions is a matter that I will address in chapter five.

Under the label of "Eastern religions" I place the religions of East Asia, including Hinduism, Buddhism, Jainism, Sikhism, Daoism, Confucianism and Shinto. Again, there is a fairly straightforward line of development for a number of these traditions. Buddhism and Jainism are direct offshoots from Hinduism; Sikhism is the result of an attempted linkage between Hinduism and Islam. There is undoubted reciprocal influence between Daoism and certain schools of Buddhism, and the Chinese indigenous religion of Confucianism has left its stamp on other Eastern cultures, particularly those of Korea and Japan.

In terms of beliefs, the Eastern traditions are more diverse than the Western ones. Monotheism is present but is in a minority compared to pantheism and polytheism. Similarly, although the Eastern religions are certainly not devoid of ethical obligations for their adherents, this area is frequently submerged in more mystical concerns. And again, while the Eastern traditions boast many great teachers and epic narratives, the emphasis tends to be on the teachings rather than on the events or the teachers. That is to say, whether there was a historical Buddha, for example, is not nearly as important as the teachings of the Buddha, and in Hinduism the events of the Bhagavad Gita are not as important as the teachings of Krishna recorded therein. In contrast, Judaism boasts of God's historical actions in redeeming his people out of bondage in Egypt, and there can be no Christianity without Christ dying on the cross. But this is getting ahead of the story.

Figure 1.1 illustrates in broad strokes the development of many of the world's religions. As one can readily see, the starting point of this scheme is "original monotheism." This is the idea that religion began with God himself, who revealed himself to human beings. Consequently, all other religions are deviations from this original starting point. The religions on the far left of the chart, the so-called Western religions, are the ones that preserved monotheism, though not without contamination, while the Eastern ones departed much more drastically. I will discuss this thesis at greater length in chapter two.

3. Beliefs in contrast to cultus. Contemporary Western scholars of religion, particularly from a Protestant Christian background, tend to focus on the beliefs of a particular religion. This stress is partially a result of the Christian emphasis on the content of belief and its faithfulness to

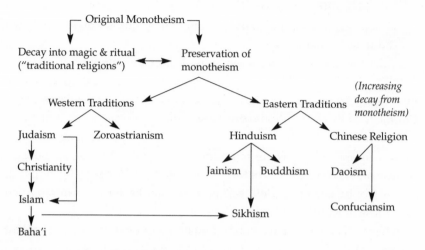

Figure 1.1. The development of the world's religions

revealed truth. However, for many adherents of a religion, what really counts is the formal observance associated with the practice of the religion. This includes such things as rituals, altars, hymns, temples, offerings and modes of prayer. This is the dimension of religion that we refer to as "cultus," and every religion has one. A traditional Western Christian cultus includes worshiping God in a building with a steeple, singing out of hymnbooks, contributing money in a collection plate, reading from the Bible and listening to a sermon. Similarly, a part of Hindu cultus is worshiping an idol in a temple by offering fruit and flowers, observing a priest chanting and waving a light before the deity, and having one's forehead marked with sacred ash. Although in theory it might be possible to have a religion without a cultus, in practice all religious groups and subgroups have one.

The relationship between a belief system and its cultus can be extremely elastic. Many times a belief system can be superimposed on an already existing cultus, or a cultus may determine the development of a belief system. Then again, two very different belief systems may have a similar cultus attached to them, maybe intentionally, as in cases of Reform Judaism and contemporary Pure Land Buddhism deliberately mimicking Protestant Christian worship forms. This will be an important consideration in discussing models relating Christianity and other world religions.

Here are some very brief summaries of the world's religions:

1. JUDAISM

Origin: Formally with Moses, fifteenth century B.C.

Essential beliefs and practices: Monotheism, obedience to a divinely revealed law.

Scriptures: The Hebrew Scriptures, containing the Law, Prophets and Writings (the Christian Old Testament); collections of interpretations of the law, particularly the Talmud.

Major contemporary divisions: Orthodox, who obey the law literally; Conservative, who obey the law, but adapt it; Reform, who do not consider the law binding.

2. ZOROASTRIANISM

Origin: Zoroaster, circa sixth century B.C.

Essential beliefs and practices: Monotheism. Conflict between God (Ahura Mazda) and the lesser evil spirit (Angra Mainyu) who opposes him. Adherents side with God through practices of ethical purity (truth and goodness) and ritual cleanliness.

Scriptures: The Avesta, the oldest part of which (Gathas) may contain writings of Zoroaster himself.

Major contemporary divisions: Although there are some minor distinctions in practice between some groups, based on their geographic location (Iran vs. India primarily), none are significant.

3. CHRISTIANITY

Origin: Jesus, first century A.D.

Essential beliefs and practices: Trinitarian Monotheism, Jesus Christ is the messiah—he is both God and human, and he made atonement for the sins of the human race by being crucified and resurrected.

Scriptures: The Old and New Testaments.

Major contemporary divisions: Eastern Orthodox, Roman Catholic, Protestant.

4. ISLAM

Origin: Muhammad (A.D. 570-632)

Essential beliefs and practices: Monotheism, revelation of God (Allah) through prophets and their books (the final one of whom is Muhammad), judgment of human beings based on their obedience to God's requirements.

Scriptures: The Qur'an and further teachings of Muhammad (Hadith).

Major contemporary divisions: Sunnite (the majority), who base their authority on the consensus of the Muslims after Muhammad's death, and various groups of Shi'ites, who trace their origin to Ali, Muhammad's son-in-law.

5. BAHA'I

Origin: Baha'ullah, initially a follower of a nineteenth-century man, "the Bab," who proclaimed himself the new gateway to God.

Essential beliefs and practices: Baha'ullah was a Manifestation of God; unity of all religions; principles that will bring about a new world order (abolition of poverty and war; education for all human beings; a universal language, etc.).

Scriptures: The writings of Baha'ullah, including *The Most Holy Book* and *The Book of Certitudes*.

Major contemporary divisions: None; some early attempts at division were eliminated.

6. HINDUISM

Origin: Circa 1500 B.C., religion of the Aryans who invaded the Indian subcontinent; numerous subsequent developments.

Essential beliefs and practices: Extremely diverse; many different conceptions of deities with approximately an equal division between theists and pantheists; most forms of Hinduism center on release from the endless cycle of reincarnation *(samsara)*, which is propelled by the law of karma (present actions have consequences for the next incarnation).

Scriptures: The Vedas, followed by the Upanishads (Vedanta). Epic myths, particularly the Ramayana and the Mahabharata (which includes the Bhagavad Gita). Numerous Brahmanas, Sutras and Puranas.

Major contemporary divisions: Monistic groups, who follow the pantheistic doctrines of the Vedanta; personalistic Bhakti groups, who devote themselves to a deity or the deity's various manifestations. Of the latter there are three major divisions: Vaishnavites, who associate themselves in various ways with the god Vishnu; Shaivites, who focus on the god Shiva and his associates; Shaktites, who worship a goddess (known by many names) in her various expressions. There are uncountable other schools and subschools as well.

7. BUDDHISM

Origin: Gautama Buddha, circa 600 B.C.

Essential beliefs and practices: Salvation consists of, first, deliverance from the cycle of reincarnations and, second, entering the state of Nirvana.

Scriptures: The Tripitaka, "Three Baskets" (also known as the Pali canon: a large tripartite collection of writings in the Pali language), the Lotus Sutra, numerous other *sutras.*

Major contemporary divisions: Theravada (also known as Hinayana), the most traditional form of Buddhism, centering on monks; Mahayana, a collection of many adaptive schools of Buddhism that make provisions for the laity, including the schools known as Zen, Pure Land (Jodo Shinshu), Nichiren Shoshu (Soka Gakkai), Vajrayana (Tibetan), and numerous others.

8. JAINISM

Origin: Mahavira, circa 600 B.C.

Essential beliefs and practices: Redemption by elimination of solid karma matter from one's soul, particularly through the avoidance of any harm to living beings. Worship of Mahavira and his predecessors, known as Tirthankaras.

Scriptures: Diverse writings, including the Angas, a collection that allegedly contains Mahavira's own writings.

Major contemporary divisions: Digambaras (in which the monks wear no clothes) and Svetambaras (in which the monks wear white loincloths and have a few other distinctive beliefs, such as a female Tirthankara).

9. SIKHISM

Origin: Guru Nanak, sixteenth century A.D.

Essential beliefs and practices: An apparent fusion between Islam and Hinduism. There is one God (the "True Name"), who is represented on earth through the holy book, the Adi Granth. There will be a state of bliss after one escapes from the cycle of reincarnations and karma.

Scriptures: Adi Granth.

Major contemporary divisions: No divisions per se. Most Sikhs identify with the Khalsa, the military society in which all men carry the surname Singh, "Lion," and women are called Kaur, "Princess."

10. DAOISM

Origin: Based on the philosophy of the legendary Laozi, many transformations turned a quietist philosophy into a religion that stresses magic and the worship of personal gods.

Essential beliefs and practices: There is an essential harmony of yin and yang in the world, which needs to be kept in balance through correct spiritual practices.

Scriptures: Daodejing.

Major contemporary divisions: By its very nature, religious Daoism[6] has tended to attach itself to other religious forms, particularly Buddhism and Confucianism.

11. CONFUCIANISM

Origin: Confucius, circa sixth century B.C.

Essential beliefs and practices: An ethical system ordering one's duties and obligations in society; includes certain religious observances but

---

[6]Please note that here and throughout this book I utilize the newer pinyin Romanization of Chinese rather than the older Wade-Giles system, according to which this religion would have been spelled *Taoism*.

does not directly address gods or rituals.

Scriptures: Analects, other Confucian writings.

Major contemporary divisions: None. Confucianism has made itself an underpinning of traditional Chinese, Japanese and Korean societies.

12. SHINTO

Origin: Japanese traditional religion with no definite point of origin, codified in the eighth century A.D.

Essential beliefs and practices: A system of practices, not doctrines, for the regular veneration of the Kami (spiritual reality that may assume the form of personal beings).

Scriptures: The Kojiki and Nihongi are collections of the ancient myths; the Amatsu Norito is a collection of prayers.

Major contemporary divisions: Traditionally divided into State, Shrine and Domestic Shinto, these are merely different dimensions of the basic orientation toward the Kami. Shinto exists more often than not in fusion with Buddhist beliefs and practices; many so-called new religions in Japan incorporate Shinto concepts, and the collection of these cultlike groups is called Sectarian Shinto.

Obviously these summaries do not come anywhere close to explaining the various religions. The point here is simply to provide a little bit of basic vocabulary. Details will, of course, be addressed throughout the course of this book insofar as they are relevant to the discussion at hand. For a complete survey of these religions, the reader must look elsewhere; some sources are cited in the notes.

CHRISTIAN PRESUPPOSITIONS

In order to present a picture of the relationship of Christianity to other religions that makes sense, it is, of course, necessary to be clear on what one means by Christianity in this context. A lot of what could come under this heading is going to be influenced one way or the other by the discussion that will follow, and so I will try to remain fairly general so as not to give away too much too soon. However, some points are essential.

   1. The authority of Scripture. My approach to this topic begins with the assumption that there is a way of deciding what is and what is not correctly included under the heading of Christian truth, namely, whatever is or is not derived from the Bible. Granted that the process of understanding Scripture can be a complex one at times,[7] evangelical Christianity nevertheless holds that whatever the Bible asserts must be considered to be authoritative and true. My point here is that in what ensues, revising Scripture in order to accommodate a theological or philosophical point is not an option (though it is a practice common in other religions).

2. The historical Christ. Jesus Christ was a historical person, and the information about his life that is contained in the New Testament, particularly the Gospels, is a reliable account of his life. He is fully God and fully a human being, as described by the historic creeds, particularly those of Chalcedon and Nicaea.

3. Mediation through Christ's atonement. Needless to say, the extent of the effects of Christ's substitutionary atonement is one of the main topics of debate for this book, so it would not do to announce a position on this issue yet. However, I want to be clear on the following point: Christ died on the cross as a genuine historical event, and in this event he provided for the salvation of human beings. His death is the substitute for the death that sinful human beings deserve, and in this way he has brought about a reconciliation between the holy, sinless God and fallen humanity.

4. Faith. The way in which a human being relates to God is by faith. Faith includes two important aspects. First, faith includes a cognitive dimension. There must be an object of faith, and the person must have some knowledge of what that object is in order to place faith in it. Such knowledge need not be unclouded or exhaustive, but it cannot be completely tacit or objectless. Second, faith involves trust. It is not merely intellectual, but it also includes the person's placing reliance on the object of faith. The primary New Testament picture of salvation is of people who know intellectually that Jesus Christ is God incarnate who died on the cross for their sins and who consciously trust Christ alone for salvation. Whether this is the *only* way in which faith works is, of course, part of what is at stake in the debate.

MODELS OF RELATIONSHIP
This book will address a number of important issues in the relationship between Christianity and world religions. As indicated above, a multidimen-

---

[7]For some of the issues involved, see my summary in "Humility and Commitment: An Approach to Modern Hermeneutics," *Themelios* 11, no. 3 (1986): 83-88.

sional understanding of this relationship in general must be open to the possibility that on specific points there may be great variety in the way in which the religions interact with each other. For now, I will simply provide some models, which I can then apply to the issues and relationships as I proceed.[8] These models describe, in a sense, the fabric of religion.

Model 1: Complete continuity. One way of looking at the relationship between Christianity and other religions is as a seamless web into which Christianity is woven along with all the other religions. In this model Christianity can be distinctive, but no more so than any of the religions are distinctive from the others. There can be both similarities and differences in the content of the religions. Some of them may be more radically different from others; but there is no categorical difference between, say, Christianity and Hinduism, or Buddhism and Islam.

This model can be considered applicable even if *(a)* not all religions are necessarily included. One could, for example, limit the cloth of religions to only the "great ones," as has been fashionable from time to time.[9] This selectivity would free a scholar from having to consider trivialities or absurdities, such as a religion that someone just decided to start and that has only very few adherents.[10] The point would still be that the identified major religions constitute the seamless web of faith. And this model could apply even if *(b)* one does not necessarily avoid all references to truth. The seamless-web view can allow for the idea that truth (as well as falsehood) can be scattered among the participating religions, so that not everything is necessarily true, but there is no major unevenness in truth. This model would require that categorically no religion has a corner on truth.

One example of a scholar holding to this model is John Hick, to whose thought I will return later in this book as well. For Hick, all religions are responses to an ultimate transcendent reality that he refers to as "the Real." The Real is ultimately beyond human concepts, so that all religions are imperfect in their ways of relating to It. And to Hick that means that they are *equally* imperfect; none has an intrinsic edge on the truth (or false-

---

[8]For a very thorough exploration of the issues, to many of which I will return later on, see Daniel B. Clendenin, *Many Gods, Many Lords: Christianity Encounters World Religions* (Grand Rapids, Mich.: Baker, 1995).

[9]Robert Hume, *The World's Living Religions* (New York: Scribner's, 1959), presents a survey of world religions accompanied by value rankings.

[10]Though one would have to be very careful in making this judgment. Almost all religions started very small. In Japan the "new religions" need to be taken seriously in order to understand the phenomenon of Japanese religion, even though many of these groups are faddish and ephemeral.

hood), but they are all on the same plane. Hick states,

> Each major tradition, built around its own distinctive way of thinking-and-experiencing the Real, has developed its own answers to the perennial questions of our origin and destiny. . . . These are human creations which have . . . become invested with a sacred authority. However, they cannot all be wholly true; quite possibly none is wholly true; perhaps all are partly true.[11]

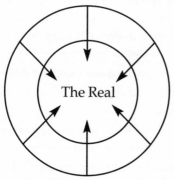

Figure 1.2. **Hick's concept of religions**

So, if one follows Hick's analysis, all religions are equal in their nature as imperfect ways of relating to the Real. There would be one cloth constituted by the fabric of religion, and it would be a somewhat shabby, perhaps patchy, piece of material. (See figure 1.2 for a diagram of Hick's concept of the world's religions.)

Model 2: Complete discontinuity. A second extreme option would be to look for an impenetrable wall between Christianity and all other religions. Christianity would enjoy a fundamental separation from all other religions in every relevant category: truth, content, values and helpfulness in life, to name some important ones. There would be nothing that Christianity actually shares with other religions, and there would not be a single tapestry, but, at a minimum, two cloths (maybe more), one of which is Christianity.

Following are two examples of how this model can be held. One would be to claim uniqueness for each religion. This has been done by J. A. DiNoia,[12] who believes that one must consider each religion within its own context rather than imposing either a general scheme or a Christian scheme on it. Looking at the world's religions this way reveals that all religions present not only different ways of salvation but also different

---

[11]John Hick, "Religious Pluralism and Salvation," in *The Philosophical Challenge of Religious Diversity*, ed. Philip L. Quinn and Kevin Meeker (New York: Oxford University Press, 2000), pp. 63-64.

[12]J. A. DiNoia, *The Diversity of Religions: A Christian Perspective* (Washington, D.C.: Catholic University of America Press, 1992). A similar point has also been made in S. Mark Heim, *Salvations: Truth and Difference in Religion* (Maryknoll, N.Y.: Orbis, 1995) and then elaborated by the same author in *The Depth of the Riches: A Trinitarian Theology of Religious Ends* (Grand Rapids, Mich.: Eerdmans, 2001). Heim does, however, ultimately classify all the end results sought for in all religions according to a trinitarian scheme, thereby allowing for a general—and even Christian—paradigm to have the final say after all.

understandings of what salvation is in the first place. Each religion exists in its own context with its own integrity and its own means of salvation geared toward its own unique ends. A diagram for this view would simply consist of a number of boxes, each labeled with the name of its religion. (See figure 1.3.)

Figure 1.3. DiNoia's view of religions

Another way of applying this model would be to contrast the unique exclusivity of Christianity with all the other world religions. Karl Barth,[13] the father of neo-orthodox theology, gave us a rather drastic example of this approach. Simply put, for Barth there is Christianity and then there is religion. In fact, for him, it is best not even to consider Christianity as a religion. The difference is that Christianity is based on God's revelation to humanity and the giving of his own divine grace by his own initiative, whereas religion is a matter of human self-effort. All religions are attempts by human beings to establish themselves as their own god, thus contradicting God himself. So the picture of the relationship between Christianity and all other religions is very simply one of total discontinuity, even opposition. The picture that seems to emerge from Barth is illustrated in figure 1.4.

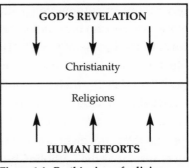

Figure 1.4. Barth's view of religions

Model 3: Continuity on the basis of superiority and inferiority. A third option would be to recognize both continuity and discontinuity. A religion such as Christianity would be categorically similar to all the others, but one could still draw distinctions between any two religions on the basis of "more or less," "better or worse," "closer or farther," etc. In other words, one could say that one religion has more truth than another, that it is better at mediating between

---

[13]Karl Barth, *Church Dogmatics*, 16 vols. (New York: Scribner, 1955), 1:280-361.

God and humanity than another or that it is closer to realizing an ideal than another, to mention just some options. Yet, that fact would not mean that no other religion could do exactly the same thing, albeit supposedly in an inferior way. All religions would, in a way, have an edge on each other. To go back to the first model, the point would be that the tapestry is not woven evenly and that the difference among sections is only the relative quality of the threads.

An interesting example of how this model can be applied is presented in the documents of the Second Vatican Council of the Roman Catholic Church. In the *Dogmatic Constitution on the Church*, the bishops declared that the Roman Church is the single true Church but that this is a matter of degree because all religions contain some of that truth as well. To be more specific, it states that "the Church, now sojourning on earth as an exile, is necessary for salvation."[14] Someone reading this statement by itself might be expecting that, therefore, Christianity (or more specifically Catholic Christianity) is completely separated from all other religions, but not so. First, the document specifies that "in many ways [the Church] is linked with those who, being baptized, are honored with the name of Christian, though they do not profess the faith in its entirety or do not preserve unity of communion with the successor of Peter."[15] And furthermore, "those who have not yet received the gospel are related in various ways to the People of God."[16] These undeclared Christians include Jews, Muslims, idolaters ("those who in shadows and images seek the unknown God"[17]) and even atheists (people who "have not yet arrived at an explicit knowledge of God, but who strive to live a good life thanks to His grace"[18]). Thus there is a clear hierarchy with the Catholic Church at the top and the benevolent atheist at the bottom. They are all linked with each other insofar as the Catholic Church has the *most* grace and revelation and the atheist has the *least*, but they all have some. (See figure 1.5 for a picture of this concept.)

---

[14]*Lumen Gentium (Dogmatic Constitution on the Church)* in *The Documents of Vatican II*, ed. Walter M. Abbot (New York: Guild Press, 1966), p. 32. It must be made clear, however, that the Council specifically warns against thinking that belonging to the Church (in the sense of being affiliated with the institution) is sufficient for salvation. An evil person who happens to be a member of the Catholic Church will be condemned.

[15]Ibid., pp. 33-34.

[16]Ibid., p. 34.

[17]Ibid., p. 35.

[18]Ibid.

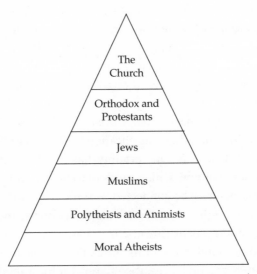

Figure 1.5. Second Vatican Council's view of religions

Model 4: Discontinuity on the whole with some commonalities. A final option for now is the idea that, even though Christianity is categorically different from all other religions, there are some areas of overlap or interrelationship. The Christian would not be obliged to give up the uniqueness of Christianity but could simultaneously recognize that—in a somewhat limited way—there may be some similarities with other world religions.

Granting that there may be points of similarity is not the same as saying that these resemblances must always be the same ones whenever Christianity and another religion have something in common. It may be that, when we compare Christianity and Islam, Hinduism or Baha'i, we will find certain similarities between any two pairs, but it need not be the same point of similarity in each instance.[19]

Without wishing to anticipate too far the eventual conclusions of this book, this last model is the paradigm in this exploration. One need not give away the Christian claims of uniqueness; in fact, if Christianity is true, it is only reasonable to expect that, wherever truth is found, it will tie into the truth of Christianity in some way. What results is a tapestry, but a highly complex one. There is a section of the cloth that is made of permanent thread, and much of the rest of the tapestry is made of thread of

---

[19]I elaborated on this scheme in a slightly different context in "The Dalai Lama and I: A Case for Natural Theology," *Bulletin of the Evangelical Philosophical Society* 6 (1983):1-11.

poor quality that may wear out and need to be replaced. But radiating
out from the permanent section are threads that pervade the entire tapestry, and much of the impermanent sections are woven into those permanent threads. As a result, there is a continuity between the permanent
and impermanent sections, even though it is not a continuity based on
intrinsic equality.

By application, this means that Christianity is first of all based on
revelation and its immediate applications. These are the permanent
threads. But then Christendom certainly has its share of impermanent
adumbrations, some of which may turn out to be very flimsy. At the same
time, other religions may be connected in some way with the permanent
threads as well, though not as directly, and, of course, they also contain
their share of impermanent threads. It is here that we may find Christianity and other religions sharing threads; that is to say, they may
manifest apparent resemblances. (See figure 1.6 for a model of this concept.) How this model will work out is, of course, the content of what follows in the rest of this book.

Unique truths;
some shared truths
and human falsehoods

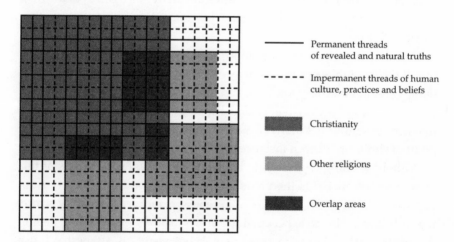

Figure 1.6. Continuity-discontinuity view of religions

2

GENERAL REVELATION
AND ORIGINAL MONOTHEISM

In the previous chapter I proposed a model according to which Christianity can be both unique and not unique. That is, in some ways Christianity could be discontinuous with other religions, while in other ways it could share various features with some religions. It all comes down to which specific issue is in view.

One such issue is the question of whether there is any overlap in divine revelation. Certainly Christianity is based on a specific revelation, namely, the Word of God both as written and as the person of Christ. But in addition, before addressing this area, we need to recognize that Christianity (and for that matter its precursor, Judaism) does not have a corner on revelation. In fact, many Christians would consider access to some revelation outside of special revelation an integral part of Christianity itself.[1]

Christian theologians traditionally recognize two types of revelation: general revelation, according to which God is known through nature in

---

[1]A very clear exception is provided by Karl Barth, who taught that any idea of a general revelation seriously compromises Christian truth. This attitude was epitomized by his writing of *No! Response to Brunner*. See the entire dialogue in Peter Fraenkel, trans., *Natural Theology: Comprising "Nature and Grace" by Professor Dr. Emil Brunner and the Reply "No!" by Dr. Karl Barth* (London: Bles, 1946). Another interesting rejection of natural revelation having anything to do with non-Christian religions is provided by Christopher R. Little, *The Revelation of God Among the Unevangelized: An Evangelical Appraisal and Missiological Contribution to the Debate* (Pasadena, Calif.: William Carey Library, 2001). Little believes that, even if non-Christians have natural revelation, that is a moot point because they all reject it. What makes Little's position unusual is that, instead of then going in Barth's direction and denying non-Christian religions any revelation at all, he claims that they do, in fact, benefit from special revelation.

such a way that all human beings have access to knowledge of him, and special revelation, which is limited to God's more direct self-disclosure in history and Scripture. Provisionally at least, I wish to stipulate an additional way in which people come to know of God. This is not a new revelation, but it is a way of acquiring knowledge about God that does not rely directly on either special or general revelation. I am referring to the knowledge of God that has persisted throughout the history of humankind. I will label it "original monotheism."[2]

I have discussed parts of the theory of original monotheism in various places.[3] I would now like to give a more expanded and complete summary than I have heretofore.

PRECURSOR—NONTHEISTIC THEORIES

The nineteenth century saw an animated debate among religious scholars about the origin of religion. An evolutionary scheme was pretty much assumed as a philosophical dogma; religion must have evolved along with the rest of human physical development, intelligence and culture. Very few writers questioned the fundamental idea that religion must have matured from primitive, even childish, beginnings to the supposedly highly advanced religions such as those espousing monotheism. The biggest question was which form of religion could have been the earliest one, and the basic strategy was anthropological: to examine the world's least developed cultures, learn about their form of religion and consider the most archaic form of religion to reflect the earliest religion of humankind.

Before getting involved in the specifics of the debate, it is instructive to comment on how ingrained the evolutionary attitude was then and in some ways continues to be today. A basic understanding that the universe was in constant evolutionary change was fashionable long before Darwin and the *Origin of Species*. The publication of alleged factual support for the process of biological evolution only added grist to the evolutionary mill, and the history of various religions was reinterpreted along evolutionary lines. Thus Julius Wellhausen,[4] taking the textual insight from previous biblical scholars, combined them with a preset pattern of evolutionary

---

[2]Wilhelm Schmidt, *The Origin of Religion: Facts and Theories*, trans. H. J. Rose (London: Methuen, 1931).

[3]Winfried Corduan, *Neighboring Faiths* (Downers Grove, Ill.: InterVarsity Press, 1998), pp. 32-35; and "General Revelation in World Religions," *Journal of Christian Apologetics* 1, no. 2 (1997): 59-72.

[4]Julius Wellhausen, *Prolegomena to the History of Israel* (New York: Meridian, 1958).

development, which he then read back into the Old Testament. The same approach was applied to various other religions as well.[5]

Over the last century a strict large-scale evolutionary scheme has been abandoned by and large. Very few scholars would actually defend a theoretical sequence of normative stages along which all religions must have evolved. Nonetheless, the application of such a scheme to specific world religions on an individual basis persists despite the loss of its philosophical foundation. For example, even though the idea of the evolution of religion, which formed the backbone of Wellhausen's Old Testament interpretation, does not find many explicit supporters these days, Wellhausen's theory is still accepted in many circles, and it continues to be taught routinely on a more popular level as though it were fact.

But then how did religion begin? During the debates of the late nineteenth and early twentieth centuries, the following theories enjoyed wide recognition:

Celestial phenomena. Some scholars held that all religion began with human beings deifying the heavenly bodies: sun, moon or stars.[6]

Natural phenomena. Other scholars, such as Max Müller,[7] attempted to derive the origin of all religion from various natural phenomena. Included in these factors would be lightning, thunder, dawn and dusk, fertility, and so forth. In all of these cases, human beings endowed the aspect of nature in question with personhood and divinity by making the grammatical mistake of confusing an attribute of nature with a god who carries that attribute.

Manism. Herbert Spencer[8] advocated the notion that religion began with the veneration of deceased human beings. The term *manism* is based not on the English word *man* (though it could serve as a mnemonic) but on the Latin *manes* meaning "ghost" or "spirit." The idea is that what was originally a fear-based cultus for the dead eventually expanded the spirits' role until they turned into gods associated with widespread religious practices that were far removed from their beginnings.

Manaism. Many traditional cultures believe in a spiritual power found

---

[5]It was very crassly applied to Germanic religion by R. M. Meyer, *Altgermanische Religionsgeschichte* (Stuttgart: Magnus, 1909).

[6]For example, Leopold von Schroeder's theories pivoted around the notion of the identification of the supreme being with sun deities (*Arische Religion,* 2 vols. [Leipzig: Haessel, 1914-1916]).

[7]For example, in Max Müller, *Natural Religion* (New York: AMS Press, 1975).

[8]Herbert Spencer, *Principles of Sociology,* 3 vols. (New York: Appleton, 1995-1997).

throughout their life-world, a power that a human being can tap into for magical energy. This power has become known in the academic world by its Melanesian name, "mana." Some scholars[9] thought they could identify the beginnings of religion in the recognition of this force.

Magic. One of the most popular theories of the origin of religion came from the pen of Sir J. G. Frazer. In his *The Golden Bough*,[10] he both analyzed the nature of magic in early religions and also tried to make a case that magic constitutes the earliest form of religion from which all others evolved.

Totemism. Émile Durkheim popularized the notion that the origin of religion lies on the societal level. He pointed to the social organization of many tribes along totemic lines (subgroups of tribes—"moieties"—each identifying with a particular animal) as the formative element from which religion originated through veneration of the totem animal and (supposedly) totemic feasts.[11] This theory influenced Sigmund Freud in his construction of religion as the result of a prehistoric totemic cult.[12]

Animism. Next to Frazer's theory of magical origination, E. B. Tylor's school on the origin of religion was the most popular for a time.[13] According to this view, religion began with the recognition of personal spirits, both ancestral and natural.

Each of the authors of these various theories intended to show that religion moved on from each of their particular beginning points in an ongoing process of evolution. One can see that they were also united in explaining religion as a fundamentally human phenomenon. They all assumed that religion, particularly in its early phases, is an imperfect attempt by an immature group of human beings to make sense of the world around them. Insofar as religion ultimately arrived at some truths (and the nineteenth-century scholars tended to reserve a special place for monotheistic religion), this achievement can be considered either a happy accident thanks to the fortuities of cultural development or a crowning success akin to the development of the natural sciences.

---

[9]Such as John H. King, *The Supernatural: Its Origin, Nature and Evolution* (London: Williams and Norgate, 1892).

[10]J. G. Frazer, *The Golden Bough* (New York: Macmillan, 1960). This work exists in many versions ranging from two volumes to ten, all produced by Frazer himself.

[11]Émile Durkheim, *The Elementary Forms of the Religious Life*, trans. Carol Cosman, abridged wth introduction and notes by Mark S. Cladis (Oxford: Oxford University Press, 2001).

[12]Sigmund Freud, *Totem and Taboo* (New York: Random House, 1948). It turns out that totem feasts are a very rare phenomenon in totemic cultures.

[13]E. B. Tylor, *Primitive Culture: Researches into the Development of Mythology, Philosophy, Religion, Art and Custom*, 2 vols. (London: Murray, 1929).

As I have pointed out, by and large these scholars were united in their commitment to an evolutionary view. This aspect of their theories is perhaps refuted most easily by recognizing that the supposed mandatory stages of an evolution of religion have never been observed in a specific culture. Religions change, sometimes drastically, but without reading some preconceived pattern into the history of a religion, it is impossible to demonstrate a linear development from supposedly lowest to supposedly highest. Nevertheless, that issue was not particularly subject to debate. The real argument concerned the question of which stage was first, and on this there was no unanimity.

As a matter of fact, people looking for reasons to reject one of these naturalistic explanations of religion need not look for them in Christian books written from a supernaturalistic perspective. They need only confine their search to the arguments brought up by the various advocates against each other. The main causes of controversy include the following:

1. *Identifying which are truly the oldest human cultures so that the equivalence between oldest culture and oldest religion can be drawn.* Some of the earlier theories made no attempt to distinguish between the ages of various cultures, and so a theory of the origins of religion dictated which culture was supposed to be early. Simultaneously, that identification of a culture as early was supposed to demonstrate the old age of the religion. In short, such arguments tended to be circular.

2. *Distinguishing between the rule and the exception.* It is all too easy to generalize from incomplete or nonrepresentative data. A good example of this fallacy would be what happened with the idea of totems. There are a few instances of totemic feasts in which the moiety consume their animal (which is normally taboo to them). From this W. Robertson Smith[14] invented the notion of a cannibalistic totem feast. This was then pressed into service as the origin of all religion. In this case, highly exceptional data were used to support shaky theories that then were expected to uphold universal truths.

3. *Allowing the theory to dictate the data.* Many of the theories in question had more of a philosophical or sociological background than an observational one. Undoubtedly there were two forces at work at times: the desire for novelty or creativity and the expectation to stay within the bounds of a particular academic school of thought.

---

[14]W. Robertson Smith, *Kinship and Marriage in Early Arabia* (Cambridge: Cambridge University Press, 1885).

LANG AND OTHER EARLY THEORIES OF ORIGINAL MONOTHEISM

The attempt to resolve the question of what was the earliest stage in the evolution of religion needed to rely on data collected by missionaries, anthropologists and explorers. As this effort progressed, an interesting phenomenon emerged: many preliterate cultures were found to have a very distinct belief in a single creator God who lived in the sky. Simply having a personal deity in any one of these cultures would go against the grain of any of the evolutionary theories just by itself, but this find was even more startling in that this belief bore a great resemblance to the God of the monotheistic traditions, thus seeming to leap to the very top of the evolutionary chain. Eventually, various writers would try to establish some significant differences between this picture of God and the God of, say, Judaism, but initially no difference was recognized, as evidenced by the fact that Tylor and others attempted to write off these occurrences to the influence of Christian missionaries. Only after that explanation became impossible to hold did disputing writers focus more on the nature of the actual content of this doctrine of God. They then tried to show that this God was, in fact, different in conception from the God of monotheism. For some others, however, this information added up to a demonstration that religion in fact began with an awareness of this personal creator God.

An early advocate of such an original monotheism was Andrew Lang.[15] This British scholar began his treatment of religion as a follower of Tylor, promoting the animistic origin of religion. In the process, he came across reports on the worship of the Creator God among certain Australian aboriginal tribes. As he investigated further, he found similar results for various tribes around the globe. A closer look at these cultures ruled out the possibility of Christian missionary influence on them (Tylor's immediate response), and, of course, the widespread geographical distribution of the cultures holding this belief made some sort of direct influence on each other totally impossible. As a result, Lang devoted himself to the promotion of the theory that the origin of religion does, in fact, lie with the knowledge of the single creator God.

The most prevalent response to Lang's theory was simply to ignore it, though one would probably do best to understand this reaction not so much as a breach of academic integrity but as the inability of the scholarly

---

[15] Andrew Lang, *The Making of Religion* (New York: Longmans Green, 1898).

community to break with the prevailing paradigm.[16] The question of how exactly religion began was far from settled, but the concept of an original monotheism was clearly not acceptable to these scholars.

At that, Lang's conclusions were far from certain. He believed that the data were evidence for an independently existing belief in a god in the sky. Other writers did not move drastically away from his insights but took a slightly different approach. For example, G. Foucart concluded that the data really proved something less: the god in the sky is actually a person-ification of the sky itself.[17] Thus his theory actually tied in to the earlier view that religion began with natural phenomena, singling out the sky as the crucial phenomenon in question. People originally worshiped the sky as divine and then postulated a god of the sky behind it. A way of estab-lishing the relative age of various cultural phenomena more precisely was needed in order to resolve this issue.

WILHELM SCHMIDT AND ETHNOHISTORY

Although Wilhelm Schmidt is popularly recognized as the leading advo-cate of original monotheism, the most important contribution he made was to provide an anthropological method for deciding the question of the relative age of cultures. He called his method ethnohistory (now common-ly called cultural anthropology), and, since he and his associates labored for a long time in Vienna, they became known as the Vienna School. A cen-tral methodological assumption is that within a particular region any spe-cific cultural innovation occurred only once; for example, a particular new style of pottery would not have been invented by two or more different tribes independently at roughly the same time. Consequently, on the basis of careful study, one can trace which cultures originated specific cultural advances and which ones picked them up later (if at all). This method, called *Kulturkreis*, or "culture circle," established a serious distinction to the accepted evolutionary paradigm in that it dispensed with the notion of a single global thread of development. In short, Schmidt's method staked

---

[16]I am applying here the picture of science as provided by Thomas S. Kuhn, *The Structures of Scientific Revolutions*, 2nd ed. (Chicago: University of Chicago Press, 1970). Kuhn himself was hesitant to endorse applying his views to disciplines outside of the natural sciences, but in cases such as this one the similarity is evident.

[17]G. Foucart, "Sky and Skygod," in *The Encyclopedia of Religion and Ethics*, ed. James Hastings, 13 vols. (New York: Scribner's, 1908-1926), 11:580-85. I am placing Foucart's contention into a conceptual sequence. As a matter of fact, in terms of historical sequence Schmidt had al-ready provided a way of resolving the issue raised. See his *Origin*, pp. 214-17.

out two things: limiting the search for a particular line of cultural transformation to specific regions (for example, Oceania, Africa and so forth) and being able to identify chronological strata within living cultures.

Using this method Schmidt was able to derive the following sequence of development among preliterate societies:

Primordial.[18] The hunter-gatherer societies are the original first level of human culture.

Primary. There are three types of primary cultures: hunters (who tend toward patrilinealism and totemism), horticulturalists (i.e., garden growers who let plants reproduce naturally, and who often become matrilineal and fertility oriented) and nomadic cattle herders.[19]

Secondary. These are agriculturalists (who preserve seeds from year to year and sow them).

Tertiary. These are early ancient city builders.

Furthermore, even among the primordial cultures it is possible to discern which cultures are the most archaic, that is, the least changed. And it is precisely these cultures that have the strongest evidence of the monotheism in question. In simple terms, these are[20] cultures that are not very advanced, living on the stone-age level. They include certain Australian aborigines, African pygmies, Philippine tribes and some specific Native American tribes—some in Central California and certain Algonquin tribes. These tribal cultures are not totally devoid of ritual or magic, but there is relatively little of it, and the religions have God as their central recipient of worship. As subsequent cultures become more advanced in terms of their overall civilization (development of agriculture, implements, etc.), the presence of ritual, magic and spirit-oriented practices increases concomitantly. Therefore, the level of religion that was held by many to be the most foundational turns out to be a development away from the original monotheism.

Schmidt recognized that when the cultures in question referred to God

---

[18]Schmidt, in keeping with the custom of his day, uses the term *primitive,* meant here in its most literal sense as "original," without any opprobrious meaning. In fact, part of what Schmidt attempts to prove is that much of the most archaic cultures are of a "higher" moral order than subsequent ones.

[19]Not to get ahead of the story, it turns out that the nomadic cultures are the ones who most faithfully preserved the monotheism of the primordial societies.

[20]In order to keep from complicating matters too much, I am using the present tense. The truth is that many, if not most, of these most archaic cultures have been eliminated in various ways, and so no firsthand research can be done any longer. However, the reports of those who had the privilege of knowing them directly are still available in our libraries.

they would use the following expressions (obviously expressed within the terms and concepts available within each culture).[21]

1. God. The majority of these cultures recognize only one being as God; thus we are not looking at one of several gods. Where more than one god appears, the culture has also moved away from its most archaic status in other respects. Of course, many monotheistic religions also acknowledge that there are various spirits in addition to God (for example, angels or demons), and this is also the case for many of the cultures under consideration, but these spirits are not gods, and they are not worshiped as gods.

2. Father. The cultures often see God as their father, individually or tribally. Cultures in which the supreme God is female have also developed in other dimensions, usually into horticulture or agriculture.

3. Skydweller. God is normally seen as living in a celestial abode. Sometimes this location takes the form of being on top of a mountain or on the clouds. In any event, God does not merely live on earth with us humans, though he may have been on earth temporarily, but is usually thought of as occupying an elevated living place.

4. Creator. Even though not all these properties are totally universal, this one is nearly universally accepted among the people groups in question. However they may conceive of God, he is definitely the one who made all there is. In fact, as I will explain below, Schmidt makes this aspect one of the bases by which the cultures came to awareness of God.

5. Superior one. God is not human; he exceeds human beings in many respects. Most importantly, he does not have a human body.

6. Everlasting one. In chapter seven I will discuss further the notion of time in preliterate cultures. For now I will make this observation: God, the Creator, is not subject to time in the same way in which human beings are. He has neither beginning nor end but is always there.

7. All-knowing one. Human beings cannot keep any secrets from God. He knows what we say or think. Thus, the meaning of this type of omniscience is essentially personal. God is not so much an encyclopedia (in contemporary terms) as he is the one who knows our hearts.

8. All-good one. God is good. Though there are cultures in which God is seen as capricious, these are later than the original cultures in which God is never seen as compromising his goodness. Furthermore, God is often (though not always) considered to be the one who made moral rules for

---

[21]Wilhelm Schmidt, *Primitive Revelation* (St. Louis: Herder, 1939), pp. 124-37.

human beings, and he is always concerned that humans should obey his rules of goodness.

9. All-powerful one. God is not limited in any way by what he seeks to do. This omnipotence is (as in most monotheistic cultures) delimited by the considerations of what is coherent or could reasonably be expected of a divine being. For example, in Christian theism God cannot cause himself not to exist or to make a stone so heavy that he cannot lift it, and neither can the God of Schmidt's original cultures.

Of course, there are many distinctions in detail from culture to culture, not only in emphasis but to a certain extent also in detail, but they are minor. The real differences from culture to culture occur not in the concept of God that is presented but in the cultus of God.[22] Some cultures pay minimal attention to God while others focus all their worship practices on God alone; nevertheless, the notion of God remains essentially the same.

ORIGINAL MONOTHEISM AND REVELATION

Now we come to the crux of this matter for the purposes of this chapter: What is the origin of these beliefs? More specifically, is there reason to believe that these beliefs originated in revelation? And if so, what is the nature of the revelation?

Among these people themselves there is no question of the allegedly revealed nature of these beliefs. They testify that the information came through special people, such as mystics or visionaries, or that it was taught by God himself. In either case they claim directly revealed propositions. In fact, one could say that the belief that these things are revealed, rather than inferred, comes with the total package of the beliefs.

Needless to say, such self-reported testimony in no way ensures the revealed nature of the beliefs, but such testimony definitely fits well with the phenomenon at hand because the data indicate that this monotheism is the earliest form of religion. Since there is no evidence of cultures slowly working their way up through various preliminary stages to more advanced stages, and since the only extant evidence exhibits the total package of traditional theism, and since similar beliefs are found in the earliest cultures all around the globe, there is good reason to believe that these theistic beliefs are based on a form of revelation.

---

[22]See some of the examples compiled by Mircea Eliade, *Essential Sacred Writings from Around the World* (formerly entitled *From Primitives to Zen*) (New York: Harper & Row, 1967), pp. 3-20.

The question remains as to the nature of this revelation. At the outset of this chapter I mentioned the two standard understandings of revelation: general, based on God's disclosure in nature, and special, based on God's disclosure in Scripture and history. Which of these sources of revelation suits original monotheism better?

It would seem that special revelation is immediately ruled out since these people definitely did not have access to Scripture, the Old Testament or the New Testament; in fact, these are completely preliterate cultures that would not know what to do with Scriptures if they found them. Nor could one say that in some way these people were a part of the stream of God's working in history as explicitly recorded in Scripture (though obviously they are part of this work in the general sense in which God works through all humankind). Thus, special revelation seems to be inappropriate for this categorization.

Schmidt, despite the attestations of direct revelation from the people themselves, favors a general-revelation approach. He believes that these beliefs had their origin when these traditional groups looked at the world all around them and asked the obvious question: Who made all this?[23] The answer then comes in the form of the monotheistic hypothesis. This approach fits well with the fact that belief in God came prior to belief in the divinity of the phenomena with which he is often associated; for example, people believed in a God in the sky long before anyone thought to endow the sky itself with deity. Schmidt does not wish to eliminate direct supernatural influence in this recognition, but he does want to locate the process of the revelation in this form of general revelation.

It would seem, however, that not all possibilities have been covered hereby. Once one has acknowledged the reality of a special revelation, one ought not to ignore the possibility of a continuity of such a special revelation through tribal memory. To be more specific, according to special revelation, the history of humanity began with the creation of human beings who had a direct relationship with God, the Creator. After the human beings disobeyed the Creator, their relationship with him was broken, but certainly not their knowledge of him. Two generations into their existence outside of paradise, they began regular worship practices, and that tradition has continued ever since. Since there is good reason to believe in the common descent of all human beings from the original pair, both on revelatory and

---

[23]Schmidt, *Origin*, p. 283.

scientific grounds,[24] it is logical that the monotheistic religions practiced by preliterate tribes do, in fact, derive from the same monotheistic beliefs and practices attributed to the earliest humans in special revelation.

The picture, then, is this: Religious belief began with the first humans and religious cultus soon thereafter with Enosh, the son of Seth, as mentioned in Genesis 4:26. As the human race expanded, contracted drastically at the flood, and then expanded again, the beliefs and practices did not slip totally from the collective memory but retained a presence within the tribes least affected by cultural development. There it was (rightly) attributed to some form of divine self-disclosure, but also (rightly) reinforced by a general revelation premised on the question, Who made it? Finally, one sees evidence of this pattern even in the more highly developed religious cultures insofar as one can find a monotheism at many of their roots. The continuity of monotheism is based on an original special revelation and reinforced by general revelation.[25]

As alluded to above, evidence exists of this persistence in the literate and more highly developed religious cultures. It seems that for almost all such cultures one can identify a monotheistic concept away from which the culture has developed. The following divinities can be found in these contexts:

Ancient Semitic. El, possibly based on the root *ul,* "to be strong," occurs in Hebrew as God in general, while *Elohim* is *the* God. In Babylonian it occurs as *ilu,* and it may be the root for the Arabic *Allah.*[26]

Chinese. Shangdi was the name of the God of heaven, worshiped by the ancient Shang (no linguistic equivalence) dynasty. Under the later Zhou dynasty, the worship of *Shangdi* was largely replaced by the worship of

---

[24]John Tierney, "The Search for Adam and Eve," *Newsweek,* January 11, 1988, pp. 46-52.

[25]Clearly I am not inventing a new type of revelation here. All that I am doing is accommodating a fairly complex pattern to already recognized forms of revelation. It is merely a matter of convenience in an effort to understand the revelatory background of many religious cultures that clearly do not have access to the Bible. Others are bolder than I am in positing more direct revelation within the context of other religions. See Gerald R. McDermott, *Can Evangelicals Learn from World Religions?* (Downers Grove, Ill.: InterVarsity Press, 2000). McDermott is willing to stipulate that God revealed himself to some people outside of the Abrahamic covenant by way of "types" that are neither special revelation (for they fall short of disclosing Christ) nor general revelation (for they do include specific religious ideas, such as faith or sacrifices). Says McDermott, "My claim is that among the religions are scattered promises of God in Christ and that these promises are revealed types planted there by the triune God" (p. 114). My response is that, by the time we have accumulated general revelation along with the persistence of original revelation, we do not need to resort to this further form of revelation.

[26]Edward Mack, "God, Names of," in *International Standard Bible Encyclopedia* (Grand Rapids, Mich.: Eerdmans, 1956), 2:1265.

heaven itself *(Tian)*, but the concept of *Shangdi* has persisted and is still the term used for *Lord* by Chinese Christians today. This example illustrates how the god of the sky was worshiped before people turned to worship the sky itself.

Indo-European. According to available information (specifically the Indian Vedas, dated roughly 1500 B.C.), there is clear evidence of an ancient monotheism, but some confusion as to its subsequent development. That is to say, there appears to be a main line and a subsidiary line. The most ancient Indian deities that are known come in two groups, which are not rigorously distinguished from each other at the writing of the Vedas. The gods that eventually become the main deities of later Hinduism (for example, Vishnu or Indra) belong to the group called *devas*, a term that may be based on the Indo-European linguistic root *div*, which means "to shine"; thus these are the Shining Ones. The same root appears in the Greek *theos* and the Latin *deus* as well as *divinitas*, and it is still apparent in the English *divine*. Among the ancient Vedic *devas*, the original God appears to have been *Dyaus Pitar* (the Shining Father), who has counterparts among the Greek *(Zeus Pater)*, the Latin *(Ju-piter)* and the Norse *(Tyr* or *Tius*—still recalled in our *Tuesday)*.

There is a second group of deities, the *asuras*, who at the point of the Vedas are not yet rigorously classified, but who in later Hinduism are seen as adversarial, demonic beings. The supreme being among the *asuras* is Varuna, the god of the sky and thus the creator and ruler of the cosmos, who appears to have an analog in the Greek *Ouranos*. The language used of Varuna in the Rig-Veda makes it seem as though possibly he, not Dyaus Pitar, was the original God, but there is a rough consensus that somewhere along the line Varuna displaced Dyaus, similar to the way in which the god *of* the sky replaced the god *in* the sky in other cultures. In any event, in the Vedas one of the *devas*, Indra by name, defeats Varuna in battle, and eventually all the *asuras* are seen as evil. Paradoxically, in Iran, which began with a pattern very similar to that in India, the process goes in the opposite direction. Here, under Zoroaster's leadership, eventually all of the *devas* (Iranian *daevas*) are declared to be evil, and one of the *asuras* (Iranian *ahuras*) is declared to be the only and supreme deity, namely, Ahura Mazda.

The point of all of this can be summarized briefly: the memory of monotheism ("persistence of revelation") can be found at the historical roots of the so-called developed religions as well, both in their earliest remembrances and in the occasional revivals of monotheism, such as under

Muhammad or Zoroaster. General revelation undoubtedly has had at least an undergirding role in these developments.

GENERAL REVELATION

General revelation consists of the avenues that God has provided in nature to provide knowledge of him. Nature is meant in a very general sense here, including not only mountains, trees and oceans, but also human nature and human psychology. Thus, for example, general revelation can be found not only by looking *out* at the world but also by looking *in* at the human conscience.

The way in which general revelation usually functions is probably not as a deductive inference but as an intuition. Intuitions are experiences of immediate awareness. They can occur in many different contexts and take different forms. In ordinary language, *intuition* is often used as synonymous with a hunch or a mystical insight that someone claims. One can also think of immediate sensory awareness as an intuition—when I see a color, experience a headache or feel hungry, I am not drawing an inference from some premises to a conclusion, but I am having a direct awareness of something that is, furthermore, consequently indubitable for me.

Perhaps more controversially, intuitions can also be legitimate shortcuts through certain inferences. I see these instances specifically as the summations of what would otherwise be lengthy inductive arguments. In an inductive argument one draws probably true inferences from observational data. They can be generalizations: All the Catholic priests I have met are celibate; therefore, probably all Catholic priests are celibate. Or they can be analogies: All the Catholic priests I have met are celibate; Rob is a Catholic priest; therefore, probably Rob is celibate.

It seems to me that frequently we cut through such inductive inferences with an intuition. We do not enumerate specific observations, let alone apply formal tests of probability, but we jump to a conclusion, as it were. Furthermore, if asked to justify such a conclusion, more than likely we would resort to a kind of transcendental form of reasoning in which we refer to conditions that must be true in order for the phenomenon in question to be true, such as, Unless all priests were celibate, I would have met some noncelibate priests by now, or Unless Rob were celibate, he would not be a Catholic priest like all the others I've met. These are clearly not very well formulated arguments, but that is the point. I believe them to be typical of the way in which ordinary human beings reason in ordinary circumstances. The fundamental mode of thinking is intuitive, not a formal inference, and in these cases, there is clearly a lot of room for error.

When I think of general revelation as an intuition, I am thinking along these terms, that is to say, a shortcut through what could be a formal inference. The following verses are the most commonly cited biblical texts with regard to general revelation:

> The heavens declare the glory of God;
>   the skies proclaim the work of his hands. (Ps 19:1)

> For since the creation of the world God's invisible qualities—his eternal power and divine nature—have been clearly seen, being understood from what has been made, so that men are without excuse. (Rom 1:20)

Both of these verses indicate that the world of nature is a source of knowledge about God. His glory, his eternal power and his divine nature (which is left unexplained at this point) can be discerned from God's creation, and the Romans passage takes the further step of asserting that, consequently, human beings are without excuse if they do not acknowledge God.

The information presented here has been used over the centuries for shaping formal theistic arguments, such as the cosmological and the teleological arguments. However, it would verge on the silly to think that formal syllogistic reasoning is what these passages have in mind. More likely, it comes down to an intuition that shortcuts through a kind of inductive reasoning process, in which the person gazing at the sky, perhaps, infers that such things as the universe simply cannot happen without someone having created them, and that, therefore, there must be a God who created the universe itself. But all of this thinking is abridged into a simple direct awareness that does not evaluate data so much as it embraces the conclusion directly. If challenged, the person can only say something along the line of, "Unless there were a God, there could not be this universe."

It might appear that I am imputing motives and thought processes here to people that I have never met and that this is purely speculative thinking. Of course, I do not mean to create speculative historical scenarios, not even as a kind of "ideal situation" as conceived by John Rawls in a different context.[27] I am simply attempting to put these two passages into what strikes me as the most reasonable construal as applied to ordinary people. If some-

---

[27]John Rawls, *A Theory of Justice* (Cambridge, Mass.: Harvard University Press, 1971). This lengthy argument is based on Rawls's development of what kind of an ethic human beings would invent if they were in a situation of separation from the world, much like a "social contract."

one wishes to argue that ordinary people convince themselves of the existence of God via formal theistic arguments, nothing of significance for this chapter is lost, though I (as well as St. Thomas Aquinas)[28] would disagree.

Similar things can be said concerning the internal side of general revelation. Again, there are scriptural references, and again it is probably best on an ordinary level to describe what happens first of all as an intuition, and only secondarily as a formal inference.

> [The Gentiles] show that the requirements of the law are written on their hearts, their consciences also bearing witness, and their thoughts now accusing, now even defending them. (Rom 2:15)

Here the general revelation goes one step further; namely, it embraces the moral dimension. Human beings not only have access to a fundamental awareness of God, but they also can receive instruction on a basic moral law, which God has implanted in their hearts. In the case of this verse, the apostle makes a specific reference to the conscience, that is to say, the faculty of the human spirit that gives us direct feedback on our moral inclinations. As people relate themselves to a particular action (either by contemplating doing it or by performing it), they experience an internal, intuitive reaction. Doing something wrong produces conscience twinges, while doing something right or redressing a wrong brings about a soothing of the conscience. This faculty comes from God, it is referred to as universal among humans, and it functions first of all on an intuitive level. Here even a further justification would again be circular; something is wrong because it feels wrong, and something feels wrong because it is wrong.

It is not just the case that there is a vague universal sense that one ought to do what is right, but there is also a sense that a fundamental set of right and wrong pervades all human cultures. I shall make a further analysis of how some of these standards play themselves out in specific religious cultures in chapter four, but here I simply wish to reiterate the reality of such a set of obligations. This does not mean, however, that all human cultures hold to the biblical Ten Commandments—far from it! But pertinent here are some fundamental categories, as asserted by Clyde Kluckhohn.[29] In different cultures people relate to each other differently with an incredible number of variations. Nevertheless, the fundamental theme of valuing human life, truth and property comes out

---

[28]Thomas Aquinas *Summa contra Gentiles* 1.3-10.
[29]Clyde Kluckhohn, "Ethical Relativity: Sic et Non," *Journal of Philosophy* 52 (1955): 663-77.

again and again. The Sawi[30] culture of Irian Jaya valued treachery against people from other tribes by befriending them and then cannibalizing them, fortunately not a very common cultural trait. Nevertheless, they expected loyalty from their own tribespeople, and they counted on truth and not falsehood in ordinary conversation.

Wilhelm Schmidt summarizes the moral values of the early monotheistic cultures with these five concepts:[31]

1. Peacefulness. Weapons primarily exist for use against animals, not people, as evidenced by the lack of shields.

2. Altruism. People are expected to put their own interests behind those of others at times.

3. Property ownership. People recognize private property and insist that it is wrong to deprive other people of what is theirs.

4. Honesty. It is expected that people speak the truth.

5. Sexual morality. There are clear standards of what is acceptable, focusing particularly on marital fidelity, even if there is a certain amount of license before marriage.

On the final point, as on the others, it is very important to keep in mind Schmidt's ranking of these cultures in terms of age and originality, for there can be no question that later cultures do not adhere to this or the other four points stated above. Schmidt states, "All those excesses are absent which are to be found so plentifully among later and more highly cultured nature peoples, and even more plentifully among civilized peoples."[32]

Thus we see two aspects of general revelation: the awareness of God and the awareness of moral right and wrong. And the objects of revelation are encountered first of all, I believe, through an intuition. However, that fact does not mean that general revelation cannot also become formalized into a natural theology.

Subsequent Reaction to Schmidt and Original Monotheism

Even though Wilhelm Schmidt did not invent the idea of an original monotheism (how could anyone?), in scholarly circles the theory and the man became strongly intertwined, both among supporters and detractors.

---

[30] As described in Don Richardson, *Peace Child* (Glendale, Calif.: G/L Publications, 1974). Both the deception and the expectation of adherence to standards come out in the course of this narrative.

[31] Schmidt, *Primitive Revelation*, pp. 109-15.

[32] Ibid., p. 111.

As was mentioned above, Schmidt's defense was most formidable because he grounded his conclusions on anthropological data and not just speculation. The ethnohistorical method demonstrated the identity of the most archaic cultures and thus allowed the historian of religion to observe directly what type of religion those cultures exhibited. Obviously, Schmidt's particular take on original monotheism rises and falls by his anthropological conclusions. If they are accurate, then his theory is well defended, but to whatever degree they can be questioned, the theory also becomes more questionable. But, interestingly, that fact has turned out not to be the main focus of the reaction to Schmidt.

Other than some people accepting his views as true,[33] one can identify two reactions to Schmidt's view. One was the demise of a general theory of the evolution of religion. Whereas, prior to Schmidt's studies, scholars had assumed that all religions crossed through a common set of stages from the lowest to the highest, with the only remaining question being to identify those stages, the discovery that the least developed cultures already possessed a monotheism put an end to that speculation. Whether one accepted Schmidt's specific conclusions or not, it was no longer possible to espouse the evolutionary theories of Frazer, Tylor and others with credibility. Theodor Gaster provided an excellent example of how far this rejection went when he issued a modern revision of Frazer's *Golden Bough*[34]—and deleted all the references to an evolution of religion.

Let me emphasize that this abandonment of explicitly teaching a general theory of religious evolution does not mean that the theory has not continued to serve as an implicit template for the analysis of religions. I already mentioned above that the evolutionary Wellhausen theory still persists as a basic assumption in many descriptions of Old Testament Judaism.[35] Some people have even attempted to revive a religious evolutionary theory, albeit a very different one from its nineteenth-century forebears.[36]

Still, the most common reaction to Schmidt has been to reject his conclusions for ideological reasons. No statement could put the matter into better

---

[33]For example, Paul Radin, *Primitive Man as Philosopher* (New York: Appleton, 1927) and *Monotheism Among Primitive Peoples* (London: Allen & Unwin, 1924).

[34]Theodor Gaster, ed., *The New Golden Bough* (New York: Phillips, 1959).

[35]See, for example, David S. Noss and John B. Noss, *A History of the World's Religions*, 9th ed. (New York: Macmillan, 1994), pp. 412-15.

[36]For example, Robert N. Bellah, "Religious Evolution," in *A Reader in Comparative Religion: An Anthropological Approach*, ed. William A. Lessa and Evon Z. Vogt, 3rd ed. (New York: Harper & Row, 1972), pp. 36-50.

perspective than this assertion by Joseph M. Kitagawa:

> In order to understand the history of a specific religion integrally and religio-scientifically, one cannot ignore the problem of its origin, which, incidentally fascinated the historians of religions of the nineteenth century. However, one must remember the admonition of [religion scholar] Tor Andrae that *the origin of religion is not a historical question; ultimately it is a metaphysical one.* Thus, the popular theories of *Urmonotheismus* [original monotheism] or the high-god, interesting though they may be, cannot be used as the basis of the religio-scientific study of religions with utmost certainty.[37]

Thus, Kitagawa tells us, even though one must always be willing to acknowledge historical factors in the origin of either a specific religion or religion in general, philosophical considerations can trump historical data when suitable. What he calls the "religio-scientific study of religions" distinguishes itself from other scientific inquiry in one important respect, namely, that a theory can supersede the facts that it is supposed to explain. Kitagawa is willing to make patronizing gestures toward historical conclusions of an original monotheism, but not to the point where the historical conclusions can have the last word in answering historical questions. Anyone who thinks that historical questions need to be answered by historical conclusions, and that metaphysical answers are the correct response to metaphysical questions, needs to rethink such a tidy arrangement. One historical question at least, namely, the origin of religion, is best answered by metaphysical suppositions. Even though this maxim has not usually been expressed quite as forthrightly, it has been the assumption in many more recent approaches to religious origins.[38]

This principle manifests itself regularly in the context of postmodern relativism in which religion is seen as essentially an outgrowth of social phenomena. For example, in an anthology of religious myths, David Adams Leeming assures us that

> when we give form to divinity, we derive that form from our own experience. We make gods in our own image because our own image marks the physical limits of our being. We cannot know the gods; we can know only our experience of them.[39]

---

[37]Joseph M. Kitagawa, *The History of Religions: Understanding Human Experience* (Atlanta: Scholars Press, 1987), p. 23 (emphasis mine).

[38]See the adroit study of the paradoxical attitude by Tomoko Masuzawa, *In Search of Dreamtime: The Quest for the Origin of Religion* (Chicago: University of Chicago Press, 1994).

[39]David Adams Leeming, *The World of Myth: An Anthology* (New York: Oxford University Press, 1990), p. 123.

Thus, it is no surprise that Leeming, as is frequently done today, places the origin of the concept of a supreme being within a particular social structure:

> The Supreme Being who emerges from the many world myths about the chief god is one who embodies the prevalent patriarchal arrangement of society. He is, in short, the embodiment of kingship, of male power, of the paterfamilias.[40]

In this sort of analysis, historical investigation is never even given a chance; ideology appears to be the only consideration.

Other scholars, Kitagawa included, would at least acknowledge the importance of historical research even if they reserve the last word on the subject for their theoretical commitments. Lawrence E. Sullivan's appraisal of Schmidt's contribution is this:

> In short, although he helped break the stranglehold of evolutionary theories and renewed serious study of supreme being, he continued a rational tradition of interpretation that found it impossible to appreciate the many existential dimensions of myth subsequently disclosed by a more profound hermeneutic of religion.[41]

But there is obviously a serious problem if the so-called more profound hermeneutic allows one to dispense with historical conclusions.

Similar conflicts arise within the works of other scholars as well. Raffaele Pettazzoni is sometimes depicted as Schmidt's ablest opponent and vanquisher.[42] He surveyed the multitudinous occurrences of supreme beings in traditional cultures and concluded that Schmidt's conclusions of an original monotheism were, at best, premature; there was far too much ambiguity in the reports on which Schmidt based his conclusions. Instead, Pettazzoni argued that most archaic cultures appear to have some awareness of a supreme being, but that it would be inappropriate to refer to this phenomenon as monotheism since the very nature of this being precluded a direct interaction with human beings. Supreme beings are typically dynamic creators as well as passive sustainers of the created order; thus, they have acted in the past but will not act in the present and, consequently, are by their very essence remote. True monotheism, Pettazzoni

---

[40]Ibid., p. 124.

[41]Lawrence E. Sullivan, "Supreme Beings," in *Encyclopedia of Religion*, ed. Mircea Eliade (New York: Macmillan, 1987), 14:178.

[42]Raffaele Pettazzoni, *Essays on the History of Religions* (Leiden: Brill, 1954).

maintained, only arises as the result of a reform movement within a culture that already has a polytheistic religion (and thus is not archaic any longer). For now one cannot go beyond simply describing the natures and functions of the various supreme beings in archaic cultures without establishing which is primary.

Pettazzoni attempted to create a bridge between extreme historicism and a purely ahistorical phenomenology, and his ideas are ably balanced between the two. In fact, Pettazzoni's main contribution among his peers was that he argued strenuously to give historical inquiry its due place. He pleaded that the study of religions ought first of all to aim at "settling the history of the various religions."[43] Nevertheless, the end result continued to be the dissolution of the data into a theory.

Kitagawa laments that "one of the most difficult problems for the History of Religions has been to maintain a *balance* between its historical and its systematic dimensions,"[44] and a little later he praises Pettazzoni for having brought off this feat. Kitagawa summarizes:

> According to Pettazzoni, the historical task of the discipline is not simply a descriptive, chronological inquiry but an attempt to coordinate religious data, to establish relations, and to group the facts according to those relations in such a way that the events in time correspond to *the internal development of religious history.*[45]

At first glance this statement may seem simply to advocate the proper reciprocal relationship between theory and data that all scientists must observe. To some extent, no scholars can ever operate without a theoretical scheme to help them interpret the data, and the data should always be able to modify the theoretical scheme. But the role of theory in this particular description is far more authoritative; it can, if necessary, speak apart from or even against the data. Two important questions arise in this context of studying the beginnings of religion: what exactly is an "internal development of religious history," and how does one achieve "balance" with it?

Let me cite one particular example. At the outset, I wish to state that I have the utmost respect for the work of the late Mircea Eliade and will, in fact, throughout the rest of the book make much positive use of his analysis of the subjective side of religious experience. Nevertheless, he commits the transgression of allowing his phenomenological analysis to determine

---

[43]Ibid., p. 216.
[44]Kitagawa, *History of Religions*, p. 303 (emphasis mine).
[45]Ibid., p. 304 (emphasis mine).

his historical conclusions. In *Patterns in Comparative Religion,*[46] Eliade, as he does elsewhere, mounts up descriptions of supreme beings from around the world and takes particular notice of their association with the sky. In the process he provides many extremely valuable insights, as well as an extensive bibliography, on this part of religion. But when it comes to chronological sequence, Eliade leaves us puzzled.

The question is simply this: what came first, the recognition of the sky as holy or the recognition of the god who lives in the sky? Eliade is willing to go so far as to allow for the possibility that among the personal spiritual powers recognized within religious cultures, the supreme being residing in the sky may have arisen first.[47] Nevertheless, his basic assumption is that before people came to see that there is a god in the sky, they were already taken up with the manifestation of holiness in the sky itself. This scheme fits in with Eliade's larger project of pointing out manifestations of the holy, which he called "hierophanies," throughout a religious person's life. One must acknowledge that Eliade is not simply talking about a personification of the sky into a sky-god, as it might have been advocated by some writers in the nineteenth century. Human beings are intelligent enough to be able to differentiate between the sky and a personal god who lives in the sky. Rather, Eliade ascribes a transcendent dimension to the sky itself in the primordial religious experience of human beings:

> There is no need to look into the teachings of myth to see that the sky itself directly reveals a transcendence, a power and a holiness. Merely contemplating the vault of heaven produces a religious experience in the primitive mind. . . . Such contemplation is the same as a revelation. The sky shows itself as it really is: infinite, transcendent. . . . The symbolism of its transcendence derives from the simple realization of its infinite height.[48]

Such a depiction potentially provides a significant amount of insight into the way in which a person might relate to the cosmos, but Eliade takes it one step further; he makes it the prior stage of a chronology of religion:

> When this hierophany became personified, when the divinities *of* the sky showed themselves, or took the place of the holiness of the sky as such, is difficult to say precisely.[49]

---

[46]Mircea Eliade, *Patterns in Comparative Religion,* trans. Rosemary Sheed (New York: Sheed & Ward, 1958), pp. 38-123.
[47]Ibid., pp. 38, 54.
[48]Ibid., pp. 38-39.
[49]Ibid., p. 40 (Eliade's emphasis).

Of course it is difficult; in fact, it is impossible. There is no particular reason to believe that it ever took place in this way. There is no evidence for such a historical sequence of events, let alone for a point in time in human cultures when this switch from sky to sky god should have been made. Even though we may be able to learn much from recognizing how the sky may evoke a feeling of transcendence in its own right (in fact, I intend to endorse this point in chapter eight), the historical evidence points to a god in the sky among the most archaic cultures, and even in cultures where the evidence for a supreme being may be vague,[50] there is no evidence for a veneration of the sky as such prior to the veneration of a personal deity in the sky. (Though it is not, of course, a primordial culture, the sequence exemplified by ancient Chinese culture in which the worship of Shangdi, the god of heaven, became supplanted by the worship of Tian, heaven-as-god, is the actual pattern for this sequence.)

Wilhelm Schmidt, in his own time, faulted his detractors (including already Pettazzoni in his earlier writings) for placing philosophical commitments ahead of anthropological investigations. He remarked concerning their pronouncements that "however dogmatically they may be expressed, all these statements are nothing more than mere opinion. . . . There is not the faintest attempt to prove by objective means any historical connexion between the individual beings mentioned and to put the particular connexions thus established together into larger culture groups. And least of all do we hear anything of the question concerning the earlier and the later."[51] To a large extent, he continues to be correct; without commitment to a method of establishing chronological sequence, simply amassing data[52] can only reinforce preconceived theories of development, but—and this sounds too obvious to need to mention—a chronological sequence based purely on one's philosophical presuppositions can never be objectively credible.

SUMMARY

In this chapter, I have attempted to show the following points:

1. There is good reason to believe that religion began with the awareness of a single creator God. Both the evidence of Wilhelm Schmidt's history

---

[50]See Eliade's appropriate warning: ibid., p. 54.

[51]Schmidt, *Origin*, p. 212.

[52]Sullivan, "Supreme Beings," would be a good example of this approach. Although he brings together a great amount of significant data, he utterly disregards historical context. Descriptions of the supreme beings in the most archaic cultures are placed right along supreme beings in highly developed religions.

of religion and the historical roots of more developed religions serve to back up this belief.

2. The God of original monotheism is identical to the God of Scripture in terms of his basic attributes.

3. One can explain the persistence of monotheism by appealing to both historical continuity with the awareness of God by the first human beings and its reinforcement in general revelation.

4. General revelation has two dimensions, an intuitive one and a rational one, which yield the same conclusions, namely, the knowledge of the existence of God, his attributes and a fundamental moral sense.

So, this chapter has been a first step in relating Christianity to other religions. Here is a belief that Christianity shares with other religions, namely, the fundamental awareness of general revelation yielding cognizance of God and the moral sense. There are two important qualifications that need to be made here:

1. Nothing has been said thus far regarding whether this belief in God has value toward salvation. This is certainly a very important issue, particularly in light of the fact that for many people general revelation may be the only access to revelation they have. I will address this matter further in chapter six. However, it may be helpful to make one point just to keep the air clear: In general, theologically speaking, there is no reason to be of the opinion that the content of general revelation in and of itself has salvific value. First of all, the New Testament makes it clear that neither belief in God per se (Jas 2:19) nor keeping a behavioral standard per se can bring a person into a relationship with God. Second, the passages in Romans, having stated the basic evidence for belief in God and the moral law, go on to clarify that the people in question have all violated those beliefs and the moral law, thus making the matter moot anyway. Later I will discuss the question of whether there are possible exceptions to this rule.

2. Agreement in general does not imply agreement in all of the details. The picture of God derived from general revelation is clearly cast into many different forms by the many cultures that evidence it. I already alluded to the fact that the basic moral foundation takes on many different variations in the fine points (and the not-so-fine points, even). The same thing is true in forming the picture of God, particularly in the names of God and some of the stories associated with him. Obviously, that fact does not mean that there is no way of determining which is correct. But to do that may require special revelation, the topic of the next chapter.

3

SPECIAL REVELATION AND
NON-CHRISTIAN SCRIPTURES

Having established some fundamental common ground between Christianity and other religions on the basis of original monotheism and general revelation, I can now turn to the matter of special revelation. According to Christianity, special revelation is located in the Bible, specifically the Old and New Testaments, as well as in Jesus Christ himself. Of course, access to Christ's teaching is now limited to the New Testament, so that insofar as revelation is a source of information, it all comes down to a book.

Let me hasten to add that (in contrast to the Islamic conception, which will be discussed later) the book is clearly the product of historical events, and the events of history have logical priority. For example, God spoke in history through the calling of Abraham, the giving of the law to Moses and the liberation of his people through Gideon as well as through prophets and psalmists. And, of course, if Christ's life, teaching, passion and resurrection were not historical realities, the written revelation would only be so much pious fiction at best, gibberish at worst. It is still the case, however, that access to knowledge of these events is primarily through what God has revealed in the book, and so this is where one must begin.

Other religions have their books as well. In fact, Islam considers itself a religion of "the book" (the Qur'an) and considers other religions with a book legitimate. See the basic listing of the Scriptures of various religions in table 3.1. The most important point I can make with regard to the table is that few things are as misleading as a table of this sort. Sure, each of

Table 3.1. The Scriptures of various world religions

Religion	Main Scripture(s): Canonical	Secondary Scriptures: Deutero-Canonical
Judaism	Tanak (Law, Prophets, Writings)	Mishnah, Talmud
Islam	Qur'an	Sunna, Hadith
Zoroastrianism	Avesta (Collection spanning many levels)	
Hinduism	Vedas, Brahmanas, Sutras, Upanishads	Ramayana, Mahabharata (including Bhagavad Gita)
Sikhism	Adi Granth	Granth Sahib as compiled by Gobind Singh
Buddhism	Tripitaka (Three Baskets), Lotus Sutra	Many *sutras*, depending on the school
Jainism	Anagas and other writings	
Baha'i	Book of Certitude, other writings by Baha'ullah	Writings by Abdul Baha, Shogi Effendi
Daoism	Daodejing, Zhuangzu	
Shinto	Kojiki, Nihongi, Amatsu Norito	
Confuciansim	Analects	

these religions has one or more Scriptures, but for each one of them, the very nature of Scripture is radically different. Before I can engage in any comparison or contrast on the truth of these Scriptures, I need to clarify what *Scripture* means in each case.

My basic point is this: quite apart from the considerations of historical accuracy and textual transmission, there is an even more fundamental set of distinctions in how Scriptures are viewed in their own settings that makes for a strong incompatibility between the Bible and other world Scriptures. I am calling the ignoring of this reality "the Protestant fallacy"—reading other Scriptures in the way in which Protestant Christians, in particular, read the Bible. Thus, I am not asserting that there is a fallacy at the core of Protestant Christianity; rather I am saying that it is fallacious for Protestant Christians to apply their understanding of the role of the Bible to other religions and their holy writings.

To observe the proper distinctions among the natures of various Scriptures is important for a number of reasons. For one, of course, it is a part of the important task of understanding other religions. Just as we need to understand different beliefs about deities, worship, afterlife and so forth, so we need to comprehend the way adherents understand the nature of their Scriptures as they are viewed in connection to those beliefs. That should go without saying. Second, in attempting to undertake a Christian apologetic toward another religion, one needs to avoid arguing against a straw man when referring to that religion's Scriptures. To focus the question a bit more before getting into details later on, can one defeat the truth of another religion by showing that its actual beliefs and practices are incompatible with its own Scriptures? In many cases the surprising answer is no.

THE PROTESTANT FALLACY

The Protestant fallacy means to view the Scriptures of other religions similarly to the way in which Protestant Christians see their Bible. I am singling out Protestants here in particular, because Christian Protestantism has championed the phrase *sola scriptura* as a part of its self-identification. As opposed to Roman Catholicism's greater flexibility in blending Scripture and tradition,[1] the sixteenth-century Reformers and their offspring have maintained that God's propositional revelation is restricted to his written Word as encompassed by the sixty-six books of the biblical canon. As Monty Python exclaims, "That's what being a Protestant is all about!"[2]

Most important, classical Protestantism maintains that the Bible itself is the Word of God and that, therefore, the actual written text is inspired by God. This means not that the paper and ink are sacred but that the very words that are expressed by paper and ink are the words that God has revealed to his church. In other words, the Bible contains the truths that God wants us to have. Furthermore, the Protestant view asserts *sola scriptura,* namely, that there is no other source of propositional revelation other than the Bible. If a statement is supposed to be a revealed truth, it had better be based directly on what the Bible declares. Otherwise, whatever it expresses cannot be considered to be a binding belief or practice for Christianity.

Thus Protestant Christians practice an extremely book-bound form of

---

[1]Although Roman Catholic theology no longer officially holds to a "two-source" view of revelation, it continues to place Scripture and tradition together on a par, as reflected in the Vatican II document *Dogmatic Constitution on Divine Revelation (Dei Verbum),* in *The Documents of Vatican II,* ed. Walter M. Abbott (New York: Guild Press, 1966), pp. 114-18.

[2]Though, admittedly, in a somewhat different context in the 1983 movie *Monty Python's Meaning of Life.*

religion. They are expected (ideally) to study the Bible on a regular basis in order to become clearer on the nature of their faith, both in terms of belief and practice. In fact, a part of the Protestant understanding of the Bible is the perspicuity of Scripture, which means that any literate human being theoretically can glean the fundamental truths of salvation from the Bible.[3] Even when Protestants read the Bible devotionally, they base their mystical encounter with God on the information conveyed by the text.

Thus, theoretically, Protestant Christianity stands or falls by scriptural assertions. Biblical declarations, if understood correctly, may contain matters affecting belief or practice, which is why Protestants will frequently engage in lengthy discussions on whether a particular text is meant as obligatory or merely as an illustration of a greater principle.[4] Conversely, any belief or practice clearly not taught in the Bible is at a minimum not binding on believers and at worst to be rejected ipso facto. Ideally, a person who has never heard of Christianity should be able to sit down with the Bible, study it thoroughly, and assert, "This and nothing else is what Christians believe." Obviously, I do not believe realistically that one can deduce, say, the conclusions of any of the great systematic theologies written over the last two thousand years from an analysis of biblical texts alone, and, even more important, I would be very unhappy with the idea of ignoring the work of illumination carried out graciously by God the Holy Spirit in guiding us into understanding Scripture. Nevertheless, in abstraction at least, Protestant Christians see Scripture as virtually self-sufficient. The Bible is the one and only propositional authority for our faith.

The Protestant fallacy consists of applying this same understanding, which is perfectly appropriate for the Bible, to the Scriptures of other religions. In other words, it means to hold that the essence of another religion can be distilled from its Scriptures just as the essence of Christian belief

---

[3]This is, of course, the principle behind the establishment of such diverse organizations as the Gideons, who place Bibles in hotels and hospitals, and the Wycliffe Bible Translators, whose goal it is to make sure that every human being can read the Bible in his or her own language. In each case, the fundamental belief is that God works directly and powerfully through his Word.

[4]So, for example, at the second meeting of the International Council on Biblical Inerrancy, one of the workshop sections became focused on the biblical text of 1 Corinthians 11:14, concerning whether a man should have long hair. The point was not, of course, to legislate on male coiffure, as might be the case in a casuistic context (Talmudic, Shari'a, Jesuit), but to expose the principle by which we should apply God's word to ourselves. See J. Robertson McQuilken, George W. Knight and Alan F. Johnson, "Problems of Normativeness in Scripture: Cultural Versus Permanent," in *Hermeneutics, Inerrancy, and the Bible*, ed. Earl D. Radmacher and Robert D. Preus (Grand Rapids, Mich.: Zondervan, 1984), pp. 217-82.

and practice can theoretically be learned from the Bible. One neither has to be a Protestant nor even accept a Protestant notion of Christian Scripture to commit the fallacy. Robert E. Hume asserts in his classic, *The World's Living Religions*, "The most important single systematic source of information among the historic religions is their canonical scriptures."[5] Robert O. Ballou must have had a similar idea in mind when he declared his intentions for *The Portable World Bible*: "The attempt here is to present the gist of each of the world's eight most influential religious faiths, as revealed by their basic scriptures, in one compact volume for the reader who has little leisure."[6] And Kenneth Kramer more modestly attempts to show that "religious meaning can best be studied through sacred texts."[7] But is this really so? I believe not. If one approaches other religions and their Scriptures by focusing on their Scriptures, one can come away with mistaken understandings, and an apologetics based on such a notion will be misleading.

JUDAISM: THE DEUTEROCANON AS KEY TO THE CANON

One of the most obvious places where contemporary evangelicals commit the Protestant fallacy is with regard to Judaism. The assumption is that to come to know Judaism one must study the "Old Testament,"[8] i.e., the Hebrew Scriptures. In fact, a stereotypical attitude is that we Christians understand Judaism better than the Jews themselves because we, after all, have a more perfect grasp of the "Old Testament" on which their religion is supposed to be based. Anyone can see, the attitude continues, that the Jews neither perform sacrifices as they were supposed to in the "Old Testament," nor have they replaced them with the atonement of Christ, as prophesied in the "Old Testament." Hence, judged by its own Scripture, contemporary Judaism would be a defective religion according to this viewpoint.

But these ideas are as foreign to contemporary Jews as they are to other people. As an evangelical Christian, I do not want to deny the notion that Christ is indeed the fulfillment of Old Testament prophecy and that the New Testament provides the correct lens through which to interpret the Old. Nevertheless, this fact has nothing to do with understanding the

---

[5]Robert E. Hume, *The World's Living Religions*, rev. ed. (New York: Scribner's, 1959), p. ix.
[6]Robert O. Ballou, *The Portable World Bible* (New York: Penguin, 1944), p. 13.
[7]Kenneth Kramer, *World Scriptures: An Introduction to Comparative Religion* (New York: Paulist, 1986), p. 8.
[8]I'm putting "Old Testament" in quotation marks here for the obvious reason that, from the Jewish perspective, the very term is both erroneous and demeaning. However, in describing the fallacious attitude of some Christians on this point, use of the term is unavoidable.

nature of Judaism as a religion in its own right. Most[9] forms of Judaism of the last two thousand years, though oftentimes giving the Scriptures a central place, interpret them in terms provided by subsequent writings.

Judaism recognizes as the canonical Scriptures exactly those books that are also the Christian Old Testament. In fact, the early church accepted those books precisely because they were recognized as inspired Scripture by the Jews of their day, including Christ himself. Among Jews, these books are referred to as the Tanak,[10] an acronym based on the Hebrew names of the three divisions: the Law (Torah), the Prophets (Nebiim) and the Writings (Ketubim).

With the fall of Jerusalem in A.D. 70, Jews began the process of writing down the later interpretive writings that had been maintained only as oral tradition. First, a rather sizeable work, called the Mishnah, was produced by a number of rabbis. Eventually (around A.D. 500) there emerged the Talmud, a huge compilation of many tractates, including and amplifying the earlier Mishnah. It is crucial for us to understand that from here on out, Judaism is Talmudic Judaism. It is the Talmud that interprets the Tanak, according to Orthodox Judaism, and, even though strictly speaking the Talmud is not inspired and is subject to expansion, it is also not subject to change or revision.[11] Furthermore, groups that added other writings, such as the kabbalistic movement's acceptance of the Zohar, did not usually disparage the Talmud; they simply supplemented it. (The Reform movement, on the other hand, expressed its disparagement of the rigidity of Orthodox Judaism primarily through a rejection of the Talmud and from there to a relegation of all Scriptures to a position of historical and advisory value only.) Thus, to repeat the crucial observation, even though the Tanak may be the only bona fide Scriptures in Orthodox Judaism, the actual governance of Jewish life—including interpreting the Tanak—is performed by the traditions recorded in the Talmud. Whether positively or negatively, the Jewish Scriptures must be interpreted through the lens of the Talmud.

---

[9]There is one Jewish tradition that denies the authority of the Talmud and attempts to base itself on Torah alone. The adherents of this tradition are known as Karaite Jews (David S. Noss and John B. Noss, *A History of the World's Religions*, 9th ed. [New York: Macmillan, 1994], p. 471).

[10]James Fieser and John Powers, eds., *Scriptures of the West*, companion pull-out volume in *Scriptures of the World's Religions* (Boston: McGraw Hill, 1998), p. 32.

[11]This point is dramatically illustrated by Chaim Potok in *The Promise* (New York: Fawcett Crest, 1969), in which his character Reuven Malter, preparing for his *smicha* (rabbinical ordination), runs afoul of his orthodox teachers because he engages in literary criticism of the Talmud in the style already made notorious by his father, a scholar who carries out textual studies of the Talmud.

This, then, constitutes a large distinction between the evangelical Christian view of Scripture and how Scriptures function in Judaism.

ISLAM: THE QUR'AN AS EVENT

In Islam we also encounter a deuterocanonical literature in addition to the central revealed Scripture, the Qur'an. The Qur'an is, of course, the compilation of what was revealed to Muhammad, recited by him and written down by his companions. Muhammad himself was illiterate, but his followers believe he received messages from God and was commanded to disseminate them among his people. The content of these messages constitutes in a sense excerpts from God's full book in heaven, the *umm-al-kitab*. Consequently, the Muslim understanding of the Qur'an fits in perfectly with a dictation theory of inspiration that is inadequate for the Christian understanding of the Bible but precisely accurate for the Qur'an. Muslims claim that the Qur'an as they have it now is precisely as it was revealed to Muhammad without any changes or corruptions.[12]

Still, despite the truly exalted status accorded to the Qur'an in Islam, it, too, became supplemented early on by a secondary literature. The Qur'an, though containing many specific commands, did not go far enough for the early Islamic community in explicating exactly how Muslims were supposed to live. What better place to turn for this information than to the sinless life and sayings of Muhammad himself?[13] Thus there emerged collections of the acts and sayings of Muhammad, called Hadith, which embodied the true *sunna*, the authoritative words of the prophet. These words, though not considered directly revealed in the same way as the Qur'an, are considered just as authoritative and binding as the Qur'an (insofar as they are genuine[14]). Thus there is clearly a secondary Scripture

---

[12]Strictly speaking, this claim is questionable in two directions. First of all, there is the historical fact that the third caliph (successor to Muhammad), Uthman by name, destroyed all copies of the Qur'an other than the one that he considered to be authentic, thus cutting the Gordian knot of textual criticism with an irreversible tour-de-force. There would be no need for New Testament textual criticism either if at some point someone had burned all variant manuscripts. Second, even at that, some textual variations of the Qur'an have appeared; they are not many and are perhaps not significant for their content, but they still raise doubt about the standard Muslim claim that there are *none*. For a summary see Toby Lester, "What Is the Koran?" *Atlantic Monthly*, January 1999, pp. 43-56.

[13]Frederick M. Denny, *An Introduction to Islam*, 2nd ed. (New York: Macmillan, 1994), pp. 158-71.

[14]And here we do have a little hitch, in that the actual process of gathering the Hadith took several centuries and was not without controversy. There is no single Hadith collection accepted by everyone. For a handy summary, see W. A. Graham, "Hadith," in *The Perennial Dictionary of World Religions*, ed. Keith Crim (San Francisco: Harper & Row, 1981), pp. 288-89.

that must be understood to do justice to the Islamic notion of Scripture. W. A. Graham states:

> After the Qur'an, the *hadith* is the basic source for "proof texts" in Islamic writing. Theologically, the *hadith* is held to be divinely inspired, albeit according to sense rather than word-for-word like the Qur'an.[15]

Islam without the Hadith could be construed as a slight on the prophet because it would ignore Muhammad's life and example.

But this is not where the true distinctiveness of the Islamic notion of Scripture lies. One would still be guilty of the Protestant fallacy even if one included the Hadith along with the Qur'an in order to understand Islam. The importance of the Qur'an in Islam has little to do with its content; the value is its very occurrence. For the Qur'an, as I observed above, is considered to be the embodiment of God's own divine word, revealed in pristine purity to Muhammad and preserved without change ever since. Islam teaches that other prophets had revealed books—Moses and the Law, David and the Psalms, Jesus and the Gospel—but all those writings were distorted by their followers. Only the Qur'an is still the perfect revelation from God. Thus, to recognize it is in a sense more important than to read it; to recite it is more important than to understand it; to practice what it teaches is more important than to study it. This statement could be understood as a criticism of Islam's understanding of the Qur'an if one were to take it to mean that Muslims should not read, understand or study the Qur'an, but that is not the point. As important as those duties are, they are eclipsed by the very phenomenon of the Qur'an itself, the divine word revealed to the world, and, by comparison, those other practices are secondary. The comparison has been made from time to time between the Qur'an and the incarnation of God in Christ,[16] in trying to show that in each case the Word of God has come into the world. It is probably best not to make too much of this supposed similarity,[17] but it does at least get at the heart of the Muslim understanding of the Qur'an as God's self-revelation.

Thus the contrast to the Christian notion of biblical inspiration is clear. The Qur'an is simply not a human book at all; it is only a divine book, and

---

[15]Ibid., p. 289.

[16]Denny, *Introduction to Islam*, p. 151.

[17]After all, this view of the Qur'an expresses only the slightest hint toward an image of incarnation, while in Christianity there are hundreds of years of nuancing the idea of a hypostatic union, and for that matter, this idea, though full of possibilities, is not a standard expressed belief in Islam.

thus its primary significance is not in what it says (as important as that is), but in its existence. Muslims do not put the Qur'an on the altar as an object of worship because that would be idolatry (the most terrible sin of *shirk*), but they do believe that the Qur'an mediates God's presence into their lives. A telling point is that even in countries where the Muslim population may know little or no Arabic the Qur'an is being recited faithfully and devotedly in Arabic. In fact, the most important function of the Qur'an in the Muslim community is just this: to recite it.

ZOROASTRIANISM: A RITUAL ACCUMULATION

The canon of Zoroastrianism also occupies a position different from that of the Bible in evangelical Christianity. Like the Bible, it is an accumulation of multiple Scriptures spanning many centuries. The collection as a whole is known as the Avesta; its oldest part, the Yasna, contains a collection of hymns called the Gathas, some of which may go back to Zoroaster himself (sixth century B.C.).[18] The most recent writing included in the Avesta is the Videvdat, composed in the Sassanid period when Zoroastrianism was Iran's state religion (A.D. 226-637). This makes it sound as though the Avesta could be a fertile source for authoritative information about Zoroastrianism.

Unfortunately, the reality is different. Even though the Gathas can be used to some extent to attempt a reconstruction of Zoroaster's teaching, they are far too impenetrable to yield much information. The language of the Gathas is simply called Avestan because, despite some affinities with the language of the Indian Vedas, it is not found anywhere else. One scholar of Iranian religion has maintained that the Gathas are so difficult to understand because they are intentional gibberish.[19] Even though this may be too harsh a judgment, it illustrates the difficulty, and there seems to be little doubt that even the magi of the later periods were clueless about the meaning of the Gathas, which they, nevertheless, recited.[20]

The fact of the matter is that in terms of its standing in its own community of faith, the Avesta is not supposed to be a source of information. It is a ritual text; its parts are recited at the various ceremonies of worship and purification. Insofar as one finds information in the Avesta, this is only a

---

[18]For the dating of Zoroaster, see my article "The Date of Zoroaster: Some Apologetic Considerations," *Presbyterion* 23 (Spring 1997): 25-42.

[19]H. S. Nyberg, *Die Religionen des alten Iran* (Leipzig: Hinrichs, 1938). See also the response of W. B. Henning, *Zoroaster: Politician or Witch-Doctor?* (London: Cumberlege, 1957).

[20]For a history of Zoroastrianism, see R. C. Zaehner, *The Dawn and Twilight of Zoroastrianism* (New York: Putnam, 1961).

bonus for the student of Zoroastrianism. I am making a point of contrast here. Clearly, much energy has been expended successfully to glean information from the Avesta by Zoroastrians and non-Zoroastrians alike. But the point is that in the context of the religion itself, this effort is only tangential to the true purpose of its Scriptures, that is, the ritual one.[21]

SIKHISM: A DAY IN THE LIFE OF THE BOOK

Another religion that is very focused on one book is Sikhism. The book in question is the Adi Granth. In order to understand the nature and function of this Scripture, one has to know a little bit about the history of the religion. Sikhism's formal founder was Nanak (1469-1539), who attempted to bring about peace between Hindus and Muslims by preaching that there is only one God, whose nature lies beyond the particularities of human reason and religious imagery. "There is no Muslim, and there is no Hindu!" was Nanak's motto. His followers revered him as a divine guru, the very embodiment of God's own light. At that, Nanak was not the first to preach this message. He was preceded by others who attempted to create harmony among the religions, including the poet Kabir and the Hindu movement called Shant, of which Kabir was a part.

Nanak was succeeded by nine further gurus, each of whom was considered to be as holy and divinely infused as Nanak himself. He and a number of subsequent gurus were productive writers of hymns and chants. The fifth guru in this line, named Arjan Dev (who also wound up being the first guru to be martyred), not only composed a number of songs himself but also created the official collection of hymns and chants, called the Adi Granth. This collection would become the standard Scripture of Sikhism.

But there is more to the Adi Granth than just being the hymnbook of this religion. The tenth guru, Gobind Singh (1666-1708), decreed not only that he was the last human guru the religion would have but that from now on the Adi Granth would be the one and only guru for Sikhism in all perpetuity.[22] From that point on, the book itself, the original of which is dis-

---

[21]In trying to understand the Avesta, it is certainly of no help that the textual integrity of this writing is highly dubious. Some scholars estimate that as much as 75 percent of the original has been lost, and the earliest manuscripts date from the thirteenth century A.D., at least 1,800 years after Zoroaster (Gherardo Gnoli, "Avesta," in *The Encyclopedia of Religion*, ed. Mircea Eliade [New York: Macmillan, 1987], 15:16-17).

[22]Gobind Singh also issued an expanded version of the Granth that included some of his own contributions, among others, but this edition is not considered to be on a spiritual par with the Adi Granth of Arjan Dev.

played in the Golden Shrine of Amritsar, has been recognized as the true and binding authority for all Sikhs. Still, its significance goes beyond its particular content and the teaching it may contain. Much more importantly, the Adi Granth is the very embodiment of God in the same way that the preceding human gurus were.

So, in today's Sikh temples the Granth functions in two important ways. First, it still is the hymnbook of the congregation, and, during a Sikh service, chants and songs are performed from its pages. But second, Sikhs venerate the book as the holy guru. In Sikh temples, the book is displayed on an altar underneath a canopy. Worshipers who enter may place some money in the offering box and prostrate themselves before the book prior to finding their place in the congregation. While a chanting service is going on, a leading member of the congregation will stand behind the altar with the open book and wave insects and impurities away from time to time. Every evening the book is put to sleep in a bed, complete with silk sheets and decorations, and every morning it is awakened and placed on the altar once again. At first glance one might think that there is a parallel between Christianity having a holy book and Sikhism having a holy book. But when one looks at the actual function of the book in the community, the similarity vanishes very quickly. The basic function of the Adi Granth is as an object of veneration, not as a record of revelation.

BAHA'I: A CANON PLUS A CANON
Baha'i is a very young religion. At its historical center is its founder, Baha'ullah, who is considered to be a Manifestation of God, the ninth in a roll call of prophets composed of Abraham, Krishna, Moses, Zoroaster, Buddha, Jesus, Muhammad and the Bab (a Persian prophet who immediately preceded Baha'ullah). Baha'ullah taught that, like himself, these other prophets were Manifestations of God; consequently their Scriptures are inspired writings, and his own writings complete this canon of world Scriptures—at least for now.

In a sense, the Baha'i understanding of Baha'ullah's writings[23] resembles the Protestant Christian understanding of the Bible. One can (in fact, Baha'is insist that one should) read the writings of Baha'ullah to get a full and accurate understanding of the Baha'i faith. However, these Baha'i

---

[23]Perhaps the two most important books are the *Book of Certitude* and *The Most Holy Book*. They are a part of what is collected in *Writings of Baha'ullah: A Compilation* (New Delhi: Baha'i Publishing Trust, 1994).

Scriptures do not stand alone because they are paralleled by the other world Scriptures, which are also thought to be inspired writings. It would not even be fair here to call them deuterocanonical; they are a part of the canon just as much as, say, Baha'ullah's *Book of Certitudes*. A typical Baha'i devotional service consists of readings from Baha'ullah along with readings from the Qur'an, the Bible, the Bhagavad Gita and so forth. Thus, the understanding of Scripture in Baha'i is very different from Scripture in Christianity because it is Scripture along with all of the world's other Scriptures.

HINDUISM: A PROTEAN CANON

As we turn to the East, the comparisons with Christian Scriptures get even less tenable. In fact, it can be argued that the whole idea of inspired writings in Eastern religions is based on the Protestant fallacy committed by eighteenth- and nineteenth-century scholars who, beginning with the assumption that all "great" religions must have a book of revelation, artificially ferreted out those writings that they believed came close to their expectations for the various religions. And even though there appears to be a superficial justification for their choices, again, the realities are quite different.

Of course, the Eastern religions do have sacred texts, mounds and mounds of them in fact. But it is verging on foolishness to believe that one can single out some of those and think that they somehow correspond to the Bible in terms of scope or authority for their particular religion. The Protestant fallacy can lead scholars to the snobbery of thinking that certain texts embody the true form of the religion (for example, the Vedas and Upanishads for Hinduism) and that what the millions of Hindus practice is actually an ignorant superstition at best. What a way of writing off virtually an entire religion, and yet a common practice! I will never forget the first time I visited a Hindu temple, freshly armed with a study of Shankara's interpretation of the Upanishads as mediated by Rudolf Otto.[24] There I was in a temple dedicated to the South-Indian goddess Mariamman, her sanctum surrounded by statues of other gods from Indian mythology, her daily worship administered by priests, some of whom were Shudras, the lowest of the four castes (i.e., not the "priestly" Brahmin caste). I realized right then and there that I needed to start over again. The

---

[24]Rudolf Otto, *Mysticism East and West: A Comparative Analysis of the Nature of Mysticism*, trans. Bertha L. Bracey and Richenda C. Payne (New York: Collier, 1932).

goings on in the temple had clearly nothing whatsoever to do with the philosophical or mystical side of Hinduism. What was dominant were the stories of the epics and Puranas as well as the rituals associated with the temple idols. Study of the supposedly main writings was not going to help me much in understanding this form of Hinduism.

According to a widely accepted distinction, Hindu sacred writings are divided into two groups, the *shruti* and the *smriti*. The *shruti* are those writings that are "seen"; that is, they were directly revealed to the semidivine *rishis* of old, who passed them on to posterity. The *smriti*, on the other hand, are only "heard," which means that they are what has been handed down as tradition only. The writings that were "seen" are essentially those composing the Vedic complex—the Vedas themselves, the Brahmanas, and the Upanishads—while the merely "heard" writings include, among other works, the great epic poems, the Ramayana and the Mahabharata (which, in turn, contains the Bhagavad Gita). This would appear to constitute a canon (the Vedic complex) and a deuterocanon (the epic poems).

As clear and straightforward as that distinction sounds, it is far more ambiguous in reality. First, there is some real question about exactly what is to be included among the *shruti*. For example, it is all very well to say that the *shruti* include the Upanishads, but unfortunately the exact number of Upanishads is uncertain (figures range all the way from twelve to one hundred and eight), and none of them was written down until the seventeenth century, 2,200 years after their initial "composition."[25] Second, can anyone (other than scholars wishing to defend theoretical distinctions at all costs) really doubt that the Ramayana and the Bhagavad Gita function in Hinduism as Scripture, not just for all *practical* purposes, but really for all purposes? In fact, one can make an excellent case that they do so far more than, say, the Rig-Veda does. My purpose here is not to defend one dogmatic position against another but to point out how malleable the idea of a canon of Scripture is in Hinduism,[26] certainly nothing like the Bible in Protestant Christianity.

---

[25]William K. Mahony, "Upanishads," in *The Encyclopedia of Religion*, ed. Mircea Eliade (New York: Macmillan, 1987), 15:148.

[26]Some modern movements, perhaps in deliberate imitation of the Western model, have adopted a more "Protestant" practice. One sees particularly the Bhagavad Gita used in this way. This is true for ISKON (commonly referred to as Hare Krishna) as well as for modern Vedantic groups. I have from time to time visited a group of educated Hindus living in the United States who have committed themselves to studying a portion of the Gita on a regular basis in order to get to know their religion better. This would be highly unusual in a traditional Hindu setting.

BUDDHISM: CANON BY SELECTION

When one thinks of the Scriptures of Buddhism, two specific items come to mind immediately: the so-called Pali Canon and the Lotus Sutra. The Pali Canon is the earliest collection of Buddhist writings. It is also called the Tripitaka, which literally means "Three Baskets," because it consists of three main sections, the first one comprises primarily the rules for the Buddhist order of monks and nuns, the second preserves the collection of teachings and sayings of Gautama Buddha, and the third amasses the philosophical elaborations of Buddhist doctrines. These are voluminous writings that span many volumes in English translations. The Tripitaka came into being in the centuries after Buddha's death, and even though they claim to contain Gautama's own teaching, there is evidence of later developments. The Tripitaka is particularly associated with the older, more traditional form of Buddhism, the Theravada branch.

The more recent and more innovative branch of Buddhism, comprising the Mahayana[27] schools, also produced its Scriptures. The chief among them is the Lotus Sutra, which lays out the basic principles of Mahayana, such as multiple Buddhas and Bodhisattvas (Buddhas-in-the making), compassion as the highest virtue and nirvana as a possibility for everyone. The central teacher of the Lotus Sutra is Gautama Buddha himself, who goes to great pains to explain away the apparent inconsistencies between his teaching here and that contained in other earlier writings. The Lotus Sutra is revered by the majority of Mahayana sects and definitely performs the role of Bible for the rationalist Tendai school.

It is precisely in the identification of Scriptures with various schools that one encounters the distinctiveness of Buddhism with regard to its writings. It would be an overstatement to say that each Buddhist school has its own Scriptures, but it is certainly the case that each major Buddhist school has its own appropriation of the canon. Look at the difference this way: In Christianity there are many, many denominations,[28] most of them claiming to have the one and only true interpretation of the Bible, thus giving us one Scripture with many competing interpretations.

---

[27]Mahayana means literally "the great vehicle" in the sense of a large raft accommodating many people. By contrast Theravada ("tradition of the elders") is sometimes referred to as Hinayana, "the small vehicle." Even though textbooks tend to state that this is a term of belittlement, I have encountered Theravadin monks who use the term *Hinayana* of themselves without apparent misgivings.

[28]Consult Frank S. Mead, *Mead's Handbook of Denominations*, rev. Samuel S. Hill, 8th ed. (Nashville: Abingdon, 1985).

In Buddhism each group either develops its own Scriptures or at least selects its favorites from existing Scriptures. There are different versions of the Tripitaka, associated at least historically with different Theravada groups. The Lotus Sutra is accepted as final authority by some Mahayana groups, mixed and matched with other writings in other groups, and ignored in yet others. For a particular Buddhist group it may be possible to point specifically to its Scriptures, but for any larger groupings, this becomes very difficult. The authority of the teacher of a group and its tradition is what determines which Scriptures are accepted as canonical, and not the other way around.

The situation is very similar in Jainism, where the two major divisions (Digambara and Svetambara) each have their own versions of the canon to suit their teachings.

CHINESE AND JAPANESE RELIGIONS

The idea of a canon of inspired writings becomes completely inappropriate for the Far East Asian religions. Again, there are Scriptures, but one is almost tempted to put the word in quotation marks. They are Scriptures in the sense that they are considered to be embodiments of wisdom and so are revered and treated as official representations of the religious teachings, but they ought not to be thought of as divinely inspired in a sense analogous to the Christian Scriptures. Specifically, they are for Daoism, the Daodejing and the Zhuangzi; for Confucianism, the Lunyu (the Analects); for Shinto, the Kojiki, the Nihongi and the Amatsu Norito.

The Daodejing contains the wisdom of Laozi, the founder of Daoism; the Zhuangzi is a collection of anecdotal essays by the teacher of the same name. The Lunyu compiles the teachings of Confucius. The Kojiki is the official iteration of the Japanese national myth, while the Nihongi provides supplemental information to it. Finally, the Amatsu Nihongi represents the standard Shinto prayers and rituals. None of these books is usually accorded status comparable to divinely revealed normative Scripture.[29] As odd as it sounds, all of these writings are in a sense deuterocanonical; that is, the true teaching is not contained in a Scripture at

---

[29]The exception proves the rule here. There were some minority groups that did in fact treat certain writings in this way. For example, the Yellow Turbans faction of China under the Han dynasty rallied around Laozi as their god and the Daodejing as their Bible. But this recognition was more symbolic than substantial, for this activist group was in its actions about as diametrically opposed to the teachings of the quietist Daodejing as one can be.

all but is revealed in the tradition itself.

The upshot of this lengthy survey is this. I have gone to pains to show that it simply will not do to line up Scripture with Scripture on the assumption that each religion has its central writings, comparable to the Bible in Christianity. Though most religions have sacred texts, in each case their self-reported nature and function within their own context is distinctive. Before going on to discuss the conceptual questions involved in comparing Scriptures, these differences had to be emphasized.

THE SINGULARITY OF THE CHRISTIAN SCRIPTURES

In light of the foregoing, the answers to some questions should be fairly obvious. Are other religions' Scriptures also Scriptures just like the Bible? The answer is clearly no. To try to make out a case of such similarity would do violence to both the Christian understanding and the understanding of the other Scripture in its own context. To say that Christians have their Scripture and, say, Buddhists have their Scripture is to commit an equivocation; they do not both have Scriptures in entirely the same sense.

It would not do to make too much of this fact since in a looser sense both religions do have Scriptures that they revere and utilize in their own way, and there certainly are many similarities. The problem is that too many people have made too much of the alleged similarity, thereby attempting to reduce all the world's Scriptures to a common denominator.[30] This, as I have shown, is highly problematic.

Thus, once one has embraced an evangelical understanding of scriptural revelation, it is neither theologically nor practically possible to accept other religions' writings as being identical to the Bible with regard to content, function or perception. So much, as I have indicated, is fairly obvious. But it is not the end of the story. There are other questions one can ask, and they need to receive far more qualified answers.

Do other religious Scriptures contain truth? The answer to this simple question is yes. If truth is what corresponds to reality, then the world's Scriptures contain many truths. If nothing else, they would harbor many innocuous true statements, such as that water is wet, that the sun is bright and so forth. But we need not limit ourselves to such inanities. There may also be many true statements that are more significant. The Qur'an declares the existence of God; the Upanishads assert the need to look beyond the mate-

---

[30]Though not uncritically, Kramer, *World Scriptures*, finds both the distinctiveness and the common ground among religions in their Scriptures.

rial realm of existence; the Analects teach us to respect other people. Surely these statements are true, regardless of where they occur.[31]

As a matter of fact, this answer is not as uncontroversial as it sounds. In providing my response I am assuming a certain conception of truth and meaning. Truth, I stipulate, is what corresponds to reality. In other words, a statement is true if there is something in reality that is captured by the thoughts that the statement expresses. The proposition "Washington's face is on the dollar bill" is true if his face does indeed appear on the dollar bill. This is the correspondence theory of truth.

But there is another way of construing truth, namely, in a coherence theory. In this version a statement is true insofar as it fits into a larger conceptual scheme, such as a worldview or a religious system. A statement cannot be considered to be true apart from the system in which it is at home. Furthermore, two similar-looking statements that occur in different systems do not actually convey the same truth because their truths are determined by the understanding encoded in their system of origin. For example, Cornelius Van Til has argued that the knowledge of even something as innocuous as a flower (and presumably propositions based on that acquaintance) is not the same for a Christian and for a non-Christian since the Christian sees the flower in terms of his whole system—the creation of a personal God who has revealed himself. The non-Christian, on the other hand, if he is consistent with his system, sees the flower as the product of the impersonal forces of matter, time and chance, and so he arrives at a very different sort of knowledge that does not share truth with the Christian view. Even the non-Christian theist, according to Van Til, does not see the same flower since the God whom non-Christians recognize is not the sovereign self-revealing God of the Bible, and hence he is a deity established by humans for their own purposes.[32]

Under such a coherence view, then, Christian or Muslim, Hindu or Confucian cannot share *any* truths since the religious environment that determines the truth would be different in each case. This is not the place to argue at length for the superiority of the correspondence view of truth.[33] If

---

[31] As I stated in the previous chapter, I do not see these as separate lines of revelation from God to adherents of other religions. For a thoughtful differing approach, see Gerald McDermott, *Can Evangelicals Learn from World Religions?* (Downers Grove, Ill.: InterVarsity Press, 2000).

[32] Cornelius Van Til, *The Defense of the Faith* (Philadelphia: Presbyterian & Reformed, 1955). See, for example, Van Til's imagery on how a non-Christian worldview is self-contained on p. 102.

[33] See Douglas Groothuis, *Truth Decay: Defending Christianity Against the Challenges of Postmodernism* (Downers Grove, Ill.: InterVarsity Press, 2000).

I were to do so, I would want to point to two factors, namely, to the experiential undergirding of the correspondence view in everyday life as well
as in theoretical discussions and to the fact that the coherence view, in
order to be applied, needs to smuggle in a correspondence view; in particular, one has to test whether in reality a belief fits into a system according
to one's view of morality. In any event, once one allows for the correspondence theory of truth, there is no reason to deny that other religious Scriptures contain (some) truths.

Do other religious Scriptures contain wisdom? The answer to this question must be more guarded, for here the particular system within which a
religious Scripture is embedded becomes more important. After all, wisdom lies in more than getting the occasional assertion right; it requires
insight into life and how to live it.

Nevertheless, I am going to answer this question with a qualified yes.
Chances are that there is going to be some wisdom in a few or many of the
non-Christian Scriptures. I am thinking of moral exhortations, perhaps
meditations on the fleeting nature of this life, advice on how to get along
with other people and so forth. There is plenty of that in other Scriptures,
and a Christian can cautiously appropriate some of it. However, there are
some clear limits on how far a Christian can go with this appropriation. I
will clarify this limit in the next section, where it is needed even more.

Do other religious Scriptures contain religious truths? Again I want to
answer in the affirmative, but I need to draw a lot of qualifications. First
of all, though, there clearly are true religious assertions in nonbiblical
Scriptures. The Qur'an contains many truths about God and Christ, such
as God's unity and Christ's virgin birth. Hindu Scriptures, such as the
Bhagavad Gita, that assert the personal nature of God (and there are
many, some even verging on monotheism) surely are asserting a very
important truth. The moral code of Confucius comprises many assertions that one ought to take to heart, and the Daodejing's counsel to rest
and not to attempt to change the world in our own power is a crucial
message.[34]

But now for the qualifications. As I stated at the outset of this chapter,
an evangelical understanding of the Bible includes the doctrine of the suf-

---

[34]This is the heart of McDermott's message in *Can Evangelicals Learn?*—a message that is well
worth hearing, regardless of how one reacts to McDermott's understanding of revelation.
Personally, I would like to say that the chapter in McDermott's book relating Christian attitudes to Daoist thinking (pp. 157-69) makes the book worthwhile.

ficiency of Scripture. The Bible is all we have, and the Bible is all we need. Thus it is not possible for an evangelical Christian to reckon other Scriptures to be revelation alongside the Bible. For the evangelical Christian there ought not even to be such a thing as deuterocanonicity. There may be many insightful and even helpful writings by Christian thinkers, but we cannot claim derived inspiration for them. Historically, though it is obvious that from time to time in various places Protestant Christians have relied heavily on one particular writer, be he John Calvin, C. S. Lewis or James Dobson, even the writer's most enthusiastic supporters would not come close to placing that person's writings in deuterocanonical status with Scripture.[35]

However, this point is not nearly as interesting as it sounds when presented in isolation as I have done above. All we need to do is remind ourselves that, certain possibly shared truth aside, the Scriptures of other religions also contain teachings that are clearly incompatible with the Bible. The Qur'an denies the deity of Christ, the Hindu writings extolling a personal God also exhort karma and reincarnation, Confucius's teachings favor expedience over self-sacrifice at times, and the Daodejing offers an impersonal universe without a personal God. In logic, the fallacy of composition argues from the properties of the parts to the whole (for example, "Every boy scout has a mother; therefore, our boy scout troop has a mother"), and it would be a crass instance of this fallacy to argue from the presence of some religious truths in some Scriptures that, therefore, these writings are inspired as a whole.

How can one recognize religious truths taught in some non-Christian Scriptures? It follows from the evangelical understanding of inspiration that only those things can be considered true that have already been revealed elsewhere. There can be no new revealed truths. Either an assertion is based on general or special revelation (as described earlier) or it cannot be more than a human insight that must be judged against what has been revealed. This can be a significant lofty moral insight, such as one

---

[35]Anecdotally, I can think back to some individual Christians in the 1960s who thought that C. I. Scofield's notes of 1909 were an intrinsic part of the King James Version of the Bible issued under his name, but these were hardly people representing any significant trend or movement in Protestant Christianity. For them, their theology of Scripture was severely assaulted in 1967 when the Scofield Bible notes were (slightly) revised. I can only imagine their horror in 1984 when the Scofield notes were added to the New International Version as well. Even at that, for these good folks, the issue would have been construed as one of canonicity and not deuterocanonicity.

that leads to the abolition of slavery or the cessation of a war, but it is still not a new revelation. So, even if there are numerous insights into wisdom and religious truths, they can never be truly novel.[36] The same thing is true, of course, for any writers within the Christian community. No matter how wise and true their writings may be, they must be judged by their conformity to the teachings of the Bible.

Consequently, the search for religious truths in other Scriptures involves the investigator keeping his Bible handy and measuring what is said in those Scriptures by what is already in the Bible. Religious truths in other Scriptures can only be duplications of biblical truth for the evangelical investigator. For example, Christians reading the Qur'an will run across the exhortation to God's people not to "despair over matters that pass you by, nor exult over favors bestowed upon you. For Allah does not love any vainglorious boaster."[37] Such a call to contentment and humility is surely compatible with similar statements in the New Testament, for example, Philippians 4. My point is that, as appreciative as Christians may be about what they see in the Qur'an (or elsewhere), they must judge the other Scripture's content on the basis of what is already stated in the Bible.

That postulation does not sound very exciting, but, despite its inane appearance, it can be a fascinating task. Two features come into play. First, the formulation of the truth in question may be different enough from the biblical phrasing that individuals can get new insights in their appropriation of the truth. Second, one must address the puzzle of how true religious insights can occur within a system that is, as a whole, opposed to the truth. The following discussion addresses this second issue.

Do other religious Scriptures contain special revelation? I already dismissed the idea that non-Christian Scriptures as a whole should be considered inspired because they contain some religious truths. But let me narrow the focus some more: Can those statements of religious truths be considered to be inspired individually?

---

[36]This is the place at which I disagree with McDermott's thesis. I just do not believe that it is necessary to invoke further distinct forms of revelation within the context of non-Christian religions (though, at that, he is very circumspect about doing so, never putting visions or dreams on a par with special revelation in Christ or the Bible).

[37]*The Holy Qur'an* 57:23, trans. Abdullah Yusuf Ali, posted on Barnes and Noble Digital in arrangement with Tahrike Tarsile Qur'an, Inc. (2000), <http://ebooks.barnesandnoble.com/index.asp>.

The Qur'an can be used as one example. From the Christian point of view, this book presents a mix of truth and falsehood. It asserts the existence of God but denies his trinitarian nature (Qur'an 5:116; 9:30); it accepts Christ's virgin birth (Qur'an 19:19-21), but explicitly rejects his crucifixion (Qur'an 4:156); it teaches a final judgment, but does not teach assurance of salvation. Could one not say, then, that those utterances that are directly in accord with the biblical story are inspired? What makes the Qur'an such an interesting phenomenon in this respect is that there is good reason to believe that Muhammad included some of these truths after he had learned them from Christians and Jews and thus, at least indirectly, from the Bible. So, is one not compelled to accept that at least some statements in the Qur'an are inspired in the Christian sense?

The problem with such an inference is that inspiration simply does not work that way. Once a statement has been detached from its larger biblical context and linked to other propositions, one can no longer attribute inspiration to it, let alone its immediate context. From the theological vantage point, verbal inspiration and plenary inspiration go hand in hand. The words are inspired, but they also have a setting in the larger text that gives them meaning and significance, and we say that the text as a whole is inspired as well. If I quote a verse of Scripture, and I set its meaning into the biblical context in which it occurs, I am citing inspired words. But if I quote the same verse and give it a new meaning other than what it carried in its original setting, then I can no longer claim inspiration for my statements, let alone allow the verse to "baptize" the new context I am giving it. To cite a silly example, as a part of his teachings Jesus told a parable in which a man was knocking on a door saying, "Sir, open the door for us" (Lk 13:25). This little statement is thus a part of the inspired corpus of divine Scripture. However, if I were to come home with one of my sons, and he had the key to the house, and I uttered the same statement, there is no way that we should construe this event as my just having pronounced an inspired proposition.[38]

---

[38]Logically speaking, this has to be so lest all sorts of nonsense arise. The following two statements are both true in their entirety: (a) Either George Washington was a race car driver, or water consists of hydrogen and oxygen. (b) If the earth has two moons, then Shakespeare wrote Hamlet. The first sentence is true because a disjunction (an either-or) statement is true as a whole as long as one of its parts is true. The second sentence illustrates the fact that any conditional (if-then) statement is true as a whole when the first part (the "if" statement called the antecedent) is false. This is the case even if the second part (the "then" statement called the consequent) is false. Thus the following statement is true as a whole: (c) If a triangle has four sides, then a square has five sides. As a result, the following statement is true

Do other religious Scriptures contain general revelation? The phraseology of this question can be misleading. If it is meant to be asking whether other religious Scriptures provide general revelation, then the very nature of general revelation forces us to say no; general revelation cannot be a book. But if it is meant as asking whether other religious Scriptures are in part based on general revelation, we are entitled to respond with a yes. In fact, it seems to me that here we come to the heart of the "overlap" between biblical revelation and other Scriptures.

There are several areas where one can discern general revelation in non-Christian Scriptures. First of all, there is the awareness of God to which many refer. As was discussed in the previous chapter, this recognition can take one of two forms. *(a)* There is the persistence of the awareness of original monotheism. This is not just an empty awareness of transcendence or the existence of a deity, but it comes with the traditional attributes of God (all-knowing, all-powerful, etc.), and it carries an ethical dimension. *(b)* There is the inference to the existence of God from various aspects of nature. In the last chapter I illustrated that this is probably a direct intuition on the most common level but that it can be expanded into rigorous arguments when one wants to give it more rationale.

Second, there is the moral dimension that is never far from religion. Chapter four will take a closer look at the moral codes of various religions in relation to biblical morality. For now, it is sufficient to stipulate that there are basic moral concerns, such as truth telling, that are revealed in the Bible but are also found in many other world Scriptures. It may be possible to trace them back to a "natural law" that is known from general revelation. This would not be a law of science, such as the law of gravity or the atomic theory, but a law of morality, such as not to lie or steal, to which all human beings are subject.

These true moral insights play several important roles in the Scriptures

---

(using biblical truth and simple logic as a measuring rod): *(d)* Either Jesus wept or Krishna is God. Now, I do not have any problems accepting the truth of that disjunction, but I most certainly do not want to recognize it as inspired even though the first clause occurs in the New Testament. Further, to think of the clause alone as inspired in this context is incomprehensible, given the larger understanding of inspiration. Similarly, the following statement is true, but surely not inspired: *(e)* If Amida created a paradise, then Jesus wept. The best way to understand this is by recognizing that you simply cannot transfer inspiration on a sentence-by-sentence basis without regard to the context. "Jesus wept" in its original context is an inspired statement occurring within an inspired text. Yanked out of context and inserted into a different text, it is not an inspired statement in a meaningful sense. It may be true, but it is not inspired.

of other religions (as well as in the Bible). For one thing, they work toward the making of a harmonious human community in which individuals can flourish and the community can thrive.[39] One could argue that some form of guidance on how humans are supposed to behave toward each other is about as fundamental a need as any human community could have. Thus, unsurprisingly, religious Scriptures usually address that need.

But there is a further aspect to the presence of moral instructions in religious Scriptures. They are, after all (with perhaps the exception of Confucius's writings), religious in nature and not just books of moral guidance. This means that the Scriptures in their own way are intended to lead a person to a relationship to something transcendent along with giving moral instructions; in fact, the moral instructions usually become part of the way in which the person is taught to relate to the transcendent. Take the Indian sutra called the Law of Manu.[40] It gives extremely detailed instructions on how to live life, but it does not do so in a vacuum. It does so in the context of living a life in keeping with the demands of the gods with the proviso that pleasing or not pleasing the gods in this regard will have direct consequences for one's future spiritual welfare. In short, the moral injunctions that are part of religious Scriptures serve to facilitate relationships with the spiritual world as well as with the temporal world.

These last two points seem almost too obvious to need mentioning. However, they lead up to a third, much more crucial point, again taking off from the observation that these are religious Scriptures, not just moral treatises. It is a given that human beings do not always follow the moral directions that they are given, so their earthly lives as well as their relationship to the world of transcendence are marred. It is here that the religious nature of the Scriptures really becomes crucial because religions in some way seek to serve to promote the relationship to the transcendent.[41]

Not all religions are redemptive in nature in the way that Christianity is (and in a later chapter this point will receive a lot more discussion). Certainly no other religion has the doctrine of depravity or original sin, which is a key aspect of the Christian story of redemption.

---

[39]This is the foundation for ethics, according to Louis P. Pojman, *Ethics: Discovering Right and Wrong*, 2nd ed. (Belmont, Calif.: Wadsworth, 1995).

[40]Some representative selections from this work are found in Fieser and Powers, *Scriptures of the West*, pp. 44-53.

[41]This is the underlying (and perhaps a little too narrow) theory of religion as worked out by Ronald M. Green, *Religious Reason: The Rational and Moral Basis of Religious Belief* (New York: Oxford University Press, 1978).

But all religions in their own way mediate between the finite human being and the transcendent reality that is that religion's content.[42] Then at one and the same time, the religion may provide a moral code that facilitates relating to the transcendent and shows the need for further devices (such as ceremonies, offerings or rituals) that make up for the failure of human beings to fulfill their moral obligations. In other words, the religious Scriptures contain moral obligations partially in order to carry out what the apostle Paul called the function of the law as *paidagōgos* (Gal 3:24), translated as "schoolmaster" (KJV), "tutor" (NASB) and "guardian and teacher" (NLT). The law teaches us our need for Christ by highlighting our failure to live up to the law's standards. Thus, general revelation as expressed in the world's Scriptures also directs human beings to a sense of their own inadequacy.

These last observations obviously need a lot of clarification. My next two steps have to be to discuss further how morality functions within the world's religions (chapter four) and then in what ways there is a means of "redemption" within them (chapter five).

SUMMARY

In this chapter I began by describing an evangelical Christian understanding of how the Bible functions as inspired Scripture. I looked at how the Scriptures in other religions occupy various different places. Then I answered certain questions on how these other Scriptures could be related to revelation. I left little room for a tie-in with special revelation, except through direct borrowing, but left more room for the idea that other Scriptures may contain information gained through general revelation.

---

[42]I am writing this fully aware that a Zen Buddhist might claim that Zen has as its purpose the opposite, namely, the overcoming of anything that appears to be transcendent. Then again, it may be that this overcoming is in fact a transcendent value in and of itself. However this debate might come out, Zen definitely fits the mold of a way of dealing with finite life by relating to something new, even if it is only further insight into life as it is.

4

MORALITY AND GUILT

It seems to be a commonplace that no matter what the differences among religions may be they all share a common set of moral values. In the United States, evangelical Christians frequently call for a return to the values embodied in the Ten Commandments as a kind of minimal code that all people should be able to agree on, no matter how much they disagree in other areas.[1] Similarly, in 1993 the second Parliament of the World's Religions issued a statement that appealed to the common moral underpinnings of not only all religious people but of all people of good faith. The document "The Declaration of a Global Ethic,"[2] after listing some of the flagrant unethical behaviors found in the world today, states:

> [These conditions] need not be because the basis for an ethic already exists. . . .
>
> We affirm that a common set of core values is found in the teachings of the religions, and that these form the basis of a global ethic.
>
> We affirm that this truth is already known, but yet to be lived in heart and action.
>
> We affirm that there is an irrevocable, unconditional norm for all areas of life, for families and communities, for races, nations, and religions. There already exist ancient guidelines for human behavior which are found in the teachings of the religions of the world and which are the condition for a sustainable world order.[3]

---

[1]For example, Norman L. Geisler and Peter Bocchino, *Unshakable Foundations: Contemporary Answers to Crucial Questions About the Christian Faith* (Minneapolis, Minn.: Bethany House, 2001), pp. 223-24. Geisler and Bocchino seem to be equating the Ten Commandments with a natural moral law.

[2]Issued on September 4, 1993, in Chicago, Ill. Published with a commentary by Hans Küng, its original author, as *A Global Ethic: The Declaration of the Parliament of the World's Religions* (New York: Continuum, 1993).

[3]Ibid., pp. 13-14.

This chapter is an examination of the question of ethics in the world's religions. Specifically, beyond the matter of whether there is a core, I will place the ethical dimension of a religion within its broader context and, once again, examine how Christianity fits into that scheme.

SOME FUNDAMENTAL DISTINCTIONS

Most, if not all,[4] religions do have an explicit set of behavioral instructions. Two of the most obvious cases in point are the Ten Commandments of Judaism and Christianity and the ten precepts[5] of Buddhism. But even where one cannot immediately identify a numbered sequence of instructions, there usually are some very clear directions on how to live, as is true, for example, in Islam. Presumably it is these norms that people have in mind when they declare that "all religions teach the same values." Furthermore, I have already several times alluded to the fact that there seems to be anthropological evidence for a very minimal, but possibly universal, set of moral values. In a celebrated article, Clyde Kluckhohn asserts:

> Every culture has a concept of murder, distinguishing this from execution, killing in war, and other "justifiable homicides." The notions of incest and other regulations upon sexual behavior, of prohibitions upon untruth under defined circumstances, of restitution and reciprocity, of mutual obligations between parents and children—these and many other moral concepts are altogether universal.[6]

However, before addressing this phenomenon directly, it is necessary to provide further perspective.

Explicit short lists of moral commandments can be very misleading. First of all, there is no guarantee that the values stated in such a list are truly at the core of that religion's moral norms. Second, there is bound to be a broader, perhaps not as clearly articulated, collection of values and instructions that amplifies, qualifies and explicates whatever is in the short list. Take the Ten Commandments of the biblical tradition. In both Judaism and Christianity, they occur within the total teaching of the Old Testament.

---

[4] It is primarily a scholar's caution that leads me to make this qualification. For one thing, I cannot claim to have knowledge of every school of every religion, and, second, some religions, for example, Zen Buddhism, might resist the idea of actually having an "ethic."

[5] There are ten precepts (listed below in the text). The first five apply to all Buddhists, and the complete ten apply to Buddhist monks only. A lay person observing a special day may abide by the first eight.

[6] Clyde Kluckhohn, "Ethical Relativity: Sic et Non," *Journal of Philosophy* 52 (1955): 672.

Then in Judaism they are interpreted by the voluminous halakic tradition, including the Mishnah and the Talmud, while in Christianity the New Testament reestablishes them in a new light. The same thing is true in other religions and their traditions as well.

Furthermore, as I shall demonstrate more clearly below, the line between ethical exhortations and religious obligations is at best a fuzzy one. Love of God and love of neighbor (or however this would need to be phrased for a particular religion) go hand in hand. The spiritual dimension cannot be divorced from the moral one.

Finally, the spiritual commandments fall into different conceptual orders. Some are very similar to ethical ones: a failure to abide by them is considered a breaking of the law or a transgression. But for others, the context is the ritual domain, and a violation would constitute defilement: either the defilement of oneself by something unclean or the defilement of something holy. (See the distinction depicted graphically in figure 4.1.) Here are three examples from the Old Testament: not to perform an obligatory sacrifice is akin to violating a moral precept, to touch a corpse is to defile oneself, and to perform a sacrifice while in an unclean state is to defile the sacrifice as well. These distinctions will be explained at greater length below. For now it is important to keep an eye out for the fact that *(a)* the distinctions are real and important, but *(b)* the two categories cannot be divorced from each other in the total world of a religion.[7]

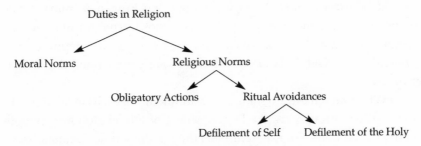

Figure 4.1. Differentiation among various religious duties

THE COMMON CORE

Beginning with a fairly minimal collection of moral exhortations, Kluck-

---

[7]Paul Ricouer developed these dimensions extensively in his phenomenological work *The Symbolism of Evil*, trans. Emerson Buchanan (New York: Harper & Row, 1967).

hohn mentions not taking someone's life gratuitously and truth telling in general. These are certainly values that appear within the moral codes of many (if not all) religions. One immediately thinks of "Thou shalt not kill" and "Thou shalt not bear false witness" among the Ten Commandments. In Buddhism, there are ten precepts that apply to monks, but five of them make up the obligations of a Buddhist layperson, and among these five precepts one finds "not to take any life" and "not to lie." There is no need to make a catalogue of all the religions that repeat these exhortations in some form or another. The Parliament of the World's Religions also stated:

> We commit ourselves to a culture of non-violence, respect, justice, and peace.
>
> We shall not oppress, injure, torture, or kill other human beings, forsaking violence as a means of settling differences. . . .
>
> We must speak and act truthfully and with compassion, dealing fairly with all, and avoiding prejudice and hatred.[8]

But this is just the beginning of the story. Another look, one that does not have to be that much closer, will start to reveal serious differences as well. Focus on the parallels between the Ten Commandments and the ten precepts of Buddhism. Table 4.1 compares the two lists, with the shaded area representing the actual points of overlap. As one can see, they encompass the four expected areas: life, sex, property and truth. However, further study reveals the following points:

1. The instructions that look the same are not necessarily the same. For example, *ahimsa*, the Buddhist principle of respect for life, is usually understood to mean not to harm any living being, human or animal, while the biblical commandment properly means not to commit murder. The slaughter of animals for sacrifices and meals is not just permitted but exhorted in the Old Testament, and armies are commanded to kill their enemies.

2. Even though there are some commandments on each side that do not have a direct counterpart, the larger context of the religion may contain similar instructions. For example, even though there is no commandment to obey one's parents among the ten precepts, such a principle is very much an integral part of Buddhism and was apparently emphasized by Gautama Buddha himself.[9]

---

[8]Küng, *Global Ethic*, p. 15.
[9]It is hard to tell which of all the collected sayings of the Buddha go back to Gautama himself, but in the Tripitaka, the early body of the Buddhist canon, many of his teachings underscore respect for your parents.

Table 4.1 Comparison of Ten Commandments with Buddhist Ten Precepts

Ten Commandments	Ten Precepts
You shall have no other gods before me.	(Buddhism recognizes many gods, though it does not worship them.)
You shall not bow down to graven images.	(Images are a part of Buddhism.)
You shall not take the Lord's name in vain.	
Remember the Sabbath day to keep it holy.	
Honor your father and mother.	(The Confucian principle of filial piety is at home in many Buddhist cultures, but it is not one of the ten precepts.)
You shall not kill.	Do not harm any life (ahimsa).
You shall not commit adultery.	Do not commit sexual immorality.
You shall not steal.	Do not steal.
You shall not bear false witness.	Do not lie.
You shall not covet.	
(The Bible encourages the drinking of wine in certain places.)	Do not take intoxicating drinks.
(The Passover meal is eaten after sunset.)	Do not eat in excess, or after noon.
	Do not attend entertainments.
	Do not decorate yourself or use cosmetics.
	Do not sleep on high or wide beds.
	Do not touch gold or silver.

3. There may be some outright contradictions between some of the principles of one religion and what is practiced in the other. The biblical commandment against graven images is opposed to the practice in Buddhism, and the Buddhist regulations on the sanctity of life cannot be accommodated to certain Old Testament requirements, such as animal sacrifices.[10]

---

[10]This seemingly obvious observation leads me to scratch my head whenever I hear people present the Ten Commandments as some kind of universal moral code. I wonder if either they do not know the Ten Commandments well enough to recognize that the first two prohibit idolatry or if they are ignorant of the fact that the veneration of images is integral to many Far Eastern religions. Rightly or wrongly, one cannot use the Ten Commandments as descriptive of a universal common ground. Nor am I, for one, prepared to ignore the existence of Buddhists (and Hindus, for that matter) simply because they are not monotheists.

This is just the relationship between two superficial renderings of some fundamental requirements within two religions. How much more complicated this picture gets if we add a third one! Table 4.2 illustrates the further complications that arise when the ethic one might glean out of the Hindu classic, the Bhagavad Gita, is added.

Table 4.2 Comparison of Ten Commandments with Hindu and Buddhist precepts

Ten Commandments	Hinduism of the Gita	Ten Precepts
You shall have no other gods before me.	There are many gods; Krishna alone needs to be worshiped.	(Buddhism recognizes many gods.)
You shall not bow down to graven images.	Images are indwelt by deities.	(Images are a part of Buddhism.)
You shall not take the Lord's name in vain.	The name of Krishna must be chanted one thousand times a day.	
Remember the Sabbath day to keep it holy.	There are many festival days.	
Honor your father and mother.	Duty to one's caste exceeds the duty to one's relatives.	(The Confucian principle of filial piety is at home in many Buddhist cultures.)
You shall not kill.	If you are in the warrior caste, your duty is to kill.	Do not take any life (ahimsa).
You shall not commit adultery.	Marriage is sacred, but exceptions are permissible.	Do not commit sexual immorality.
You shall not steal.	Do not steal.	Do not steal.
You shall not bear false witness.	Tell the truth.	Do not lie.
You shall not covet.	Do not become attached to material realities.	

In a sense, then, the point is very straightforward and seemingly simple: religious ethics occur in religious contexts and are an integral aspect thereof. But much truth hinges on this simple point; namely, it cautions us to be wary of a facile identification of a supposed common ethical core. Not that it may not exist, but if it does then it always comes thickly embedded in religious and metaphysical conceptualizations.

To put it in no uncertain terms, the first commandment of the Decalogue renders the other nine possible; they have meaning and authority only insofar as they are rooted in the God who has revealed himself. The

Buddhist ten precepts make sense only within the context of a religion given over to the twin goals of achieving nirvana or accumulating merit until the achievement of nirvana becomes a possibility. And the lifestyle enjoined in the Bhagavad Gita only makes sense when it is based on the fundamental premise that Krishna does indeed provide release from the detrimental effects of karma on one's life. Consequently, the dividing line between moral exhortations and religious instruction, though helpful for theoretical discussions such as this one, is always artificial within the actual content of the religion.

THE CEREMONIAL DIMENSION

So far, I have tried to make the point that at times moral and religious mandates are indistinguishable within the framework of a religion. But often the integration of the two goes further. At times seemingly moral regulations are deeply religious at their very core, namely, when they are a part of the ceremonial dimension of the religion. Then one is dealing with ritual purity or defilement, complicating things further.

The best way to distinguish between ritual norms and moral norms is on the matter of intention. For moral norms, intentions are decisive, whereas for ritual norms, they can become irrelevant. Take the following simple case in point. Say that in the Old Testament context a man named Aram killed Obed, his neighbor. Is Aram guilty of a sin? Well, the answer is, of course, dependent on circumstances or intentions. Did Aram kill Obed out of envy or to gain his property? Then Aram is guilty. Did he kill him in self-defense because Obed was attacking him? Then he is not guilty.

Looking at a different scenario, say that Obed has died from natural causes, and Aram walks into his house and finds Obed's corpse lying on his mat. Thinking that Obed is only sleeping, Aram taps him on the shoulder in order to wake him up. Only then does he realize that he has just touched a corpse and thereby defiled himself. It does not matter that he did not mean to do so; Aram is now ritually unclean and must purify himself in order to escape from that state. So, the two exhortations, "Do not kill," and "Do not touch a corpse," though grammatically very similar, are very different in their nature. The one pivots around the distinction between right and wrong; the other entails the separation between clean and unclean. And, interestingly, whereas moral prohibitions usually focus on actions that may cause overt harm to a community or an individual, ceremonial observances frequently focus on some very trivial-seeming areas that would not matter a whole lot outside of the religious system, such as touching a corpse or eating a certain type of food.[11]

Most religions maintain this ceremonial distinction in some way. In certain cases it is a very pronounced presence. For example, in the Zoroastrianism of the Sassanid Empire in Persia (A.D. 226-637), the concern for ritual purity became a preoccupation of obsessive proportions due to the belief that any defilement left one vulnerable to the attacks of the evil spirits, the *daevas*. Perhaps on the other end of the spectrum is the prohibition of pork in Islam. Of course, not to eat pork is a very important rule within Islam and to touch anything that had contact with pigs will defile someone, but, at least according to theoretical accounts, intention does matter, and unintentional defilement does not carry the penalty of an intentional violation.

As mentioned above, ceremonial prohibitions can point in two different directions, preserving one's own sanctity or preserving the sanctity of something holy. The following might come under the first heading: dietary laws, rules concerning corpses or diseases, ordinances related to rites of passage (such as preparing for circumcision) or directives on human discharges (including menstrual fluids, semen or waste products). Regulations geared to protect the sanctity of something holy might include not touching an object used in worship or respecting the totem animal of one's group. [12]

The line between these two orientations may become diffuse when one looks at particular cultures, and frequently they are grouped together under the general heading of taboo. In ordinary language we often refer to any important prohibition as a taboo, but in a more technical sense, the term refers to these ritual proscriptions. And once again, as observers of the religious world we find ourselves looking at a paradoxical phenomenon. On the one hand, the distinction between moral laws and ritual taboos is a very helpful one in that it aids us in understanding the elements of different religions. At the same time, we must realize that in the minds of the adherents of a certain religion, this distinction does not exist. All three of the elements described now—moral, religious and ceremonial—will exist side by side in the world of the religious person, and the adher-

---

[11] As always, the exception proves the rule, and there are occasions where one can identify clear advantages to a ceremonial system. For example, dietary rules (such as those in the Old Testament) may serve to prevent diseases, and prohibitions against incest clearly avert genetic problems.

[12] In the widespread practice of totemism, a tribe is subdivided into two or more phratries, each of which can contain further moieties. Each group is associated with a particular animal, and in many totemic cultures, the group will not eat their totem animal.

ents may not recognize the distinction even though they may implicitly make use of it.

CASE IN POINT: CHRISTIANITY

Before proceeding with further comparative analysis, I will pause here to take a brief look at these three elements—moral, religious and ceremonial—in Christianity. In the process, I will refer to biblical notions as well as phenomena from the broader world of Christendom.

Merger of moral and religious issues. Christianity is not an ethical religion as, say, Judaism or Islam are, but it is a redemptive religion. By this I mean that, in contrast to Judaism and Islam, while Christianity does contain a moral code, the heart of Christianity is not the code but a historical event, the death of Jesus Christ on behalf of the sinful world, which in turn gives rise to a further event in the life of a human being who comes to Christ by faith. Thus Christianity focuses on the redemption by God of the individual, and the moral code only plays a supporting role—albeit an important one—in the total scheme. Judaism and Islam, on the other hand, look to the code of behavior as the center of the religion.[13]

Although there will be much disagreement in the details, many biblical Christians would embrace the following categorization of the roles of the law in Christianity. First, the law operates as a general practice of government. A fundamental moral law makes life on earth something other than a purely barbaric existence. An example would be the directions given by God to Noah after the flood, which included the admonition to carry out capital punishment for murder. Much of the law that God gave to ancient Israel also comes under the heading of creating a functioning and just society.

Second, the law functions as a "schoolmaster" (using the KJV appellation). In Galatians 3:24 Paul refers to the *paidagōgos* the slave of the ancient world who prepared his master's son for adulthood by teaching him all necessary skills. When the boy had mastered his subjects, he was fit to become officially adopted into his birth family. Similarly, the law prepares us for Christ and adoption into God's family. However, there is a great paradox here. Whereas the "guardian and teacher" works to continually improve his charge until he has attained a sufficient level, the law works

---

[13]At the risk of belaboring the obvious, I am certainly not saying that this is all there is to these two religions. However, keeping the code is at their center, while redemption is at the center of Christianity.

to show us that self-improvement to the point where we might be acceptable to God is impossible. The harder we try to keep the law, the more the law demonstrates our inability to keep it. Thus, when we have come to the point of knowing that we can never be good enough for God, our only recourse is to turn to Christ in faith, not works of the law. Thus in this second use of the law, the moral code carries out the paradoxical function of making an exhibition of our moral failures. By doing so it witnesses to our incapacity for fellowship with God in our natural state since it is impossible for God and sin to coexist (1 Jn 1:5).[14]

The third use of the law in this categorization focuses on life after a person has come to Christ in faith. Now there is a possibility of a person keeping God's commandments, but this possibility has a supernatural grounding. Evangelical theologians disagree about how exactly sanctification occurs,[15] but they all agree that regeneration by the Holy Spirit and his enablement are essential for a person to live up to God's standards. This thought leads to the crucial point for this discussion: the moral code is not an end in itself. Our failure to keep it results in a separation from God; our ability to keep it results from God's own redemptive work and his endowment of us with a new capacity for obedience. In short, Christian ethics apart from a Christian supernatural setting is pointless.

Thus in the case of Christianity, Christian religion and Christian ethics are completely intertwined.[16] A Christian way of life is thoroughly dependent on having and nurturing the supernatural relationship to God. If one removes the theological underpinnings, all that is left is an impossible moral code. Although it is also the case that if one were to remove the moral exhortations one would be stuck with an empty piety, for the purposes of this discussion, it is more crucial to observe that the moral system within Christianity is ultimately a theological system. For example:

- Love of our neighbors is predicated on our love of God and his love of us.

---

[14]The Lutheran theologian Mueller declares that "it must be borne in mind that the Law itself does not lead to Christ, but only to despair. But it serves the coming to Christ by pointing out to the sinner his need" (John Theodore Mueller, *Christian Dogmatics: A Handbook of Doctrinal Theology* [St. Louis: Concordia, 1934], p. 478).

[15]Melvin E. Dieter et. al, *Five Views on Sanctification* (Grand Rapids, Mich.: Zondervan, 1987).

[16]I made reference above to the multiplicity of Christian views on ethics and sanctification. So that what follows now shall not die the death of a thousand adumbrations, I shall make more explicit use of my own view that sees sanctification as a process of which the Holy Spirit is the agent and the law the standard by which we gauge how much the Holy Spirit has accomplished in our lives.

- Life in the Christian community is predicated on believers being a part of the body of Christ (Rom 12:5; Eph 5:30).
- Specific vices are denounced because they "grieve the Holy Spirit" (Eph 4:30).
- The moral code displays our sinfulness from which we are redeemed.
- The righteous life is an expression of the work that God has done within the believer.

The list could go on, but the point should be clear that in Christianity even redemptive history is primary over the moral code; one cannot divorce the theological realities from the ethical obligations.

Ceremonial aspects of Christianity. From its very beginnings, Christianity took a stand against many of the ritual prohibitions that were an integral part of its Jewish and Gentile host environments. Jesus clearly communicated that ritualized observances, such as public displays of prayer (Mt 6:6) or repetitious prayer (Mt 6:7), were detrimental to true piety. He also struck at the heart of the rabbis' preoccupation with clean and unclean foods by declaring all foods clean and indicting the inner sinful life of those who are troubled by external things such as food (Mk 7:19). This theme was also taken up in the book of Acts when Peter received a vision commanding him to eat animals that were formerly considered unclean (Acts 10:9-16).

The only place that I can think of in the New Testament where there seems to be a clear notion of ceremonial purity is in regard to the Lord's Supper. In exhorting the church at Corinth with regard to their practice of Communion (1 Cor 11:17-34), Paul reminds them that the elements represent[17] Christ's body and blood and that to eat and drink of them "unworthily" (1 Cor 11:27 KJV) can have serious detrimental effects, such as death. One must respect the body of Christ. Now, as I understand it, the admonition here is not, as it is usually represented, so much a command for personal holiness prior to partaking of Communion[18] as it is a mandate to understand Communion correctly and thus to treat it with proper respect.

---

[17]I am not intending any specific theological orientation here; I am just making a minimal statement that I am hoping is acceptable in a Zwinglian interpretation on one end of the spectrum just as much as in a Lutheran one on the other end.

[18]In fact, it seems to me that the common counsel not to come to Communion without first having eliminated the sins from one's life denies the very nature of Communion, namely, as a celebration of the forgiveness we have received through Christ's death. One thing is clear: there was plenty of unconfessed sin in the church of Corinth at the time that Paul was instructing its members.

The Corinthians' sinfulness, as Paul addresses it here, was not the presence of unconfessed sins in their lives but that they had turned the Lord's Supper into drunken parties where the rich people dined and drank while the poor people looked on. The very nature of the observance and the elements used in the process was in question, and Paul's admonition has to do with this issue. The Communion elements are taboo in the sense that mistreating them at the time of the Communion service could have debilitating effects on a person.

In the history of Christendom, items of ceremonial purity became engrained in various traditions. In contemporary American Christianity, some of the following items may have taken on a cast of ceremonial purity:

- treating the main room for worship, the sanctuary, as holy ground
- wearing special clothes on Sunday mornings
- treating the Bible in particular ways, such as not placing it on the floor or underneath any other book
- eating food only after having blessed it by "saying grace"

ETHICS IN THE RELIGIOUS UNIVERSE

Having shown the Christian perspective on moral, religious and ceremonial issues, it is now possible to compare them to the corresponding elements of other religions. Judaism and Islam are relatively similar in that they both stress the need to observe a strict moral code as the proper religious expression.[19] Both of them believe that their fundamental code was revealed by God to a prophet (Moses or Muhammad) and that it is contained in the central Scripture (the Torah and the Qur'an). Beyond the central Scriptures, both religions have also developed various supplemental writings, the whole Tanak (the Christian Old Testament) for Judaism along with the Mishnah and the Talmud, and the Hadith with the Shari'a that is based on them for Islam. There are even great similarities in the specific commandments enjoined in both religions. Of course, Muhammad probably learned these from Jews with whom he had contact, but they immediately became an integral part of Islam. They include the prohibition

---

[19]With obvious exceptions, such as those constituted by some Hasidic movements in Judaism or the Sufi movement in Islam. In some of those circles, a theology of the mystical presence of God takes precedence over the observance of the rules and commandments; nevertheless, they do not dispense with the code of behavior either. In fact, paradoxically, the Hasidic movement in Judaism, which began precisely as an attempt to liberate Jews from the barrenness of a purely legalistic form of religion has now become known for its rigorous adherence to the law.

against eating pork, praying several times a day while facing a particular city and those ethical standards that seem to be a part of the universal core, such as not to lie or commit murder.

But there are also serious differences between Judaism and Islam. Judaism carries a far longer history, including several distinct phases (such as the period prior to the temple, the temple period and the present period without a temple). In consequence, Judaism contains a far greater set of specific obligations than Islam does. For instance, Orthodox Judaism has the injunctions for men to wear side curls, skull caps and fringes; the Qur'an merely enjoins modesty. Similarly, even though some of the Islamic dietary restrictions are comparable to Jewish ones, they appear severely truncated compared to Jewish kosher laws.

Even more important is the distinction in the way the commandments are seen as functioning in the overall theological context. Although Judaism certainly has a tradition of believing in a heaven, keeping the commandments is seen primarily as an expression of a given relationship with God, not as earning that relationship. Although such thoughts are not totally foreign to Islam, the primary reason for living according to Qur'anic standards is the hope of thereby qualifying oneself for heaven after death. Furthermore, Jewish standards apply only to Jews; the Gentiles are not obligated to fulfill all the commandments of the law since they are not the chosen people. On the other hand, Islam maintains that its standards are ultimately applicable to all human beings.

Zoroastrianism is very similar to Judaism and Islam in its understanding of its various obligations. Again, there is a law that was revealed to a prophet (in this case, Zoroaster). Zoroaster apparently stressed many fundamental moral values, particularly living according to truth and not falsehood. I already commented above on the fact that Zoroastrianism in its period of greatest flourishing became occupied with ceremonial purity more than ethical purity, but that observation should not be taken to mean that the moral obligations were simply superseded.

In the Indic religions (Hinduism, Buddhism and Jainism), the most outstanding feature is a two-tiered arrangement. In each case, there is a clear distinction between two groups of people, those who work within the general system and those who have transcended it. In Hinduism, the former group is constituted by the vast majority, those who are living within the perimeters of the various schools of Hinduism, particularly temple worship; the latter group are the *sannyasin*, those who have renounced everything in favor of their quest for liberation. *Sannyasin* have given up their names, their families and their former stations in life in order to live alone and pursue the path of true enlightenment. In Jainism and Buddhism, the two groups have more formal status and are constituted by the laity and the monks. The lay people may achieve merit in their religious efforts and, thereby, improve their next incarnations, but it is only the monks who have a real possibility of reaching salvation.

The key to the Hindu code is the caste system. All duties and obligations are in some way tied to one's caste. There are responsibilities that apply to the top three castes, the "twice-born,"[20] and other responsibilities that apply to the Shudras, the caste that exists to serve the top three. Then, of course, there are duties specifically for each of the castes, encompassing all three categories of religious, moral and ceremonial regulations. In a central passage of the Bhagavad Gita, Krishna informs the warrior Arjuna that he cannot harm his karma by killing his kinsmen because, as a warrior, that is his duty. Presumably for someone else, it could have serious repercussions.

One of the guidelines that the three top castes share is to follow the four stages of life prescribed in the Law of Manu, a central Hindu text. The four stages begin when, around age ten, a boy is officially initiated into his caste by receiving the "thread of the twice-born," a cord slung diagonally over his shoulder and torso. Now he is supposed to be a student of the Vedas. The second level is the stage of householder, which spans the entire time a man works in his occupation and raises a family. Once the children are grown and have children of their own, the time may have come for stage three: withdrawal. Now the man and his wife start to focus far more on their religious life, possibly by leaving the village together. The sequence culminates when the man becomes a *sannyasin*. The woman returns to her family in the village. At this point the man renounces everything, including his name, wife, family, caste, even his previous religious activity in order to seek his total release from the world. The fascinating feature of this state is that the *sannyasin* is completely oblivious to all former duties and obligations. His only goal is the realization of *moksha*, "release, liberation," and he does everything he must to attain this goal, particularly meditation and ascetic exercises. But the old rules no longer apply to him.

In Jainism and Buddhism, the pattern goes in the other direction; that is, there are more rules and obligations for those who seek final redemp-

---

[20]Brahmins—the priests, Kshatriyas—the rulers and warriors, and Vaishyas—the merchants and property owners.

tion. In both of these cases, the laity has a standard to live by, but, since they are not eligible for the ultimate step into nirvana, it is not as strict as the one that applies to the monks. Lay people are primarily custodians of the religious cultus, including worship practices in the temple and at home. They must live by standards that are fairly similar in both religions: tell the truth, do not harm any living being, do not steal, do not misuse sex and do not partake of intoxicants. In order to make these standards work, Jainism adds supplementary rules, such as, do not travel far, limit your possessions and give alms to the monks. In both cases, the rules are not onerous, and the larger religious context gives them meaning.

But the monks in both religions (Buddhism and Jainism) are under much greater obligations. Similar to the Hindu *sannyasin,* they have to renounce their previous existence to devote themselves to the full-time pursuit of enlightenment. However, now a plethora of rules takes over, geared to the attainment of enlightenment. In Jainism, the rules under which the monks live are radical versions of the rules for all Jains. The first rule is not to take any life. For lay people that means a vegetarian diet and no unnecessary killing of plants or animals, but for monks it entails not even the risk of killing any insects and not eating any food unless it was destined to be discarded. The second rule enjoins lay people always to tell the truth; it places monks under the obligation always to qualify their statements with the term *syadvada,* "maybe," and, at times, to make opposing statements with this qualification, just to make sure that one does not unintentionally utter a misleading assertion. The ascetic life culminates with the expectation that a monk will eventually starve himself to death and thus, perhaps, attain salvation.

Buddhism considers itself the "middle way," and it stays away from the harsh asceticism of Jainism. In fact, the story of the Buddha includes a period of a few years when he lived an extremely ascetic lifestyle, but this did not bring about enlightenment. Buddhism teaches that asceticism can be just as much of a spiritual hindrance as a life of luxury because it focuses unnecessarily on one's physical life. Nevertheless, Buddhist monks live far from a comfortable lifestyle. The five precepts for the laity are expanded to ten, as mentioned earlier in this chapter. In addition, monks spend grueling hours in meditation exercises and beg for their daily food.

Finally, Confucianism is yet a very different example. Confucianism is a code of behavior first and foremost. It includes social and metaphysical presuppositions, and it is integrated to a certain degree into a religious system, but these things are secondary. In fact, the religious system into which Confucianism is integrated is not Confucianism itself, for it is not a religious system per se. Where Confucianism has established itself, it has amalgamated itself with the dominant religious systems. Thus in China it exists within the Chinese synthesis of Daoism and Buddhism, while in Japan Confucianism has made itself at home together with Shinto and Buddhism. The important point here is that Confucianism came to exist *within* the religious establishment, not just *alongside* it.

Confucianism is primarily about human relationships. The fundamental premise is that proper behavior on the part of individuals will resolve problems in society. Confucius created five categories of human relationships (father-son; ruler-subject; older brother-younger brother; husband-wife; older person-younger person), each with its respective pair of virtues. In addition, individuals must comport themselves in very specifically defined ways depending on the situation; for example, one's posture and facial expression in front of nobility must be very different from that in front of one's equal. In these ways, Confucius hoped to create an ideal society.

The proper Confucian society will include the appropriate religious practices, particularly those that are associated with ancestor veneration. But, as was established above, Confucianism does not carry any specifically religious doctrines.[21] However, in the history of Confucianism Confucian philosophers did work out some of the metaphysical assumptions that make the Confucian code plausible. Specifically, the discussion focused on the characteristics of human nature underlying the Confucian project. In a gigantic overstatement, let me point out two main concepts: (1) a fundamental optimism concerning the possibility of human beings living a perfected life[22] and (2) a theory of powers *(xi)*[23] that give the

---

[21]It needs to be kept perfectly clear that Confucianism is not about the worship of Confucius, although, of course, Confucius received the veneration due an exalted ancestor. However, in Chinese religion ancestors can be so distinguished that they can become promoted to the rank of deity, and this took place in China during the Han dynasty when there were many temples devoted to Confucius. Even today one can see his statue in some Chinese temples. Nevertheless, these matters are completely peripheral to what Confucianism is all about, namely, the Confucian system of relationships and code of behavior.

[22]In particular, this is the teaching of Mencius, a Confucian teacher who lived and worked several generations after the great master.

[23]Also written as *chi* (popularly) or *ch'i* (Wade-Giles), it originally represented the transcendent power of the human breath. But it became known more and more as a spiritual power in its own right. See Michael Diener, ed., "ch'i," in *Lexikon der Östlichen Weisheitslehren* (Munich: Scherz, 1986), p. 74.

human being the ability to live above the restriction of circumstances.

Obviously, this survey could be extended indefinitely and be refined with far greater detail in order to do more justice to the teachings of the world's religions. However, at least the main options have been delineated, and it is time to bring them together again by setting them in their religious contexts.

Violations and Their Consequences

So, what happens when one keeps or breaks the rules indigenous to a religious tradition? In a sense, answering this question would involve recapitulating everything that a particular religion is about, a task that obviously exceeds the intent of this book. But perhaps it is possible to identify a few patterns that will help create some order for understanding.

As I mentioned in the introduction, there are two main trajectories in the world's major religions. The Western or Abrahamic traditions include Judaism, Zoroastrianism, Islam, Baha'i and Christianity, while the Eastern or Indic traditions encompass Hinduism, Buddhism, Jainism, Sikhism, and, by extension, Daoism and other aspects of Chinese and Japanese religions. One evident difference between these two streams is their conception of sin. In the Western traditions, the nature of sin is primarily a matter of offending God and thereby breaking the human being's relationship with God. The Eastern tradition, on the other hand, holds to a notion of karma, the accumulation of positive or negative effects on one's life. Let us examine each in greater detail.

In the monotheism of preliterate tribes, God is not always the direct source of the moral commands, but he is always their proprietor. In many cases, he issued the rules by which the people are expected to live, but even in those where the rules come from somewhere other than God, God expects human beings to abide by the rules and punishes those who do not. Frequently lightning is his tool of enforcement.

In the literate monotheistic religions, there is no question that God is the source of moral rules by way of his personal revelation. Consequently, a trespass of the law is not only a violation, but it is an offense against God himself. Thus the character of the moral law is *pre*scriptive and *pro*scriptive, similar to a governmental law, not *de*scriptive as a natural law would be. And as a result, the violation of such a law engenders punishment. This is not to say that descriptively a violation does not also frequently bring about harm (e.g., the sin of lying damages the liar's own character), but this result is secondary to the more important consequence of having affronted God, the owner of the law. The more serious consequence is that God will punish the sinner in some way.

Punishment may take several forms.[24] It may consist of a warning in which God tells the person that more dire results could occur at another time. Sometimes punishment has a primarily salutary function of producing moral growth and greater virtues in a person. At other times, punishment could be intended to make the person an example to others. More seriously, however, God delivers the sinner to a state outside of fellowship with him, culminating in the possibility of permanent suffering.[25]

The central aspect that I want to highlight is that punishment in the literature of Western religions is the result of the decree of a personal God. The operative image is that of a judge who imposes a sentence. One should not take this imagery too far; obviously, there is not a trial held every time someone breaks God's law—the actual judgment comes about either after a person's death or at the end of the world. Nevertheless, the punishments incurred are God's judgments on the sinner. The flip side of this idea (and ultimately the most important reason for stressing it) is that a personal judge can also provide mercy or grace, something that the impersonal laws of nature cannot do. There is no gracious exemption from the law of gravity.

On the other side of the world and the religious ledger, in the Indic traditions the results of violating a law are much more akin to breaking a law of nature. These religions share the concept of karma, which is not directly tied to a personal deity. For illustrative purposes, and thus at the risk of oversimplification, I will sketch three different understandings of karma and align them with Hinduism, Buddhism and Jainism.

In a broad-brush Hindu conceptualization, one can discern the idea of both good and bad karma. *Karma* initially (in the Vedas) meant action, and in a religious sense it referred to the actions of a Brahmin priest in carrying out the Vedic sacrifices,[26] thus carrying relatively little metaphysical baggage. But by the time of the Upanishads, it had taken on some very distinc-

---

[24]See the interesting delineation by Marilyn McCord Adams, "Redemptive Suffering: A Christian Solution to the Problem of Evil," in *The Problem of Evil: Selected Readings*, ed. Michael L. Peterson (Notre Dame, Ind.: Notre Dame University Press, 1992), pp. 169-87.

[25]For a defense of the legitimacy of the Christian doctrine of hell, see Robert A. Peterson, *Hell on Trial: The Case for Eternal Punishment* (Phillipsburg, N.J.: Presbyterian & Reformed, 1995).

[26]J. P. McDermott, "Karma," in *The Perennial Dictionary of World Religions*, ed. Keith Crim (San Francisco: Harper & Row, 1981), pp. 401-2.

tive meaning, namely, the idea that all human actions, both good and evil, carry direct consequences. Tied into the idea of *samsara*, the cycle of reincarnations, this meaning became stretched further into the notion that the consequences of actions will be manifest in the next existence. Consequently, one's present existence and state of life are the direct outcome of what one has done in one's previous life. If you are born a Brahmin priest, you must have accumulated a great amount of good karma; on the other hand, being reborn as a worm shows that there was a lot of bad karma accrued in your previous lives, and it may take many generations of wormhood to work it off.

There are five important points to keep in mind when looking at this doctrine in Hinduism. First, it is not intrinsically deterministic or fatalistic. One's karmic destiny is under one's own control. Whatever state I may be in, it is the result of what I personally did before, and by fulfilling my present duties, I can work toward a better incarnation in my next life. Second, karma works automatically. It is usually[27] not a kind of judgment passed by a deity; rather it is an automatic process, a law of the universe that even the gods (usually) cannot get around. Third, the idea of karma is a negative, pessimistic one. The proper way to view it is not as an opportunity for indefinite chances at self-improvement but as a destiny of perpetual suffering.

Thus, and fourth, the final goal of most Hindu schools is not to accumulate the greatest amount of good karma but to get off the wheel of reincarnation altogether. To achieve this end one must not only focus on building good karma, but one must also master whatever specific avenue of escape is provided, such as utter devotion to a particular deity or the techniques of Yoga. Fifth, there is provision (at least in some schools of Hinduism) for divine intervention in the process. This is the message of the Bhagavad Gita: The person who clings steadfastly to Krishna alone will have all his karma erased. Thus, a supreme deity can supersede the universal law. But this is clearly not a feature of all Hindu schools.

In both Buddhism and Jainism, the negative features of karma are even more pronounced. Reincarnation in Buddhism is a touchy subject. The Buddha taught that there was no such thing as a central individual soul but that each person was actually an aggregate of effects rooted in the illusory notions of "dependent origination," a house of cards in which insub-

---

[27] As with everything in Hinduism, the exception proves the rule of course. In some forms of theistic Hinduism, karma is seen as wielded by the highest form of God.

stantial cards are propped up against each other. At bottom, there is nothing, not even a soul or an ego; instead of the Hindu *atman*, there is the Buddhist *anatman*. So how can karma be passed on from generation to generation if there is no ego to bear the fruit of karma? What is passed on is akin to a blueprint that is imposed on the next-appearing non-ego, or an impression similar to an imprint made by a signet ring on wax.

There is a further wrinkle to karma in Buddhism. Just as in Hinduism, one can distinguish between good and bad karma, and just as in Hinduism, the effects of one's actions are most likely manifest in one's next life. But in Hinduism, good karma can be seen as having positive value in improving one's chances in the next existence, eventually leading to release. However, in Buddhism, good karma can be as harmful as bad karma; good karma, like bad karma, demands to be worked out in future lives. Thus, theoretically, someone who otherwise might be ready to escape *samsara* and head for the state of nirvana might be hampered, not by bad karma but by good karma that compels the person back into another existence. The ideal then is ultimately to have no karma at all and to withdraw from all actions.

In Jainism, this conception is exaggerated. First of all, the conception of karma is given a unique twist, in that all karma is a kind of dust that accumulates on one's soul. Every action (and, thus, every karma) adds to the store of dust that one accumulates: the more actions, the more dust; the worse an action, the more dust. Only a complete abnegation of life will bring about release. "He who has entered the road leading to the destruction (of Karman), who controls his mind, speech, and body, who has given up his possessions and relations and all undertakings, should walk about subduing his senses," preaches Rishabha the first Tirthankara (one of the mythical teachers of Jainism).[28] Not that there are not tremendous differences between good actions, such as withdrawal from the world, and bad actions, such as hurting a sentient being, but both accumulate karmic dust. Thus, it is not surprising that the recommended outcome for a Jain monk's life is to do nothing, and thus at the end to starve himself to death.

Obviously, none of this should count as a comprehensive survey of karma in Indic religions. There is much more that can and should be said,

---

[28]Mircea Eliade, *Essential Sacred Writings from Around the World* (New York: Harper & Row, 1967), p. 559. A Tirthankara (lit. ford-finder) is one of the twenty-four exalted teachers of Jainism, the last of which (and probably the only historical one) is Mahavira, the founder of Jainism. See the discussion of Jain history in chapter seven. Rishabha is supposed to have lived in a time so long ago that one can have no conception of it.

but I have tried to provide enough detail to show that the Western concept of sin and punishment is drastically different from the Eastern concept of karma. The notion of sin is at home in a decidedly personal theistic framework; karma belongs in a less personal system in which the divine beings can never be more than peripheral.

But there is an additional complication with regard to Christianity, for in Christianity there is a doctrine of "original sin."[29] To someone unacquainted with theological distinctions, this doctrine can seem an awful lot like a doctrine of karma in this sense: it appears to suggest that we human beings are, without our own personal moral fault, born into a state of condemnation. Obviously, the doctrine of original sin includes no idea of reincarnation, but it looks as though the bleak impersonal side of karma—I can perform good acts or bad acts, but whatever I do, I stand condemned—is implied by this view.

To some extent, one cannot avoid this picture. Original sin is a negative doctrine; that is the whole idea. However, one must be clear about where the negativity lies. A common popular misunderstanding attributes our sinfulness to our finitude, and even as astute a theological writer as Paul Tillich[30] made this fundamental mistake. The idea behind this erroneous notion is that, having been born into the finite world, we have no choice but to sin. Then, in the final analysis, our sinfulness is ultimately a function of our birth condition, and that is where the tie-in to the doctrine of karma seems to be the strongest.

However, a full-blown (perhaps Augustinian) understanding of original sin directs us back to God, the Creator and Lawgiver. There is no a priori reason why finite creatures must be alienated from God, for they were created with the capacity of fellowship with him. Adam and Eve were not compelled by their creaturehood to eat of the forbidden fruit, and Jesus Christ demonstrated in his incarnation that a human being can in fact live without sin. The heart of sinfulness, both for Adam and Eve and for us, lies in a direct violation of God's standards. Our first parents, by their will,

---

[29]For purposes of this discussion, I have used the most popular, and possibly least accurate, phrase to refer to this doctrine. Either "fallenness" or "total depravity" would be more appropriate. But these terms come laden with a lot of specific weight, which I would like to slide by at this point. Furthermore, it is precisely the phrase "original sin" that can cause the confusion that I wish to clarify here.

[30]Paul Tillich, *Systematic Theology* (Chicago: Chicago University Press, 1951-1963), 1:44 and 2:187. Clearly Tillich was far from orthodox, but, at that, his writings were usually carefully thought out and rigorously defended. Nevertheless, Tillich wound up equating our finite actual state with our fallen state. Perhaps his total system left him no other option.

acted contrary to what God had commanded, and we, too, are living in a state of rebellion against God, of which we give evidence by our sinful actions. Thus, original sin describes our broken relationship with God, not our immersion in the world.

HEALING THE BREACH

In the next chapter, I will look more extensively at the nature of redemption as it occurs in Christianity and other religions. But it is helpful, while on the topic of the moral order, to make a reference to at least a theoretical scheme of how morality and salvation function together.

Ronald M. Green has provided a helpful overall scheme for understanding the role of morality in religion.[31] Following Immanuel Kant,[32] Green begins with a rational understanding of morality in human life. He distinguishes among four senses of reason:

1. "Theoretical reason" is our conceptualization of the world around us. We create for ourselves a picture of the world in order to make sense of our existence.

2. "Prudential reason" is our capacity for living successfully in the world as we understand it. We use it to fulfill our drives and desires as we struggle through our existence. Its exercise demands that we make certain choices in order to make sure that we can eat, stay healthy, produce offspring, etc.

3. "Moral reason" places our prudential reason in the context of a larger community. It demands that we subordinate some of our choices to broader principles that further the good of the community rather than our own. Thus, I may be required not to eat, not to pursue my own health or not to produce offspring because the greater good of the community demands it.

4. "Religious reason" attempts to reconcile the inevitable conflict between prudential reason and moral reason. It does so by, first of all, providing

---

[31]Ronald M. Green, *Religious Reason: The Rational and Moral Basis of Religious Belief* (New York: Oxford University Press, 1978) and *Religion and Moral Reason: A New Method for Comparative Study* (New York: Oxford University Press, 1988).

[32]Immanuel Kant, *Critique of Practical Reason,* trans. Mary Gregor (New York: Cambridge University Press, 1997) and *Groundwork of the Metaphysics of Morals,* trans. Mary Gregor (New York: Cambridge University Press, 1998). Kant held that there was an inherent tension between "ought" (our rational moral obligations) and "can" (our actual ability to live on the basis of our duties). This inevitable tension needs to find reconciliation within a form of "highest good," which demands that we postulate a God who carries out this reconciliation function.

its own "theoretical reason," namely, an enlarged world picture in which the secular world picture as well as prudential and moral reason can all be threaded together.

Thus, Green attempts to explain all of religion on the basis of this dialectic in which the thesis of prudential reason and the antithesis of moral reason are reconciled in the synthesis of religious reason. What it shows, in simple terms, is that in all religions, moral reason contributes to the nature of the religion.

To provide an oversimplified example, as a Western Christian I have been brought up in a society that values the freedom of individuals but that also recognizes that the freedom of individuals needs to be protected by the society as a whole by such things as education and military defense. This point of view would be one item under the heading of theoretical reason, a part of my total understanding of the world. Second, let us say that with my prudential reason I carve out for myself a comfortable material existence by teaching, speaking and writing a book every now and then. Unfortunately, let us go on to imagine that one year when my taxes are due, I find that I do not have enough money to pay them, and I decide that since the revenue service will probably never notice and since the amounts are too small to matter anyway, I will not declare my book royalties on my income tax form. So, my prudential reason has found a way for me to protect my (perceived) self-interest. Nevertheless, what I am doing is wrong, and thus, third, my moral reason tells me that my selfish behavior is harming the community; if everyone paid taxes at their convenience, our society could not endure. Thus these three forms of reason—theoretical, prudential and moral—have established a tension for me. My selfish prudential interests are at war with my moral obligations.

Now, to do justice to Green's scheme would require a much more subtle and comprehensive analysis. It is not just a functioning community but a total worldview that constitutes theoretical reason; prudential reason extends to all areas of my life; and it is not just an outright breaking of the law that constitutes a violation of moral reason. Regardless, in this little vignette I am trapped in the conflict between prudential and moral reason. A religious system provides categories to help me understand the conflict and achieve personal reconciliation. Thus, as a Christian I understand that my behavior is sinful, the result of the shared human condition of fallenness in which human beings will chronically put their self-interest ahead of their community obligations. Notice that I have now taken my specific case and have placed it into a larger abstract interpretation. And then, of course, my religion also teaches me that I can receive forgiveness for my sins because of Christ's death on the cross. So, I not only have an interpretation, but I also have a means of regaining harmony with myself and the community thanks to my religious orientation.

Green works out his hypothesis in a careful and rigorous manner, and it would be going too far here to deal with his examples in greater detail. Instead, I am going to mention two aspects of Green's scheme that demand clarification lest we are left with a purely reductionistic pattern in which all the other dimensions of religion are ignored.

First, we must not lose sight of the fact that moral precepts come to us deeply embedded in their religious context and that moral reason in some neutral sense does not precede religious morality. This was part of what I tried to show earlier in this chapter. Even though we may be able to point to some commonalities in the moral duties of various religions, we must see each of them as they are defined and function in their specific setting. They are not universal moral precepts *simpliciter.*

Second, we must also recognize that to locate redemption only in the moral dimension would be overly reductionistic. To do so we would have to turn the conception of ceremonial purity into moral righteousness, and that (as we have seen) is not proper. And then we would have to ignore the fact that in too many cases, salvation however else conceived, turns on matters that exceed the moral universe, where the moral issues are only a manifestation of the cosmic issues. Both the Buddhist and Jain need to be redeemed from their good deeds as well as their evil ones. And in (Augustinian) Christianity, even a person who would theoretically never sin by his own deeds would still be condemned on the basis of the very fallenness of his human nature.

Here, then, is the point of all this. Religious systems usually include moral systems. These moral systems sometimes show similarities to those in other religions, but they are religious at heart because in any particular system moral duties appear side by side with religious obligations and ceremonial taboos. The same comprehensiveness appears on the level of the violation of such duties. Impurities or sin lead to negative consequences, but, again, the nature of the consequences varies drastically from religious system to religious system, as shown by the drastic differences between the Western concept of sin and the Eastern concept of karma. Consequently, we can continue to expect such diversity when it comes to the question of providing a way out of the human condition: the concept of redemption.

RESPONSE TO THE WORLD PARLIAMENT STATEMENT

I will close out this chapter by addressing the declaration issued by the Parliament of the World's Religions of 1993, given some of the insights raised in this chapter. Here, once again, are some of the key phrases, [33]

> The basis for an ethic already exists.
> A common set of core values is found in the teachings of the religions, and . . . these form the basis of a global ethic.
> There is an irrevocable, unconditional norm for all areas of life, for families and communities, for races, nations, and religions.
> There already exist ancient guidelines for human behavior which are found in the teachings of the religions of the world and which are the condition for a sustainable world order.

It seems as though there should be no question that all persons of good will should be willing to put their names to statements such as these calling for peace, tolerance and equality. And, one might argue that if one cannot induce the religions of the world to contribute to this effort, then religion is not as beneficial a commodity as one might hope.

Furthermore, as I have argued, there is no good reason to doubt the reality of a minimal ethical code that is found in most, if not all, cultures. Just as it is possible to overemphasize supposed similarities, I think there may be times when we get too carried away by staring at possible exceptions; we recognize that there may not be universality, so we do not acknowledge the overwhelming majority. There may be cultures whose codes of conduct seem to defy the fundamental rules with such actions as infanticide or torturous puberty rites, but these examples do not say all that much *de*scriptively about religious codes of ethics, let alone *pre*scriptively. The exceptions do not need to determine the rule; there is an overwhelmingly accepted minimal code of ethics to which one can appeal.

Of course, one must pay attention to the religious settings in which these codes are housed. They are significant, and they ought to keep us from speaking too freely of a single common code taught in all religions. Only the most minimal code (truth-property-life-sex) seems to be fairly universal. And, even then, there are strong connotations barnacled to these

---

[33]Küng, *Global Ethic*, pp. 13-14. A little more context for these quotations is provided at the outset of this chapter.

commandments. Nevertheless, in some cases the barnacles can be ignored, particularly when speaking to global issues. Should Christians and Buddhists refuse to unite in condemning genocide because the Christian commandment and the Buddhist precept against taking life are different in many respects?

However, the problem with a document such as this declaration lies as much in what is not said as in what is said, particularly when it comes to the desired outcomes from this declaration. Even when we can agree on a fairly acceptable common core of ethical values, how do we intend to apply them? Two issues mentioned in the declaration stand out to me.

First, the declaration asserts: "There should be equal partnership between men and women." What does this mean? For many people it means complete androgyny, that is to say that no difference whatsoever between the sexes should be acknowledged. For others, say Muslims, it means that men and women are equal partners, but that their equality manifests itself in each sex carrying out extremely distinctive roles. If one endorses the Parliament's declaration, which idea is meant? They are different, and one cannot mean both and still think that one has said something meaningful. Either it is empty as a *des*cription of what religions do teach, or it is surreptitiously advocating a specific agenda of what religions should teach *pre*scriptively. Hans Küng, the original author of the document, says in his explanation that "what is said in this section about *equal rights for women* doubtless presents a challenge not only to some Muslims and Hindus but also to more conservative European and American Christians."[34] So, it is clear, for him at least, that the statement goes beyond *des*criptively expressing a consensus among religious believers and— rightly or wrongly—advocates a particular *pre*scriptive stance that actually puts adherents of certain religious views outside of the bounds of the statement. My point here is not so much what the statement says in this respect as that it really does not express common ground as it claims.[35]

Second, as strange as it sounds, I am troubled by the part of the declaration that enjoins "avoiding prejudice and hatred." If one reads this state-

---

[34]Ibid., p. 69.

[35]My take is that the assembly was eager to condemn gender discrimination in the Western world while trying not to give offense to the Third World representatives. In other words, while wishing to speak out on questions of whether a woman has an equal place in today's secular business world, they were not willing to confront directly those regions of the world in which women continue to be essentially owned by their husbands and treated as objects of defilement to the rest of their society.

ment in one sense, not to sign on to it seems unthinkable: We ought always to respect the humanity of all people and never treat them as anything but creatures who bear the image of God, no matter what our differences with them may be. However, in contemporary culture, *prejudice* and *hate* have taken on a further connotation, namely, as words describing serious disagreement on matters of worldview and morality. Thus, evangelical Christians are sometimes accused of prejudice and hate when they state that certain behaviors such as homosexuality are immoral, or when they declare that there is no salvation outside of faith in Jesus Christ. Many Christians maintain that these are matters that can and should be subject to honest and open debate,[36] which can and should be done with mutual respect, but that in the final analysis some things are clearly wrong and not all worldviews have ultimate truth. If the disavowal of prejudice and hate includes forbidding objective truth claims and moral exhortations as well, then an evangelical Christian would have to respectfully disagree. The same thing would apply for other religions that carry specific ethical commandments that may not fit into a preassumed ethical pattern. Again, we can let Hans Küng, who originally penned these words, clarify his own meaning. He asserts concerning apparent advances in peace for the Middle East:

> But this was a peace towards which the religions and their representatives—the representatives of Judaism, Islam and Christianity—should have made a greater contribution than they had done previously, by each opposing the fundamentalists in its own ranks. For there can be no peace among the nations without peace among the religions.[37]

In other words, no matter how good his intentions may be, Küng's recipe for finding unity among the religions includes the suppression of those religious views that would obstruct his higher political goals. And so, again, the appearance of expressing a religious consensus is illusory; the statement expresses the opinions of many, but not of all.

In sum, the 1993 Declaration of a Global Ethic has much to offer. It affirms a universal moral code, and it locates it where it belongs, namely, in a religious context. Furthermore, it calls attention to the commonalities among religious ethics that enable people of different faiths to cooperate

---

[36]And, of course, I cannot deny that there are prejudiced and hateful Christians for whom these are not objective issues but are matters of venting their hostility against those who are different from them. But that is clearly not the case for many others.

[37]Küng, *Global Ethic*, p. 43.

with each other. However, it leaves a lot of questions about what that cooperation will actually look like. The specific goals, though noble-sounding on a superficial reading, also leave questions about whether they really do apply to all religions and, more specifically, whether evangelicals can affirm the statement as it is meant by its authors.

5

CREATION AND REDEMPTION

In the course of the previous chapter an important thought emerged: In reviewing the consequences of disobeying moral injunctions in various contexts, it becomes apparent that in some religions the notions of phenomenal existence and the need for redemption intertwine. By "phenomenal existence" I mean the fact of being a human being in the world, a fact that includes being finite and material.

These two categories (phenomenal existence and the need for redemption) must be held separate in Christianity because here there is a distinct doctrine of creation, followed by a separate doctrine of the fall, followed by God's plan of redemption. Thus redemption is the deliverance from a fallen order and not simply from the order of creation, and it is a serious mistake in Christianity to equate phenomenal existence (and even our finitude) with fallenness. However, in some religions this is not so because the need for redemption comes concurrently with being a part of the universe. By definition, in those religions phenomenal existence itself is in need of redemption. In those cases, the first key to a contrast with the Christian doctrine would be on what it means to be an entity in the world rather than primarily on what it means to be sinful.

So, when we take a look around the world of religions, we shall oftentimes have to link phenomenal existence and redemption together. And when we say "phenomenal existence," that term, at least implicitly, invokes the idea of creation. It is a temptation to start talking about the doctrine of creation in other religions, but this is something we need to be very careful about. All religions have some sort of conception of phenomenal existence, even if it is just relegated to the realm of illusion; many of them have a cosmogony, that is, a belief on how phenomenal existence originated, though many do not necessarily have a doctrine of creation in the sense of a god or gods creating phenomenal existence.[1]

Similarly, the term *redemption* is not intended to limit the discussion to a Christian meaning of the term. No other religion has a concept of redemption quite like Christianity. But then again, the same thing can be said for the concept of redemption in Jainism; no other religion has quite the same concept as the Jain one. So, in order to think intelligibly about this issue, I am including in the term *redemption* all the various end-goals of the various religions that can be shoehorned in. Some religions, particularly traditional or tribal ones, do not have a recognizable concept of redemption. The spectrum is wide: personal salvation may be a part of it, but so may be the salvation of the entire cosmos.

THE CREATED ORDER: WHAT WENT WRONG AND WHAT WENT RIGHT?

One can begin by pointing out two fundamental attitudes toward what I am calling creation: creation as a positive work and creation as something unfortunate. In the latter case, whatever *redemption* means is going to be mainly an escape from phenomenal existence, while in the former case it is going to have to address whatever may have become defective within phenomenal existence, such as perhaps a person's own soul.

In very broad terms, the two categories that I am addressing align themselves with the division into Western and Eastern religions. But these terms are indeed broad because there are plenty of exceptions on both sides; particularly, many of the Western mystical writings seem to fall into the category in which phenomenal existence causes the need for salvation.

In general, the Western traditions see creation itself as something good, and, consequently, phenomenal existence in its pure state is also good. Insofar as redemption is necessary, it is something that most directly affects the human being. Any cosmic redemption only comes attendant upon human salvation.

The clearest example of such a basic Western view is probably Islam

---

[1]Examples of these might be the Samkhya school of Hinduism or Jainism, neither one of which allows for a creator of the universe. Furthermore, even in Hinduism where the god Brahma, the Creator, is a constant presence, it would be wrong to see him as the actual creator of the totality of all that exists. In the final analysis, he himself is a finite part of the total cosmic order. (Brahma, the personal creator God, is not the same as Brahman, the ultimate infinite Reality of Vedantic Hinduism.)

because it has no doctrine of systemic sin; that is, it lacks both a cosmic fall and human original sin. The world as created by God is good, and this goodness also includes human beings. According to Islam, every child is born a Muslim because theoretically every child recognizes (at least implicitly) the existence of God and the need to obey him. Thus an infant comes into the world uncontaminated by sin, and the same thing was true for Adam as the first human being on earth. He, too, was created in a state of purity.

The origin of sin, for Islam, lies in the human free will. Even though persons are born initially in a state of purity, their free will brings sin to their lives. Despite their tacit knowledge that should lead them to do otherwise, boys and girls will make choices that go against Allah's commands and thus are sinful. Similarly, Adam chose to eat of the fruit,[2] thereby breaking faith with God. But neither of these is a cosmic disaster. Nothing is fallen in the sense of now being in a permanent state of alienation from God. Human beings have disobeyed God with their will; they can also return to God with their will. After a suitable interval, God (being all-beneficent and all-merciful) simply forgave Adam, and any human being who seeks to follow God can do so without any need of prior redemption or regeneration. All it takes is the sincere declaration of the fundamental creed of Islam ("I confess that there is no God but God,[3] and that Muhammad is his prophet") for a person to become a Muslim and thus be on the road to restoration with Allah. And further, according to Islam, even apart from such a declaration, a Christian or Jew who lives according to the precepts of the Qur'an has a chance at heaven.[4] In sum (and in very general terms): phenomenal existence is good and remains good, sin is brought into the world through human free will, and sin can be eliminated by human free will. A further act of redemption, such as

---

[2]Qur'an 2:35-37, trans. Abdullah Yusuf Ali, posted on Barnes and Noble Digital in arrangement with Tahrike Tarsile Qur'an, Inc. (2000) <http://ebooks.barnesandnoble.com/index.asp>.

[3]*Allah* is, of course, the word used in Arabic. However, this is simply the word for "God," and not a proper name.

[4]Qur'an 2:62. A crucial issue, but one that would constitute a side track here, is one that always comes up in the context of "works" religion, namely, how much is enough? How many good works are necessary to become acceptable to God, and so to earn heaven? This is a particularly problematic concern in Islam where there is a strong belief in the goodness and mercy of God, but this belief is balanced by the utter sovereignty of Allah, so that any claim to assurance of one's salvation is ultimately unacceptable since only God can finally decree who is saved (Suzanne Haneef, *What Everyone Should Know About Islam and Muslims* [Chicago: Kazi, 1979], p. 37).

an atonement or a special spiritual technique, is simply not necessary.[5]

The general picture for Judaism is a little more complicated, but not categorically different. Again, created reality is good,[6] and evil is the result of the misuse of human free will. And again, there is no specific mechanism of salvation in Orthodox Judaism, let alone in the more liberal (Reform or Conservative) branches. In simple terms, Jews expect to enter the world to come as a reward for keeping "the commandments," a phrase that refers to the 613 commandments of the entire Torah, not just the Decalogue.[7] Again, there is no original sin that must be abolished first.

However, the picture is not as simple as the above paragraph makes it look. There is no original sin, but there is systemic damage to the world order. Sin brought death, a corruption of nature and a general corruption of humanity as well. And so the non-Jewish nations exist in a state in which corruption reigns: they neither worship God nor keep God's law; in fact, they seem to go out of their way to break the law and to harm those who keep it. However, the solution does not lie in the mass conversion of Gentiles to Judaism. In the traditional Orthodox scheme, the Torah applies only to Jews and not to Gentiles.[8] The Jews bear the special burden of the law that comes with the privilege of being God's chosen people, and that burden also entails a special liability for judgment.[9] Thereby Israel shoulders the task of being a unique witness to God's righteousness in a decadent world. The Gentiles, on the other hand, have no special calling, thereby no special blessing but also no special obligation. Even though they are manifestly sinful, they are held to a lesser standard for salvation. In order to be counted as righteous, a Gentile need not first convert to Judaism and take up the full measure of the law. Gentiles are not expected

---

[5]Exceptions abound as soon as one looks at many smaller traditions, such as Sufism or certain Shi'ite groups.

[6]At this point, the obvious (and fairly widespread) exception is kabbalah, the mystic tradition in which creation is frequently seen as the withdrawal of God's being, and thus of God's goodness. Consequently here, as in Eastern religions, there is a clear need for a salvation that severs one from material phenomenal existence. See Gershom G. Scholem, *Major Trends in Jewish Mysticism* (New York: Schocken, 1946).

[7]Thus, let it be said clearly, Judaism does not teach salvation on the basis of sacrifices (or, for that matter, on the basis of any specific ritual). The frequent question by Christians, "How do Jews think they can be saved, now that they no longer have sacrifices?" misses the holistic approach of contemporary Judaism, which seeks to encompass all of life.

[8]With a proper (and sometimes reluctant) provision being made for Gentiles who wish to convert to Judaism.

[9]Dan Jacobson, *The Story of the Stories: The Chosen People and Its God* (New York: Harper & Row, 1982), traces the highly paradoxical nature of the burden of chosenness.

to rise out of their state as Gentiles but are responsible for general commandments only, such as not to kill and not to lie. Yet again, Gentiles are counted as righteous primarily through what they do, not on the basis of a salvific scheme. Thus, in a very general summation: Judaism, similarly to Islam, teaches a good phenomenal reality, sin on the basis of free will and return to God on the basis of human actions. However, the expected human actions have at least two layers (Jew and Gentile).

The Western system gets even more complicated in the dualism that has (at times, at least) been an integral part of Zoroastrianism. There is good reason to believe that the original religion, as taught by Zoroaster himself, was primarily dualistic in only an ethical sense. Human beings are caught in the opposing forces of God (called Ahura Mazda) and Satan (called Angra Mainyu or Ahriman) and must aid the one and repudiate the other based on their actions. Salvation for the human being depends purely on what the person does in response to God. But there is no doubt that Ahura Mazda alone is Creator and that what he created is good. Thus, if this understanding of the earliest form of Zoroastrianism is correct, the original scheme is not all that different from Islam or an idealized Judaism.

However, the subsequent development of Zoroastrianism introduced a different dualistic outlook, namely, that reality itself, not just human actions, can be divided into good (derived from Ahura Mazda) and evil (derived from Ahriman), even to the point of having Satan be a counter-creator so that, for example, when Ahura Mazda creates beauty, Ahriman creates ugliness. On this basis, then, the redemptive objective of the religion has changed as well: No longer is it enough to keep oneself morally pure; one also needs to aspire to metaphysical purity by avoiding contact with the negative side of reality. Not to do so would render one unclean and subject to the evil spirits (daevas), thus in turn leading to further evil. This approach, which has remained a constant presence in traditional Zoroastrianism, has made it the religion of ritual purity and taboos. Such things as hair or nail clippings, not to mention entire corpses, are spiritually dangerous, and contact with them must be avoided strenuously.

Given these factors, it is not surprising that salvation in Zoroastrianism is ultimately one of universal purification of all human beings. But it is not easy to achieve. First, right after death, a person goes into a state of either bliss (paradise) or torment (hell) based on the person's deeds. However, at the end of time, when Saoshyant, the last prophet, comes, he will preside over a complete engulfing of the entire world by a flood of hot molten metal. To the pure and faithful it will seem as a bath in warm milk, while to the evil and contaminated it will be a horribly painful experience. Nevertheless, all persons will emerge from the event in a pristinely pure condition. Thus, in very simplified terms, Zoroastrianism perceives that creation could have been pure were it not for the evil brought about by God's opponent, Ahriman. During the present time period, the war between Ahura Mazda and Ahriman is fought by humans who must strive for both moral and metaphysical purity. Still, at the very end, the originally intended purity of both reality and human beings will be accomplished.

And yet, Zoroastrianism, even in its dualistic forms, is not a rejection of physical existence. It is physical existence that can fall into the two categories of good and evil: good physical reality that was created by Ahura Mazda and evil physical reality that was created (or contaminated) by Ahriman. It is neither the fact of physical existence nor that of being created that makes something evil; rather its origin or its association with God's evil counterpart determines evil. Zoroastrian dualism is categorically different from those worldviews in which something is considered evil purely by virtue of its physical state. This is the sentiment advocated by gnosticism, neo-Platonism, Manichaeism, so-called Christian Science and some Eastern religions, but *not* Zoroastrianism.

To sum up this oversimplified description: Despite their diversity, the major Western traditions teach the idea that phenomenal existence is in and of itself good since it was created by a good God. Corruption is brought about by the misuse of the human free will (possibly with the assistance of nonhuman spiritual beings), and the object of redemption is primarily the human being, who must exercise this free will again in order to be restored to God. Obviously, all of this needs to be refined significantly in order to be fair to any specific religion, but an understanding of the overall pattern will facilitate the discussion here.

As already advertised above, in the Eastern, Indic traditions the picture is usually very different. Again, there are significant exceptions, and all that can be done here is set up a general picture. In broad strokes, the predicament from which one needs to be redeemed is phenomenal existence. Sin as expressed in the concept of karma is not a fall from a state of original innocence but the mechanism by which persons keep themselves mired in the unfortunate circumstance of phenomenal reality. Consequently, the outcome of redemption is not just the attainment of a spiritual state but an escape from the predicament caused by the very nature of reality.

In Hinduism this scheme is most evidently represented in Vedantic monism.[10] The starting point is the predicament: the continual existence of a soul *(jiva)* in the present world. This world is *maya*, a realm of existence whose reality is only secondhand, and the soul that exists in this realm will, without a doubt, suffer. Thus, as long as that state continues, the soul needs to be rescued. In the present state of a soul, it exists severed from its true identity as Brahman, the pantheistic understanding of God. Only if it should ever come to recognize that at its deepest level, called *atman*, the soul is identical to Brahman, can it return to its true state. But instead it exists in the realm of *maya*, secondary or derived reality, and that adds up to a life that, no matter how good, is a life of suffering.

There are two further problems to overcome. First of all, there is the continual cycle of reincarnations *(samsara)* that keeps the soul anchored in its present state, so that, when people die, they simply commence another life. This process repeats itself *ad infinitum.* The level of life (human, animal, demon, etc.) is determined by the karma one accumulates, and in each successive life one either adds more karma by committing disruptive actions *(klesha)*, or one scrubs off a certain amount of bad karma through suffering. But there is little hope of ever getting off the cycle.[11]

If that were not enough, there is a second negative factor, namely, ignorance. Not only is the soul entrapped in an undesirable state; it may not even comprehend its deplorable state. In fact, it may even think that it likes this state because it is oblivious of anything better. In particular, it may not be cognizant of its true identity as *atman*-Brahman. Thus, the path to salvation has to begin with the removal of ignorance and the instillation of knowledge *(advaita).*[12]

Note the two core elements in this much generalized depiction of Vedantic Hinduism:

1. The achievement of salvation is through knowledge. To be sure, this knowledge is something more than pure intellection, the acquisition of

---

[10]Even among adherents of this school, there are many important differences. All I can do here, once again, is present a generalization. See Stuart C. Hackett, *Oriental Philosophy: A Westerner's Guide to Eastern Thought* (Madison: University of Wisconsin Press, 1979).

[11]As many Westerners have added a quasi-Hindu worldview to their own, the underlying hopelessness of this view has often been pushed aside, and the belief of *karma/samsara* has become an optimistic doctrine of unlimited second chances. In its original setting, it is a doctrine of inescapable entrapment from which only very few can flee.

[12]Rudolf Otto, *Mysticism East and West* (New York: Collier, 1960). This is an important study of Vedantic mysticism in its own right, emphasizing the *advaita* theme, as well as a comparison to the similar thought of Meister Eckhart.

factual information. But it is knowledge, nonetheless, in the sense of a direct awareness of one's true nature that brings about salvation.

2. The nature of salvation consists of release from the bondage of phenomenal existence, specifically the cycle of reincarnation (*samsara*) and the karma that propels it. The two words that typically describe this salvation in Sanskrit are *moksha* or *mukti*, both of which literally mean "release." In other words, to make this contrast clearer, salvation is not so much salvation *to* something, such as a state of bliss or heaven, as it is salvation *from* something, namely, phenomenal existence. In this sense, then, this Indic conception stands the Western emphasis on its head. Certainly both frameworks contain a *to* and a *from* aspect of salvation, but in the Western context the *to* is more important, whereas in the Eastern sense the *from* is more important.

The same thing is true in other schools of Hinduism, though they are not as abstractly metaphysical in their orientation. For example, the schools of Bhakti Hinduism and the popular forms of Hinduism loosely derived therefrom look to personal deities to provide salvation, not to a pantheistic soul-God identity. A good case in point would be the forms of Hinduism basing themselves on Krishna and the Bhagavad Gita.[13] The method of salvation—devotion to a deity, namely, Krishna—is very different from that of *advaita* Vedanta. However, the effect of salvation remains the same, namely, release from the suffering engendered by existence in the realm of *maya*.

What is true for Hinduism is also true for the two religions most closely related to it, Buddhism and Jainism.[14] Certainly, the nature of the plight caused by phenomenal existence is explained differently in these religions, and consequently the understanding of salvation is also geared to these different explanations. In Theravada Buddhism, for instance, the straits we are in are caused by the delusion that we are substantial entities. In contrast to the Hindu Vedantic goal of uncovering our identity as *atman*, the true Self, the Buddhist goal is to accept the fact of non-Self or *anatman*. Only when

---

[13]Krishna says, "But those who dedicate all their work to Me, serve Me as the only goal, worship Me, and concentrate on Me exclusively, and stay possessed by Me, are quickly retrieved by Me from the death-ridden ocean of the phenomenal world. Fix your mind on Me, direct your Reason to Me and you will, without doubt, live in Me after death." (Bhagavad Gita 12:6-8 in *Mahusudana Sarasvati on The Bhagavad Gita*, ed. Sisir Kumar Gupta [Delhi: Motilal Banarsidass, 1977], pp. 221-22).

[14]Also, though I am not going to discuss it here, in its own way this patterns applies also to Sikhism.

we have recognized that we do not exist can we stop clinging to this realm of existence,[15] and only then can we escape its chains. Thus, here too, we have the same understanding of salvation as release from the present realm.

Within its own backdrop, Jainism plays by the same rules. Again, the nature of the human condition is described differently. This time it is the case that we exist in this present realm due to accumulated karma (understood as actual physical matter clinging to our souls). The source of this continued infection with karma matter lies within our own actions, particularly in anything we may do that results in harm coming to other living beings. Thus, to bring about our salvation we need to act in such a way that we stop powdering our souls with karma dust, and Jainism has a rigorous list of instructions, most prominent among which are the precepts never to harm any living being and always to tell the truth. However, one ought not to gloss lightly over the fact that this process of salvation begins with knowledge; it is no accident that Mahavira, the founder of Jainism, is credited with omniscience. The soul that knows the truth and then acts on it is the soul that gains release from the cycle of reincarnations.

Chinese and Japanese traditions in and of themselves do not entertain a notion of salvation. In both cultures Buddhism has stepped in, so to speak, and supplied the ideas of reincarnation and how one's actions determine the consequences for future existence.[16] Thus, it is fair to say that in both those cultures Buddhism has provided both the need for and the means of salvation. In Japan and China, Buddhism has flourished in its own right as well as linking itself with the local religions. In China it has become a part of the highly protean popular religion, an amalgam of Dao-

---

[15]This is a notion that is oftentimes described with the term "desire" (*tanha*). One must realize, however, that in English *desire* can be used as pretty much synonymous with *wanting*, whereas the concept in question here goes far beyond mere intellectual intention (which is, as a matter of fact, a part of Buddhism—one must resolve to seek enlightenment) and includes the idea of making oneself dependent on the phenomenal universe.

[16]I would have to concede that it is possible to read a kind of salvation into the Daoism of the Daodejing, namely, the attainment of the state of the "uncarved block," which is to say a state of pure and pristine nature, unsullied by human actions. However, what is missing here, and what is supplied eventually through Buddhist influence, is the idea that the attainment of this state has long-range spiritual consequences for the human being. Subsequent to the period represented by the Daodejing (possibly 500-200 B.C.), Daoist philosophy became the foundation for alchemy insomuch as it was used to provide a theoretical framework for the attainment of personal immortality. But even here, although this may sound like the Daoist philosophy approaches a concept of salvation, that is not really the case. This search for immortality was more akin to, say, a modern person's attempts to procure immortality through gene replacement therapy than a Christian's expectation of everlasting life in heaven.

ism, Confucianism and Buddhism, while in Japan, Buddhism married itself to Shinto, thereby begetting "two-sided" *(ryobu)* Shinto.

CHRISTIANITY

What sets Christianity apart conceptually from everything discussed so far is the doctrine of original sin.[17] In the context of the discussion above, this doctrine makes Christianity distinct from both Eastern patterns and other Western patterns. In contrast to the Western religions (Islam, Judaism, Zoroastrianism), original sin rules out any idea of human neutrality because human beings are perceived as being tainted by sin from the moment of their birth (indeed, their very conception). However, in distinction to the Indic model, this depravity is not something that simply comes with being a creature; it is the result of being a fallen creature. According to the Western understanding, a creature is not in need of redemption just because it is a creature, but a human creature needs to be redeemed because it is in a state of fallenness.

To develop this a little further, in the biblical scheme of things, Adam[18] was created an innocent creature who had the knowledge of God but who was able to sin. I think it is fair to say that Adam's state at this time was pretty much what Islam attributes to all human beings—a good person with the capacity to make morally significant choices.[19] Now, as everyone

---

[17]I am employing the most frequently used designation for this doctrine. This phrase implies a certain orientation, derived specifically from Augustine, which may not be the most felicitous understanding. Personally, I prefer "fallenness" or "total depravity," but it is more likely that others would consider these terms (particularly the second one) even more objectionable. So, I will use the most popular one and let subsequent refinements take care of possible misconceptions associated with this term.

[18]Over the next few paragraphs I am focusing on Adam as both historical individual and representative of the human race. Obviously, Eve was involved in the entire episode as well, but it is Adam in particular who has taken on the emblematic function. As the apostle affirms, "just as sin entered the world through one man, and death through sin, and in this way death came to all men, because all sinned—for before the law was given, sin was in the world. But sin is not taken into account when there is no law. Nevertheless, death reigned from the time of Adam to the time of Moses, even over those who did not sin by breaking a command, as did Adam, who was a pattern of the one to come" (Rom 5:12-14).

[19]One's answer to the question of whether Adam at this point was in a truly neutral condition will ultimately be affected by one's view of God's providential involvement in Adam's life before the fall. It could be possible to argue that, since God could have prevented the fall but not only did not but provided opportunity for Adam's transgression, that God was already slanting the scenario in the direction of Adam's eventual sin. This is a view that could be attributed to Augustine. Then it could be said that God did not provide Adam with an even playing field, and he never really had a fair choice in the matter. Nevertheless, this conception (which I take to have some merit) addresses Adam's circumstances, not his nature, and it is his nature with which I am concerned for the moment.

knows, Adam made the wrong choice when he ate of the forbidden fruit. The question is, what was the result of this action? In contrast to the other Western religions, Christianity affirms that in a very serious way Adam not only disrupted the world order but even destroyed himself. From this point on, he was subject to death, both physically and spiritually. The latter, according to Christian theology, needs to be understood as a state of separation from God, his Creator, and this constitutes the fundamental need for salvation.

Christian theologians are divided over how exactly to describe all of the implications of the fall of Adam. The biggest disagreement concerns the question of how the fall has influenced the human will. Whereas before the fall, Adam had a choice between obeying or not obeying, some Calvinistic theologians claim that now Adam no longer had a free will, whereas other Arminian Christian thinkers maintain that Adam, beset by sin though he may have been, had not lost his capacity for free choice. And, of course, these differences have been worked out with great detail and subtlety, but all orthodox Christian theologians agree that Adam did not have it within himself to restore his own relationship to God. Adam was in need of redemption.

A further important point is that Adam's fall had metaphysical implications. When he turned away from God, the act of severing this most important relationship corrupted his own nature. What before was simply human nature created in the image of God now became fallen human nature, still in the image of God but suffering from corruption. Consequently, if there is going to be any redemption, it needs to involve a regeneration of the human being's nature as well. Once again, there is plenty of room for disagreement among Christian theologians on the question of whether restoration of the will needs to precede restoration of the human spirit or vice versa.[20] But the need for an act of regeneration is a given.

Finally, to complete this bleak picture, Christian theology holds that all human beings suffer from the same fallen condition as Adam. We are all estranged from God; we all are similarly in need of redemption. Of course the fall also had negative implications for the universe and for the human social order, but the most important consequence is that all human beings are equally considered a part of the fallen human race. Further, human beings also give evidence of being members of Adam's race by continuing

---

[20]Compare my discussion in *Handmaid to Theology: An Essay in Philosophical Prolegomena* (Grand Rapids, Mich.: Baker, 1981), pp. 167-79.

to make wrong moral choices, but the most fundamental problem is that of the class of beings to which we belong, namely, fallen ones.

So, in contrast to the other Western religions, Christianity emphasizes the fall of the human race. The fall also provides the most important point of contrast to the Eastern religions. The pattern of Indic religions described above is that the human soul needs to escape the predicament of imprisonment in the natural order with its never-ending cycles of reincarnation, propelled by karma. At its core, there is a state of purity: *atman* equals Brahman in Vedantic Hinduism, the soul can rid itself of karma matter in Jainism, and, in the negative mirror of Buddhism, the soul ultimately is identical with the nothingness of true reality (*sunyata*—the Void). Thus, the need for redemption is primarily a need for release out of negative circumstances that hinder the soul from enjoying its pure state. By contrast, then, in Christianity the human soul itself is the culprit. If the cosmos is corrupted, it is so because the human soul has brought it about.[21] Redemption cannot just be yanking the soul out of its present environment so that all will be well, but it needs to involve the restoration of the soul to its proper relationship with its Creator.

This proposition of restoration poses a conundrum. In order to be healed, the soul needs to be restored to its proper relationship with its Creator, but the soul cannot restore itself to this relationship unless it is healed first. The upshot for Christian theology is that salvation cannot occur apart from mediation.

Now, mediation is something more than just help. All religions aim to provide assistance to their adherents in whatever spiritual quest they are pursuing. Else, there would be no point in having a religion. So, by means of prayers, sacrifices, rituals, etc.—in short, the entire cultus of a tradition—a religion seeks to provide for human beings whatever they need for spiritual benefit. Furthermore, most religions believe that their measures are to some extent indispensable. However, mediation in Christianity means something more than that—it means that God himself performed those actions that the human being ideally should have done, but could not.

More specifically, in orthodox Christian theology, mediation occurs by

---

[21]Well, strictly speaking, I probably need to take things one step further back and start talking about the fall of angels and the havoc they have wrought. Let me just say this: Presumably one can take whatever I am saying here about human creatures and apply it back to angelic creatures. The problem is that we know virtually nothing about these events, so, with the stipulation that things *could* be taken back further, I will leave it with the humans for now.

way of the atoning death of Christ.[22] At the heart of this conception is the notion that in order for human beings to be restored to God, the penalty for sin must first of all be paid. Human beings, finite creatures that they are, can never do enough to atone for the seemingly infinite chasm created by human sin; however, God himself stepped in and, in the ultimate show of love, sacrificed his own son, who willingly gave his life for our atonement on the cross.

And so Christ becomes the mediator for human beings. In order for individuals to be saved, they have to rely on Christ and him alone for redemption. There is nothing that a human being can do in order to merit salvation (Eph 2:8-10). One can only come to Christ and trust in him and his work. This is what Christianity understands by saving faith—complete reliance on God. In fact, the attempt to supplement faith with various religious works undercuts faith and makes it worthless since it is impossible to both trust and not trust at the same time (Gal 5:2-4).

Salvation entails numerous facets, but I will briefly summarize only a few here.

1. *Justification.* God declares the sinner to be righteous on the basis of the work of Christ.

2. *Regeneration.* God implants a new nature in the person. With this new nature, the individual is able to live a righteous life.

3. *Conversion.* The sinner turns away from his sin, trusts in God and begins to live in righteousness.

4. *Adoption.* The new believer is made a member of God's family; that is to say, the person now can know God as father (Gal 4:6) and Christ as brother (Heb 2:11).

5. *Indwelling.* God in the person of the Holy Spirit comes and takes up residence within the believer in Christ (Jn 14:16-17).

6. *Glorification.* Very importantly, the end result of the whole proceeding is not just the restoration of the believer back to the same state that Adam and Eve were in. The final destiny of the person in Christ goes beyond the original innocence to a state of glorification. In simple terms, heaven is more than the Garden of Eden, and being permanently in the presence of God is greater than the relationship with God that Adam originally enjoyed.

---

[22]Once again, I am writing in full awareness of the fact that there are many different ways of conceiving of the nature of the efficacy of the atonement. I believe, however, that the concept of a substitutionary atonement is the most appropriate one and, *pace* Aulen, the biblical one as well. See Gustaf Aulen, *Christus Victor: An Historical Study of the Three Main Types of the Atonement* (London: SPCK, 1970), p. 20.

Finally, I must point out that, even though the Christian understanding of saving faith precludes that faith can be supplemented by works, a person's saving faith will *result* in good works (Jas 2:14-18). Faith that does not manifest itself in subsequent works is not genuine faith. Thus Christians will perform good works, not in order to procure salvation but in order to give evidence of their salvation and to give thanks to God for this salvation.

I began this brief summary of salvation in Christianity by introducing the concept of mediation. God himself provides for our salvation in Christ. And thus mediation is directly linked to the concept of grace. Since it is God who does all that is necessary for us to be saved, human beings can only accept this salvation as a free, unmerited gift from God.

GRACE IN OTHER RELIGIONS
As a matter of fact, Christianity is not the only religion that includes belief in salvation by grace alone. Before looking at some examples, I need to make an important clarification, however. One must distinguish between grace and mercy (as well as numerous other cognates).

Virtually all religions have a concept of mercy, and it usually is a very important aspect of that religion. So, for example,

- Islam consistently invokes Allah as the All-Beneficent and All-Merciful.
- Judaism holds that God is characterized by *hesed*, "loving-kindness."
- Bhakti Hinduism and its modern popular derivatives focus on the love of the central god or goddess of a particular school in making redemption available to their devotees.
- A central idea in Buddhism is the compassion of Buddha himself, as well as the many other Buddhas and, in later developments, particularly the multitude of Bodhisattvas, "Buddhas in the making," who have foregone their own enlightenment in order to make the redemption of all human beings possible.
- In contemporary Chinese popular religion, one of the most popular goddesses is Guanyin, the goddess of mercy; she even has it in her power to avert an otherwise certain negative fate that might beset someone.

There are many other examples.

It must be made clear here that even though in all of these cases there is a strong emphasis on mercy and compassion, these are not true examples of grace. By *grace* we should mean that human effort simply does not contribute to the individual's state; grace is entirely the result of the divine person's (god's, Buddha's, etc.) actions, and this is clearly not the case in the examples mentioned above. In each of these instances, the divinity makes it possible for humans to do what is necessary to contribute to their salvation,[23] but the human contribution is still instrumental. Thus:

- In Islam, it is considered presumptuous to assert certitude of one's salvation;[24] one can never know if one has truly done enough to please Allah.
- In Judaism, God's *hesed* is displayed, at least to some extent, in that he makes the law available so that human beings can live by it.
- Bhakti Hinduism is usually premised on the idea that the love of the deity is a response to the human being's acts of devotion.
- The Buddhas and Bodhisattvas make salvation easier, but they do not usually eliminate the need for human actions.
- In order for Guanyin to reverse a person's fortune, she has to be entreated with worship and offerings.

These express the concept of mercy or compassion, but not grace.

However, there are two classic examples of grace in the world's religions in addition to Christianity.

1. The cat school of Bhakti Hinduism. The southern school of devotion to Rama in Hinduism (cat school) teaches that just as a mother cat carries her kittens in such a way (in her mouth) that the kitten makes no contribution to its transportation, so Rama saves us through his actions alone. There is nothing that human beings can contribute to their salvation, just as the kitten can make no contribution to its transportation. All works of devotion are expressions of gratitude, not means toward salvation.

Rudolf Otto[25] has provided a very helpful treatment of this phenomenon in the history of religion. The following is a summary of his discussion. One of the most eloquent defenders of Vaishnavite Bhakti Hinduism

---

[23]At best, then, these cases would be instances of what in Christianity we would call "semi-Pelagianism": God supplies the grace, and human beings put it into effect (surely a self-contradictory notion).

[24]Haneef, *What Everyone Should Know,* p. 37.

[25]Rudolf Otto, *India's Religion of Grace and Christianity Compared and Contrasted,* trans. Frank Hugh Foster (New York: Macmillan, 1930).

was Ramanuja. He referred to Vishnu as Ishvara, the Creator,[26] and also worshiped him as the redeemer who through his love and grace alone gives a person redemption. Otto makes the following points concerning the nature of this personal redemptive version of Hinduism:

- It makes a distinction between a worldly and a spiritual life.
- Devotion to God is characterized by singleness of aim; ultimately it is a matter of trust and reliance on God.
- Redemption of the individual human being is possible only by the fact that the person's decision has been preceded by an offer of grace and an act of divine election.
- The natural state of the human being is fallenness, which must be overcome by God's grace.
- The devotee of God manifests his devotion through the religious expressions associated with temple worship and personal acts of piety.
- The person who has received God's redemption experiences a state of blessedness in this present life.

As in Christian theology, the relationship between grace and works has occupied much discussion in Vaishnavite Bhakti Hinduism. Otto gives a brief historical tracing of one line of development on this issue. (a) At first, as exemplified in the Bhagavad Gita, the need for some works of devotion was stressed over against the virtual antinomianism which seemed to be the goal of the Vedantic sage (the *sannyasin* who has renounced all ties with the world, including religious ones). (b) In subsequent development, the works of devotion were seen primarily as signs of surrender to the deity. (c) Then *bhakti*, the very idea of devotion, was seen as nothing more than a manifestation of faith. Even at that, some people went on to stress that this very faith was no more than an acceptance of what God had done already. (d) Eventually, these Bhakti thinkers, particularly the devotees associated with Ramanuja, split into two groups: the northern "monkey" school, which believed that at a minimum the *bhakta*, "devotee," is required to cling to his God as an exercise of the will, just as a baby monkey needs to cling to his mother, and the southern "cat" school, which, using the way in which a kitten is carried by his mother as a metaphor, claimed that all work is done and all initiative is taken by the God on behalf of the believer.

---

[26]In terms of classical Hindu mythology, the creator is, of course, Brahma, usually pictured with four heads. Ishvara is a more general term, applicable to different persons of the Hindu pantheon, usually when the creator is seen as an object of devotion. In this context, it is Rama, the incarnate Vishnu, who preeminently carries this title.

Thus, the cat school promoted an all-absorbing form of grace while the monkey school permitted a free-will decision by the devotee. Otto states,

> The sum of the whole difference is:
>   The North: The soul gains God for itself.
>   The South: God gains the soul for himself.[27]

The parallels to the Christian concept of grace seem overwhelming. Otto rejects the possibility that the Bhakti schools may have arisen out of direct influence from whatever Christians may have been present at the time in India,[28] and thus, it would appear that there is an astonishing case of convergence in religious thought. Just as a doctrine of salvation by grace through faith came into being with Christianity, so a very similar doctrine apparently arose in India with the Bhakti movement.

2. *The Jodo Shin-shu school of Buddhism.*[29] This, the most popular school of Buddhism in Japan today, teaches that salvation can be had entirely through the grace of a Buddha named Amida. He is not the same Buddha as Gautama, the founder of Buddhism, but a different person, whose life is supposed to have paralleled that of Gautama in many ways. According to the mythology, in the remote past[30] he was a king who learned about Buddhism through the teaching of another Buddha (named Lokesvararaja). He assumed monkhood under the name of Dharmakara but vowed that he would not actualize his own enlightenment until he had made the same possible for all other creatures. This he would do by creating a pure land or paradise in which all would live in supreme bliss and enter the state of nirvana in their next subsequent rebirth.

When Amida had achieved sufficient merit and spiritual as well as mental powers, he attained enlightenment and now took on the name Amitabha (Sanskrit) or Amida (Japanese), which means "Infinite Light." He turned to the western quadrant of the universe, and here he brought about this ideal land that he had worked toward for many billions of years. There is nothing particularly unique in later Buddhism in the idea of a Buddha creating a paradise, but what makes this special are two factors. First, in contrast to the other pure lands, which excel in only a few perfections, Amida's pure land is said to combine all perfections, and, second, as

---

[27]Otto, *India's Religion of Grace*, p. 58.
[28]Ibid., pp. 138-39.
[29]"Jodo-shin-shu," "Jodo-shu," "Reines Land" and "Reines-Land-Schule," in *Lexikon der östlichen Weisheitslehren*, ed. Michael S. Diener (Munich: Scherz, 1986), pp. 306-7.
[30]See the discussion of time in chapter seven.

will be explained below, it is very easy to be reborn into it.

Even though Amida is not a part of very early Buddhism, he did become an important and pervasive figure subsequently. Eventually in various settings, particularly in Korea and Japan, invoking his name turned into a widespread popular practice. As a Buddha who had distinguished himself through his great compassion, there was much to be gained by repeating the mantra, *Namu Amida Butsu*—"I (bow down to) worship the Buddha Amida," usually shortened to *nembutsu*. In the twelfth century A.D. the monk Honen elevated this practice to the core of a school of Buddhism, called Jodo-shu, the "School of the Pure Land." He taught that Amida will allow anyone who is truly devoted to him entry into the pure land. Such a devout person is reborn into this utopian setting as a male human; he will lead a truly blissful existence for a time and then, in his next existence, cross over into nirvana with no hindrances, thus attaining the highest goal of Buddhism. Honen maintained that, in addition to visualization techniques, the most effective way of building one's faith in Amida was to recite the *nembutsu* frequently. He encouraged people to take on monkhood in order to achieve their goal.

For the purposes of this discussion, the most important development occurred in the next generation after Honen when another monk, Shinran by name, declared that Amida's compassion was even greater than Honen had imagined. He founded the school, known as Jodo-shin-shu—"the *True* School of the Pure Land." According to Shinran, there is nothing that a human being can do to earn entry into the pure land other than to trust in Amida's work. Ultimately all that is necessary for salvation is for a person to utter the *nembutsu* once—and even then only as an expression of gratitude rather than as a means of earning one's salvation. Similarly, the good life that a person should lead, including temple worship, is not a condition of salvation but a manifestation of one's thankfulness to this Buddha. There is no monkhood in Jodo-shin-shu since there is no point in it; one need not take up asceticism (or do anything else, for that matter) in order to become worthy of Amida's compassion. Thus, in Jodo-shin-shu there is a clear concept of the grace of Amida.[31]

---

[31]We need to make sure not to criticize a "straw man." It is better to concede what is obviously there and then to deal with it than to deny that there is a concept of grace in Amida Jodo-shin-shu. See my article "Buddha, Shiva, and Muhammad: Theistic Faith in Other Religions?" in *Who Will Be Saved? Defending the Biblical Understanding of God*, ed. Paul House and Greg Thornbury (Wheaton, Ill.: Crossway, 2000), pp. 129-43.

CHRISTIAN RESPONSE

So, in Christianity salvation comes by grace through faith in Jesus Christ, while in the cat school of Bhakti Hinduism, salvation is by grace through faith in Rama/Ishvara and in Jodo-shin-shu by grace through faith in Amida Butsu. What is the difference? The difference lies, of course, in the first half of this chapter. There is no need to dispute the appropriateness of applying the concept of grace in these two traditions. Within their respective contexts, both of them definitely offer a bona fide concept of grace.

However, the key to the matter lies in the reference to the context. I have already pointed out that the entire framework of what *redemption* means is very different in Christianity and both of these Eastern religions. A part of the thesis of this book is that Christian concepts and similar concepts in other religions sometimes overlap, and clearly, this is a case in point insofar as there is a genuine understanding of grace in both of these religions. Nevertheless, it should also be clear that this convergence cannot have particular significance by itself because the surrounding context makes it so obvious that other than the presence of a belief in grace there is no further similarity, as I explained in the comparative section earlier in this chapter. Salvation by grace through faith they may be, but salvation in the context of Christianity means something radically different from salvation in Bhakti Hinduism and in Pure Land Buddhism.[32] Salvation in Christianity centers on the atonement Christ made for our sins, and without it, any concept of salvation—with or without grace—cannot possibly be accepted as valid.

I shall consider some of the implications of this stance at length in the next chapter. At this point, though, it may be helpful to address the question of what makes the idea of Christian salvation, complete with atonement, qualitatively different from other concepts of salvation. Why should one person's grace be better than another's? Why choose the Christian teaching over the Hindu or Buddhist teaching?

The distinguishing feature lies in the grounding of Christianity within actual history. This is not only true in the present context since neither Ishvara/Rama nor Dharmakara/Amida have the remotest connection to his-

---

[32]I will add here that consequently I find Clark Pinnock's rejoicing at having found grace in other religions puzzling, to say the least. It may be grace, but it is the wrong context for it. See his "Toward an Evangelical Theology of Religions," *Journal of the Evangelical Theological Society* 33, no. 3 (1990): 359-68. See also Otto's thorough criticisms of such a position in *India's Religion of Grace*, pp. 59-108.

torical events, but it is also what distinguishes Christianity from other world religions, both in general and in connection with the matter of salvation. In fact, Christianity is the only religion whose truth depends strictly on historical events.

This is not to say that historical events, particularly in the Western traditions, have no important role to play in other religions. I said in the first chapter that a robust notion of history is part of the standard framework of Western religions. But it is not a crucial role. Consider this question: Can anyone imagine Islam without Muhammad? At first thought, that seems to be impossible. After all, Muhammad, who definitely was a historical person, is esteemed as the final messenger from God, the one who has received the Qur'an, which is still supposedly recited in the same unblemished form as it was revealed to Muhammad. Islam without Muhammad seems unthinkable.

But wait! Muhammad himself was able to think of Islam without himself. In fact, it is one of the core teachings of Islam that the same message has been proclaimed by prophets and messengers numerous times.[33] Islam had been practiced at many times and places before Muhammad, and if it had continued to be practiced properly, Muhammad would not have needed to come as the final prophet. So, Muhammad plays a very important role in Islam, but not an essential one. The essence is the proper belief about God and the resulting proper actions; wherever this is done, Islam is present.

Similarly in other Western religions, the message and practice of the religion are more important than the founder and the historical events associated with them. Both in Judaism (and I am thinking here primarily of rabbinic Judaism since the fall of Jerusalem in A.D. 70) and in Zoroastrianism, the beliefs and practice are decisive. The origins of the religion, though important for the total legacy, are not crucial.

Furthermore, what is true for the Western religions is true all the more in the East. It is reasonable to believe, for example, that there was a historical Buddha and that to some extent his life did indeed coincide with the events described in the standard myth about him. We cannot depend upon a lot of reliable historical information, but there does not seem to be any

---

[33]The Qur'an gives several nonexhaustive lists of previous prophets. Some of these men are also found in the Bible, for example, Adam, Noah, Abraham, David and Jesus, but some come out of a nonbiblical Arabian context, for example, Hud, Shu'aib and Salih (Qur'an 3:33-34; 4:163; 6:83-86; 7:66-93).

good reason to dispense completely with at least a historical kernel to his legend. Surely it is plausible to believe that he was the founder of Buddhism. However, despite the veneration that the Buddha receives from his followers, the religion itself makes it very clear that, other than as someone who has taught these beliefs, the Buddha is neither unique nor essential. There were many other Buddhas (countless ones according to the Mahayana schools), all of whom taught the same path toward enlightenment, including Kasyapa, the one who is said to have taught the Buddha himself innumerable lives ago. For that matter, there will be others in the future as well. As in Pure Land Buddhism, the focus of devotion is on Amida, not Gautama, and in Zen, disparagement of the Buddha is at times practiced in order to make the point that the historical Buddha cannot provide salvation on behalf of anyone.[34]

Jainism is in a somewhat similar position in that the founder, Mahavira, was most likely a historical person, but he was nonessential for the actual teaching, for, again, he was preceded by other Tirthankaras like him, and there will be more to follow eventually, all of whom teach the same principles. For Hinduism, there is no historical tie-in whatsoever. Presumably, some of the events of the Hindu epics could be associated with occurrences of a long time ago, perhaps the conquest of the subcontinent by the original Aryan invaders, and sometimes Hindus that I have talked to make such a claim. However, one must understand that when they say such things, the point is not to root the events in history but to stress the antiquity of the teachings, for the teachings themselves are what counts. Whether, for example, there was a historical Krishna (and, in contrast to the Buddha or Mahavira, there is no particular reason to assume that there was) has no bearing whatever on the religion of those who devote themselves to Krishna as their *bhakti* deity.

With Christianity, the situation is radically different. Christianity includes teachings, but it goes far beyond its teachings. In fact, if you take the historical setting away from the teachings, the teachings become impossible moral exhortations and occasional platitudes, but not much of a basis for a vital religion. Without the historical events related in the New Testament, there cannot be genuine Christianity. To enumerate: without a historical Christ, without his life and teaching, without his death on an actual cross, and without his actual resurrection from physical death,

---

[34]A good example: Stephen Mitchell, ed., *Dropping Ashes on the Buddha: The Teachings of Zen Master Seung Sahn* (New York: Grove Press, 1976).

Christian claims are empty. How can one trust in an atonement that never happened?

A helpful—and highly telling—passage in this context is found in 2 Peter 1:16-18. Peter makes the point here that his proclamation of Christ is based on eyewitness experience. He contrasts other religious claims (including, no doubt, those of the false teachers against whom he directs himself) with his own on the basis that the others are speculations while his are grounded in direct experience. "We were eyewitnesses of his majesty," he says, speaking of the transfiguration (v. 16), "when we were with him on the holy mountain" (v. 18 NASB). Peter is stressing that his preaching is based on events that actually occurred and at which he was physically present.

Interestingly, this verse occurs in the context of a book whose authorship is disputed by many writers[35] who do not believe that Peter was the author of this epistle. In that case, the author's claims in this passage (unless it was either James or John calling himself Peter for no intelligible reason) are downright fraudulent. The whole point of the assertion is that the teaching of the power and majesty of Christ is based on direct experience of actual events. And, even though one might theoretically be able to accept the idea that someone else might have written an epistle covering various topics in Peter's name, having this unknown writer claim to have been an eyewitness when he surely could not have been would have been inexcusable.[36]

Because this is such a crucial point, let me stick to it just a little longer. For example, the very popular and esteemed author William Barclay addresses this issue.[37] First, he joins the many scholars who reject the Petrine authorship of 2 Peter and lists the common arguments on their

---

[35]A very cogent analysis of the authorship of 2 Peter is presented by Michael J. Kruger, "The Authenticity of 2 Peter," *Journal of the Evangelical Theological Society* 42 (1999): 645-71.

[36]In the article cited in note 35, Kruger makes the important point that, on the whole, claims that the early church would have had little trouble accepting a pseudepigraphic epistle because it was allegedly such common practice have little to go on. The single most important criterion (if not at times the only one) for sorting out which books did or did not belong in the canon was that of authorship. It was only because there was ultimately acceptance of the authorship of this epistle as Peter's that 2 Peter did become a part of the canon. If it had been agreed that Peter did not author the book, it would not now be in our New Testaments. The early church—and one thinks this need not be said—was loath to accept eyewitness testimony from those who were not eyewitnesses.

[37]William Barclay, *The Letters of James and Peter*, rev. ed. (Philadelphia: Westminster Press, 1976). It is precisely because he is such a good expositor and so many Christians have been helped by his teaching that Barclay's lapses on some issues are so disappointing.

behalf.[38] Then he opts, as many others do, for the idea that someone else wrote it in Peter's name in order to use Peter's authority against the illegitimate authority of the false teacher whom this epistle is combating. But when it comes to the passage in question, 2 Peter 1:16-18, Barclay needs to get around the eyewitness claims because presumably he does not wish to impugn the integrity of the author. He does so by suggesting that the word used here for being an eyewitness *(epoptēs)* is derived from the mystery religions in which a person has an inner vision of his god.[39] Thus, his experiences are in and of faith, not of the physical world. But, surely, even if the word *epoptēs* had some use referring to spiritual vision in the mystery religions, this would be a most peculiar use of it. For one thing, the specification of being "on the holy mountain" seems to rule out a purely spiritual experience. But even more importantly, this impostor who is trying to assert that his teachings are different because they are not just based on speculation and spiritual insight would now be putting a purely spiritual insight to use in order to defend his point; he would be doing exactly the opposite of his claim! Thus, he would not just be a pretender; he would be a very incoherent pretender.

My point here is that we have two different strains of thought at odds with each other: the one grounding faith events in historical events and the other creating an autonomous role for faith, making the belief system independent of the actual events of history. But it is the former position that is taken by the New Testament, whereas the latter would align Christianity with other religions, thereby depriving Christianity of its distinctiveness. And, of course, for William Barclay this is only an occasional lapse in his otherwise very beneficial writings,[40] whereas so-called liberal Christianity from Schleiermacher on has for two centuries now attempted to maintain a Christianity severed from its historical moorings.[41]

The Christian doctrine of salvation stands out from the rest of the world's religions because it is closely tied in with actual events in history. Clearly, this fact brings with it both an asset and a liability. From the credit

---

[38]Ibid., pp. 283-89.

[39]Ibid., pp. 310-11.

[40]Perhaps it is because Barclay takes the text so seriously that his infrequent blunders stand out so glaringly.

[41]B. B. Warfield used to make the point that, in the final analysis, the so-called search for the historical Jesus led to the idea that the person of Jesus himself is irrelevant to Christianity. In other words, the discovery of a historical Jesus would yield for us a nonhistorical faith. For example: "Christless Christianity," in *The Person and Work of Christ*, ed. Samuel C. Craig (Philadelphia: Presbyterian & Reformed, 1950), pp. 265-319.

side, it gives Christians the ability to speak confidently of their faith because it is anchored in reality and not myth or speculation. Of course, the debit side is that in the final analysis Christianity could always be disproved with sufficient historical information. Hypothetically, if it could actually be shown that there was no such person as Jesus Christ, that he was definitely not crucified or that his dead body is still in the tomb, then the Christian doctrine of salvation would be falsified. Other religions cannot be so falsified, but then they cannot be shown to be plausible on the basis of historical data either.[42] In short, the Christian understanding of salvation stands out from the others, not just by having a unique conceptual wrinkle but by being established in the time-space continuum of history.

COSMOS AND MYSTICISM

And now, to confuse things a little. Up to now I have focused on broad patterns in order to clarify categorical distinctions. But anyone with any awareness at all of Christian theology will know that in the total picture of Christianity things are not as clear-cut as the description above could lead one to believe. To be sure, I do not intend here to belabor various departures from Christian orthodoxy, as important a topic as that may be, because those occurrences in and of themselves are not germane to the topic of this chapter. Rather, I now wish to emphasize that on a secondary level, some of the same elements that are constitutive of salvation in other religions obtain also in Christianity, though (from the point of view of orthodoxy) not as central to salvation.

Mysticism. First, what comes to mind is the mystical tradition that seems to stretch across both Eastern and Western religions.[43] Even though it is best not to think in terms of one single mystical phenomenon, it is undeniable that in virtually all religions there are mystics who witness to experiences that resemble each other a great deal. The essence of the mystical experience is that the person participates in an unmediated link with something absolute. Usually this means some sort of union with the divine. More specifically, here are some typical instances of mysticism:

- the Sufi in Islam who experiences the closeness of Allah
- the kabbalist in Judaism who sees God on his throne in an experience entitled *devekuth*

---

[42]John Warwick Montgomery, *Christianity and History* (Downers Grove, Ill.: InterVarsity Press, 1964).

[43]See my *Mysticism: An Evangelical Option?* (Grand Rapids, Mich.: Zondervan, 1991).

- the Vedantic Hindu who realizes the total absorption of his *atman* in Brahman
- the Bhakti Hindu who has direct vision *(darshan)* of his deity
- the Buddhist who comes to the awareness resulting in nirvana
- the Daoist who has yielded all to the Dao

The list could go on indefinitely. Furthermore, for such a list to be truly meaningful beyond just some general pointers, one would have to start to become much more specific and make note not only of the resemblances in general but of the many significant differences. I shall not do so since I am not compiling a description of mystical traditions but merely giving some minimal examples of mysticism. Nevertheless, here is the important point. Even in as brief a list as the one above, there are clear differences in the meaning of the experiences in their home contexts. More to the point, once again the East/West distinction applies. In the Eastern examples, mystical experience is closely tied to the Eastern paths of redemption, whereas in the Western ones, the experience should only be seen as *enhancing* the total spiritual picture. As in Islam or Judaism there is not a clear-cut notion of a redemptive experience, so the mystical experience cannot fulfill a redemptive function either, though it could definitely add to the spiritual qualities of an individual, which may eventually result in the person's attainment of heaven. In the East, however, where redemption centers on the soul in various cosmic settings *(samsara, sunyata,* etc.), the mystical experience is frequently the key to the consummation of the soul's release.

Clearly there is no shortage of Christian mystics of many different descriptions. Many of the great Christian thinkers have been mystics. Augustine had a quick glimpse of God's unchanging nature; St. John of the Cross experienced the marriage of the soul to Jesus; even Martin Luther issued an edition of the mystical *Theologia Germanica*.[44] Many of the best writings on the mystical side of Christianity have been done by women, such as Teresa of Ávila and Margaret Porette.[45] And one cannot deny that the descriptions Christian mystics give of their experiences often appear very similar to those given by mystics in other religious contexts. A number of writers have seen this similarity as evidence for a "perennial philos-

---

[44]See my chapter "Mysticism in Christendom," in *Mysticism: An Evangelical Option?* pp. 97-115. Also, my "A Hair's Breadth from Pantheism: Meister Eckhart's God-Centered Spirituality," *Journal of the Evangelical Theological Society* 37 (1994): 263-74.
[45]See my article, "The Gospel According to Margaret," *Journal of the Evangelical Theological Society* 35 (1992): 515-30.

ophy" in the sense that Christians and non-Christians alike link up with the same ultimate reality, which they approach through their mystical experiences.[46]

Let me make the following summary statements concerning mystical experience in the Christian context.

1. If one takes the actual testimony of Christian mystics seriously, there is no good reason to infer that they did, in fact, encounter the same reality as non-Christian ones. The following are some subordinate points under this premise: (a) Writers on mysticism like to speak of the unanimity of mystical experience, but this unanimity is an artificial invention of secondary writers. A good example of how their analysis works is found in W. T. Stace's well-known book on mysticism. Stace wishes eventually to make an argument from the unanimity of mystical experience, and so, in order to bring about his goal, he first of all divides up types of mysticism, those that are "typical" and thus a part of the mystical core and those that are not. When he refers to the unanimity of mystics, he then restricts himself to the core that he had previously created.[47] But if he took all of mystical experience into account equally, he could not establish such a core. (b) Mystics do not encounter Reality, but they encounter Jesus, Allah, Brahman, etc. It takes a conceptual tour de force to inform the mystics within a particular tradition that, even though they may think that they encountered Jesus or Shiva or Allah, they really encountered Reality. (c) Given the actual diversity of claims by mystics, and given the fact that mystical experiences can also be created by artificial means, such as electronic stimulation of the brain or ingestion of drugs, there is no warrant to infer from the mere testimony of mystics that there is an actual spiritual reality that they encountered. On this basis, one cannot rule out that there might be a reality to which, say, a Hindu mystic joins himself, but one cannot infer it either. Adjudication of truth claims needs to be done on some other basis than simply the report of an experience.

2. Insofar as there are mystical experiences in Christianity, one must be very careful not to ascribe too much significance to them. For one thing, there is, biblically speaking, no good reason to believe that a mystical experience must either accompany or be the result of saving faith. Mystical experience is not a part of the Christian theology of redemption. Nor is it

---

[46]Perhaps most notably, at least in terms of popularity, Aldous Huxley, *The Perennial Philosophy* (Cleveland, Ohio: World, 1962).

[47]W. T. Stace, *Mysticism and Philosophy* (New York: Tarcher, 1960), p. 46.

a particularly important aspect of the Christian life; if it were, surely the New Testament would have encouraged Christians to seek such an experience, but, other than reporting on a few occasions where such an experience may have occurred,[48] it does not occupy itself with the topic. And, of course, anything that is intrinsically opposed to New Testament Christianity, such as pantheism or private revelations, cannot possibly be accommodated.

3. Nevertheless, in a modest sense, there is room for a fairly trimmed-down version of mysticism in New Testament–based Christianity. When one considers particularly the indwelling of the believer by God, the Holy Spirit, one comprehends a genuine direct link that the believer has with God. However, it is a mystical *reality* that is given to everyone who believes in Christ, and a mystical experience is not necessary to bring it about. On this basis, Christians are empowered by God to live a supernatural life—even if they are not aware of this fact!

Cosmic Redemption. One other category needs to be added to this discussion on redemption. So far, I have focused almost entirely on the redemption of individual human beings, regardless of which religion I have considered. And this is the right thing to do since this is the priority of the religions themselves. However, the religion that seems on the whole to have the least preoccupation with individual salvation leads in another direction. I said above that, even though it does not have a doctrine of original sin, Judaism does frequently stress the fallen nature of the present world order. This brings me to this last topic: the cosmos, too, stands in need of redemption.

This observation may sound at first contradictory to what I have said earlier, namely, that in Christianity what is in need of redemption is the individual fallen human being but that God created a universe that is good in its own right and that for Christianity the need for redemption is not the need to be released from present reality, as it is in Eastern religions. Of course, these statements are true; in Christianity, redemption is not the liberation of the human soul out of a negative set of circumstances. However, in Christian theology, the direction arrow continues the other way. The human fall has negatively influenced the cosmos (Gen 3:17-18), and the cosmos is in need of redemption because of the state brought about by rebellious creatures. So we read in Romans 8:19-22 of the universe groan-

---

[48]Specifically, Paul's experience, as he alludes to it in 2 Corinthians 12:2-4.

ing, waiting for its redemption to occur. When God finally brings things to a close, he will create a new heaven and a new earth. Thus, there is a cosmic dimension to the issue of salvation in Christianity after all.

And, in looking at how this issue compares with other religions, one again must take note of the East-West split. There is a clear consummation of history in the Western religions: the kingdom of God in Judaism, heaven and hell in Islam, and, most dramatically, the cataclysmic reclamation of the universe in Zoroastrianism. But the Eastern traditions do not know of such an end. Even though in the temporal cycles of the Eastern religions there may be periods of destruction of the cosmos, followed by re-creation, there is no end in sight for this process. The cosmos may be renewed, but it is never finally redeemed.

In this chapter, I stressed particularly the uniqueness of the Christian doctrine of redemption. Even though there are similarities on certain points in both the Eastern and Western traditions, Christianity, with its emphasis on mediation by God in the historical atonement, presents a unique soteriology. Apparent crossovers in mysticism or the idea of cosmic redemption do not detract from this conclusion either. Now I can turn to the all-important question of whether, then, faith in the atoning Christ is necessary for a person's salvation or whether someone who remains in an explicitly non-Christian belief system can receive the benefits of Christ's atonement as well.

6

THE GRACE AND
REDEMPTION DEBATE

In the previous chapter I made the case that salvation in other religions is drastically different in both purpose and content from Christianity. For example, release from the karmic cycle of reincarnation can hardly be equated with reconciliation with God based on Christ's atoning death. To put it another way, the goal of salvation in Christianity cannot be achieved by the means provided by other religions because salvation in those religions is such a different thing altogether.[1] Even if I had the proper technique for dissolving myself into Brahman, how could that achievement result in my being reconciled to a personal God and spending eternity with him?

But recognizing that salvation cannot come *through* other religions is not the same thing as saying that salvation cannot come *despite* or perhaps *alongside* other religions. A Buddhist may not be saved in Christian terms on account of his Buddhist beliefs and practices, but is it not possible for the Buddhist to be saved regardless of his current beliefs and practices? Is salvation in Christ limited to those who consciously

---

[1]Clark H. Pinnock has tried to demonstrate parallels to Christianity in several other religions, but as I have shown, those claims cannot be substantiated. See his article "Toward an Evangelical Theology of Religions," *Journal of the Evangelical Theological Society* 33 (1990): 359-68, and his book *A Wideness in God's Mercy: The Finality of Jesus Christ in a World of Religions* (Eugene, Ore.: Wipf & Stock, 1992), pp. 100-101. See my critical comments in "Buddha, Shiva, and Muhammad: Theistic Faith in Other Religions?" in *Who Will Be Saved? Defending the Biblical Understanding of God*, ed. Paul House and Greg Thornbury (Wheaton, Ill.: Crossway, 2000), pp. 129-43.

acknowledge him as Savior, or can it be extended to those who have no explicit faith in Christ?

This issue can be formulated in a number of different ways if one wishes to become more precise, and undoubtedly the way in which one phrases the question will be based to a large extent on how one intends to answer it. Here are some possibilities:

- Epistemologically: Is Christianity alone true?
- Metaphysically: Do the effects of Christ's atonement extend only to those who are believers in him?
- Ethically: Is a human being required to express faith in Christ in order to be eligible for salvation?
- Subjectively: Is it possible to have faith in Christ without consciously knowing it, and if so, is this kind of implicit faith in Christ that expresses itself in actions but not in words as valid as an explicitly stated faith?
- Theologically with reference to God himself: Does God's saving love extend to those who do not know of Christ?
- Socially: Are those who have never heard of the gospel without hope of salvation?

As one can see when looking at all these questions lined up in this way, there are both points of overlap and points of difference. The overlap in each case obviously has to do, to a large extent, with the fundamental question of the fate of the non-Christian. However, there are also clear differences. The question on the extent of the atonement does not necessarily make assumptions about the necessity of any faith at all while the question on implicit faith clearly does so. The question that targets human requirements for salvation seems to take a very different line from the question on God's love. The last question, on the truth of Christianity versus other religions, goes in a radically different direction. After all, who is to say that knowing truth is necessarily relevant to being redeemed?

Over the last twenty years, many books have been written within evangelical Christianity on this topic. Undoubtedly, the writers of these books have been motivated by the increasingly pluralistic nature of our society and the need for evangelical Christians, along with almost everyone else, to think about members of other religions in terms other than the time-honored foreign-missions paradigm. The resulting meditations reveal authors with strong opinions running in both directions: those who see a greater openness toward salvation among non-Christians and those who believe that only those who actually confess Christ are saved.[2]

In what follows, I would like to address the issues with the intent of leading up to a particular position. I will allude to some of the conclusions of previous chapters without necessarily arguing for them all over again, and I shall make use of other sources, both positively and negatively, in the course of the discussion, but I shall attempt not to fall into the pattern of producing essentially a literature review.[3]

SOME BASIC CATEGORIES AND THEIR EXAMPLES

Before proceeding any further, it is necessary to establish the basic categories among Christian thinkers who address this issue. There are three terms and their synonyms that have come into common use. Even though at first glance these three positions seem to be fairly straightforward, there are variations within them, and the boundaries between them are not necessarily distinct.

- Exclusivist: Also called restrictivist and particularist,[4] this position holds that salvation comes only to those who hold explicit faith in Jesus Christ.
- Pluralist: In this view, all ways are equally legitimate roads to salvation.
- Inclusivist: This understanding begins with one particular form of salvation, as held in a specific religion, as paradigmatic but then maintains that all other forms of salvation are really just part of the paradigmatic one.

I would like to explore some examples of these points of view. Again, I would like to stress that this will not be a review of all the relevant literature but simply a look at some typical examples by way of illustration. After some relatively straightforward examples, I will be able to focus on some more complex ones.

Exclusivism: Ronald Nash. A good example of an exclusivist is Ronald Nash. In fact, Nash is so convinced that exclusivism is the correct biblical

---

[2]See, for example, the "select" twelve-page bibliography in Daniel B. Clendenin, *Many Gods, Many Lords: Christianity Encounters World Religions* (Grand Rapids, Mich.: Baker, 1995), pp. 159-71.

[3]Daniel B. Clendenin provides an excellent bibliography as well as solid analysis in *Many Gods, Many Lords*.

[4]At one point, Pinnock lets down his guard and refers to the exclusivist position as "narrow-minded" (*Wideness in God's Mercy*, p. 186, n. 12).

position that he feels that simply refuting competing views is virtually all one needs to do; the exclusivist view will then stand on its own as the most natural model for the teaching of Scripture.[5] With regard to verses like John 14:6, Acts 4:12 and Romans 10:9, he avers:

> I know no one who denies that evangelicals commonly understand verses like these to teach that since the death and resurrection of Jesus, explicit personal faith in Jesus is a necessary condition for salvation.[6]

No personal faith in Jesus—no salvation. Obviously, what I am summarizing here, Nash develops not in isolation but in dependence on other scriptural teachings.[7] Nevertheless, there is no hedging in the position that Nash advocates.

Pluralism: John Hick. The position that there are many legitimate ways of salvation can be construed a number of different ways as well. One would be to take a purely psychological approach. If one believes that religion is only a subjective phenomenon and that people pursue religion only for the sake of psychological fulfillment, then, of course, it is easy (though not necessary!) to argue that one religion is as good as any other. In fact, holding to no religion may be just as useful as being religious, depending on how one's psychological needs are being met. Another way of construing pluralism is by allowing that there are fundamental realities to which all religions relate themselves. This latter tack is the one taken by John Hick.

Hick's position is very widely discussed.[8] Here is a summary of his argument:

1. Hick concerns himself primarily with those religions that began roughly in the sixth century B.C., frequently called the "axial age." These religions (Judaism, Hinduism, Buddhism, Jainism and Daoism, along with their many subsequent offshoots) have as their goal for human beings to relate correctly to an ultimate reality ("the Real") and thereby have their lives transformed. People will move from "self-centeredness" to "reality-centeredness." For example, they will become more virtuous.

---

[5]Ronald H. Nash, "Restrictivism," in *What About Those Who Have Never Heard?* ed. John Sanders (Downers Grove, Ill.: InterVarsity Press, 1995), pp. 107-10.
[6]Ibid., p. 108.
[7]Ronald H. Nash, *Is Jesus the Only Savior?* (Grand Rapids, Mich.: Zondervan, 1994).
[8]For example, there is a collection of articles pro and con prefaced with an article by Hick himself in the very useful volume *The Philosophical Challenge of Religious Diversity*, ed. Philip L. Quinn and Kevin Meeker (New York: Oxford University Press, 2000), pp. 54-192.

2. Despite certain differences between the ways in which religions go about their business of transforming people, it would seem that, empirically speaking, no religion holds an edge in how well it does its job. The degree to which any given religion succeeds in having its adherents transformed seems to be about the same around the globe.

3. On the pragmatic evidence, then, all religions do about an equal job, and so it stands to reason that they are equal ways of leading their followers into a relation to the Real.

4. Clearly, when one looks at the actual content beliefs of these religions, one sees many doctrines that are inconsistent with each other. Thus, it would appear that they cannot all be true.

5. However, as divergent as these religions may be, they all share this much: they claim that their ultimate Reality—God, Brahman, nirvana, Dao, etc.—is actually beyond human words and concepts. Consequently, one can say that all these religions have a common basis in their affirmation of the Real, this ultimate, absolute actuality that lies behind all of them and legitimizes all of them.

6. Therefore, all (post–axial-age) religions are equally legitimate ways of relating to the Real.

Thus Hick attempts to provide a way of letting each religion be true, not finally because of its uniqueness but because it, like all other religions, has its own way of relating to the Real. Virtually all comers seem to be welcome, whether their view of God is personal or impersonal, whether they are redemptive or mystical, or whether they understand themselves in this way or not. The only exceptions are traditional religions that are based strictly in an immanent plane and do not direct their adherents to a transcendent Real and those that claim exclusive truth for themselves. These latter are not false in their claims to providing salvation, but they are not truly exclusive, even though they may see themselves that way. In other words, Hick deals with the thorny question of how an exclusive religion can be one of several legitimate ways to God by insisting that they are wrong in their avowal of exclusivity.[9]

---

[9]"Each major tradition . . . has developed its own answers to the perennial questions of our origin and destiny, constituting more or less comprehensive and coherent cosmologies and eschatologies. These are human creations which have, by their association with living streams of religious experience, become invested with a sacred authority. However they cannot all be wholly true; quite possibly none is wholly true; perhaps all are partly true. . . . Insofar, then, as we accept that salvation is not confined to Christianity, we must reject the old exclusivist dogma" (John Hick, "Religious Pluralism," pp. 63-64).

Inclusivism: Karl Rahner. If one does not wish to be an exclusivist, it is probably easier to be an inclusivist than a pluralist since it is easier to supply a model for inclusivism than for pluralism. Has not John Hick actually resorted to inclusivism by making all religions conform to his scheme (which, by the way, is really the pattern of a theosophical mysticism, very much akin to Vedantic Hinduism)? The inclusivist typically begins with a design of salvation, namely, that of his own religion, and then applies it to all other religions.

A very famous such attempt is given by the twentieth-century Jesuit theologian, Karl Rahner, with his doctrine of the "anonymous Christian."[10] According to Rahner, most of the people of the world have an implicit faith in God, which is sufficient for their salvation. It is important for understanding Rahner to recognize that he does not present a simple deductive chain in which he infers from the universal love of God to a universal saving will and from there to the idea that, therefore, God will make sure that all people will be saved, whether they want to be or not. Instead, he works out a highly complex scheme by which any human being, in the process of coming to know anything or making any moral decision, makes implicit reference to God.

For example, when I come to know an object, that object is represented by an image in my mind. In order to recognize the nature and reality of this object, my mind must form certain judgments concerning this object as represented by the image, most fundamentally that it exists. But I cannot infer that the object exists unless my mind reaches out to being itself as the ground for the existence of anything. But being itself is none other than God. Thus, by coming to know an object, I am implicitly expressing my very dependence on God.

A similar thing is true for making moral decisions for Rahner. If I judge an action to be wrong or right, I am implicitly saying by my decision that it is meaningful because there is an ultimate frame of reference. This frame of reference brings with it a sense of hope based on the idea that such decisions carry an ultimate worth, which can only be derived from God. Again, in making the moral judgment, none of those ideas may consciously occur to me, but I am implicitly affirming them in the process.

Thus, both in knowing and deciding, my human nature makes an implicit reference to God. Rahner believes that this process can only be

---

[10]Karl Rahner, *Schriften zur Theologie,* 16 vols. (Einsiedeln: Denziger, 1965), 5:183-221.

explained on the basis of divine grace. Consequently, two of the most fundamental things that I do as a human being—knowing and deciding—are already grounded in God's grace. And, even though I may have no idea of this, whenever I authentically exercise my human faculties, I am in a relationship with divine grace.

Furthermore, according to Rahner, God in Christ has assumed not just *a* human nature, but human nature in general, and thus any human being potentially participates in God's grace as disclosed in Christ. As a result, almost all of humanity, those who profess a religion as well as atheists, so long as they do not deny their true humanity, are anonymous Christians. Only those who directly pervert human nature are excluded from salvation.

This line of thought is behind the pronouncements of the Second Vatican Council in the document on the church, entitled *Lumen Gentium*.[11] Here we learn that virtually all people, from Protestant Christians and Eastern Orthodox through Jews, Muslims and idolaters, even sincere atheists, are partakers of God's grace and thus in some unexplained way related to the church. For the purposes of this discussion, it is important to realize that this development in Roman Catholic theology in the twentieth century was based not on a lame inference of what a loving God must be expected to do since he is good but on metaphysical reasoning, as developed by Rahner and others.[12]

The preceding are examples of the three main positions: exclusivism, pluralism and inclusivism. Of course there are seemingly infinite variations possible. Describing all of them would require this entire chapter, even the whole book. So, I will continue to refer to them for illustrative purposes only, and let other works take care of the extensive literature review. I can now proceed to answer the questions raised earlier, beginning with the question of truth.

IS CHRISTIANITY ALONE TRUE?

Of course, there is truth in other religions. Why shouldn't there be?

---

[11]*Dogmatic Constitution on the Church (Lumen Gentium)*, in *The Documents of Vatican II*, ed. Walter M. Abbott (New York: Guild, 1966), pp. 32-35.

[12]Consequently, evangelicals who wish to subscribe to Vatican II's conclusions without buying into the reasons why the council said what it did are in a sense holding goods to which they are not entitled. An exceptional analysis of the epistemological issues underlying Roman Catholic inclusive thought is provided by Ronald McCamy, *Out of a Kantian Chrysalis: A Maritainian Critique of Fr. Maréchal* (New York: Peter Lang, 1998).

Many non-Christian religions contain propositions that strike me as true, ranging from the trivial ("There is a material world"; "It is wrong to lie") to the profound ("True devotion to God should not be based on expected rewards"). When we ask whether a religion is true or not, we are not asking simply whether it contains truth—chances are that it does in some way—but whether the religion as a whole is true. The question, in order to be meaningful, must direct itself to the entire complex of beliefs and practices—and their justifications—that make up the religion. Needless to say, there is nothing trivial about this question and its answer.

Heretofore in this book, I have not shied away from the issue of truth, for example, in the discussions on original monotheism, general revelation and Scriptures. But at this point I need to address the more fundamental issue of truth in general. What is involved in a religion making truth claims about itself? How do these claims square with the truth claims made by other religions? I am going to try to answer this question through the back door: by looking first at the arguments of two writers who deny the unique truth of Christianity.

As was noted above, pluralists would say that all truth claims (at least of religions in a certain class) are equally adequate. For example, Hick allows that all religions[13] put their adherents in touch with the Real, thus making them all true in this ultimate sense but false in terms of their specifics. Hick's pluralism is an aggressive one. For the Christian making exclusive truth claims, Hick has only unkind words.

> Insofar, then, as we accept that salvation is not confined to Christianity we must reject the old exclusivist dogma. This has in fact now been done by most thinking Christians, though exceptions remain, mostly within the extreme Protestant fundamentalist constituencies.[14]

In other words, in the light of Hick's insights, exclusivist Christians need to revise their theologies. And the same thing is true for anyone in another religion wishing to make a similar claim. Exclusivist claims fall before the sickle of Hick's scheme.

---

[13]I have pointed out above that Hick's range of acceptable religions is limited to the ones derived from the axial age and have qualified my statements several times along that line. From here on out, I shall not continue pedantically to issue this qualification each time but shall assume that the reader is aware of it by now.

[14]Hick, "Religious Pluralism," p. 64.

Many criticisms have been leveled at Hick's aggressive pluralism.[15] From the standpoint of an analysis of truth, it is either false or arbitrary. The simple reality (of which Hick is certainly not unaware) is that most religions do not teach that theirs is simply one way among many other equally valid ones. And no religion teaches in the manner of Hick's theory that theirs is merely one of many valid avenues to be transformed by the Real.[16] As a matter of fact, there are good grounds to challenge Hick's notion that only a few recalcitrant extremists, who hopefully will soon be brought in line, see their religion as exclusively true. I believe that, quite to the contrary, most religions, because they see themselves as addressing the ultimate of all questions, do make exclusive claims to the effect that they occupy a unique position of having genuine truth. From their vantage point, even if there may be some religions that have some truth, possibly even enough to attain salvation, they do not have the real truth, as espoused in one's own religion. A simple survey of religious literature and practice would confirm this assessment.

Nevertheless, even though Hick skews the data somewhat to support his conclusion, this really is not news to him. He recognizes both that specific religions see themselves as ultimate and that their claims are incompatible with each other. So, how can he advocate his scheme according to which, in the final analysis, they are all simply different legitimate ways to the same goal of the Real? Sumner B. Twiss[17] makes the point for him: One must recognize that there are two different orders of interpretation. On the first level, one simply describes religions as they are; here there can be no question of finding Hick's scheme exemplified, and Hick does not claim that it does. But there is a second, higher level, that of providing an overarching explanatory theory. And, since a higher-order explanation by definition is a general theory rather than just a summary, the fact that it is not found in the religions themselves constitutes no problem.

---

[15]For example, Ninian Smart, "A Contemplation of Absolutes," in *The Philosophical Challenge of Religious Diversity*, ed. Philip L. Quinn and Kevin Meeker (New York: Oxford University Press, 2000), pp. 99-108; Paul R. Eddy, "Religious Pluralism and the Divine: Another Look at John Hick's Neo-Kantian Proposal," in *The Philosophical Challenge of Religious Diversity*, ed. Philip L. Quinn and Kevin Meeker (New York: Oxford University Press, 2000), pp. 126-38.

[16]Certainly there are inclusively oriented religions, particularly Baha'i and certain schools of monistic Hinduism, but even there the more detailed sets of beliefs differ significantly from Hick's description. Hick's theory resembles Vedantic Hinduism in principle but not in details.

[17]Sumner B. Twiss, "The Philosophy of Religious Pluralism: A Critical Appraisal of Hick and His Critics," in *The Philosophical Challenge of Religious Diversity*, ed. Philip L. Quinn and Kevin Meeker (New York: Oxford University Press, 2000), pp. 67-98.

It seems, however, that Twiss makes things a little too easy for Hick. In order to be meaningful, an explanatory theory must draw its life from the data it is meant to explain. If the data do not support the theory, one cannot simply claim immunity from the data for the theory on the basis that it presumably occupies a higher position in the cognitive order. Such a theory would be nothing more than an arbitrary invention. In other words, if Hick's theory is based on the facts within religions, it is wrong; if it is not so based, it is arbitrary.

In the second century Irenaeus made a similar point with regard to an unnamed gnostic teacher and his system of mystical emanations. This teacher claimed that transcending all things was a primary Tetrad, which he called Monotes, Henotes, Monas and Hen. Irenaeus responded by saying that this was all arbitrary; he proposed his own Tetrad of Gourd, Utter-Emptiness, Cucumber and Melon. These, in turn, gave rise to the

> remaining multitude of the delirious melons of Valentinus. For if it is fitting that that language which is used respecting the universe be transformed to the primary Tetrad, and if any one may assign names at his pleasure, who shall prevent us from adopting these names as being much more credible, as well as in general use, and understood by all?[18]

The same question can go to Hick. If our description of the Real is not tied in to first-level descriptions of the Real, why is the Real better than Gourd? And Gourd would have the advantage of at least making quite clear what we are talking about.

Furthermore, counting against the separation between the first-order descriptions and the second-order explanatory theory is that Hick, in the case of Christianity at least, has for a long time argued for the accommodation of Christian theology to his scheme. That is to say, he requests that Christianity ought to rewrite itself in order to eliminate those beliefs that stand in the way of the Real hypothesis. For example, he proposes that Christians should abandon the doctrine of the incarnation.[19] Twiss ingenuously writes this inconsistency off to the fact that Hick happens to pursue two separate careers, one in philosophy and one in Christian theology, and that one must keep the conclusions that he reaches in each of these careers

---

[18]Irenaeus *Against Heresies* 11.4, in *The Ante-Nicene Fathers: Translations of the Writings of the Fathers down to A.D. 325*, ed. Alexander Roberts and James Donaldson (Grand Rapids, Mich.: Eerdmans, 1979), 1:332-33.

[19]John Hick, ed., *The Myth of God Incarnate* (Philadelphia: Westminster, 1977).

separate from each other.[20] But surely this is straining one's credulity beyond the permissible, especially since Hick himself closes an essay advocating his pluralism with a gentle call on Christians to rethink how they can accommodate their belief systems.[21] Again, Hick cannot separate and not-separate phenomenal religion from his Real hypothesis at the same time.

Now, the point is this. There is no legitimate way of dealing with the question of the truth of a religion other than to take it at its face value. As soon as one does what Hick attempts to do, namely, to discuss the truth of a religion in terms of some higher-order conceptual scheme, one either does violence to the religion or one trivializes it. Thus, if the New Testament teaches that Christianity alone is true, we can accept that claim or reject it, but we cannot legitimately modify its own teachings in order for it to come out as one of many other true religions.

Whereas Hick's is an aggressive and reductionistic pluralism, William P. Alston has advocated what I wish to call a bashful pluralism.[22] His argument, in brief, runs like this:

1. Christians who are basing their beliefs on their mystical experience of God are justified in holding those beliefs.
2. Similarly, adherents of a different religion basing their beliefs on their experience within their religion are also justified in holding those beliefs.
3. Even though there is no way of adjudicating between the different belief systems since they are each coherent and productive, Christians are entitled to maintain the truth of their beliefs.
4. However, as things stand, persons of another religion are also entitled to the truth of their beliefs since their system is coherent and productive as well.

I call this a bashful pluralism because it hides behind the skirts of an apparent exclusivism. After all, the argument does give Christians the right to hold their own views with all the commitment they feel necessary. Thus, Alston's argument seems to look very similar to, say, Plan-

---

[20]"But this is an illusion fostered by Hick's dual career" (Twiss, "Philosophy of Religious Pluralism," p. 77).

[21]Hick, "Religious Pluralism," p. 65.

[22]William P. Alston, *Perceiving God: The Epistemology of Religious Experience* (Ithaca, N.Y.: Cornell University Press, 1991), pp. 255-85; and "Religious Diversity and Perceptual Knowledge of God," in *The Philosophical Challenge of Religious Diversity*, ed. Philip L. Quinn and Kevin Meeker (New York: Oxford University Press, 2000), pp. 193-207.

tinga's, who also makes a case for the idea that Christians are within their epistemological rights to claim the exclusive truth that comes with their system (but who allows the exclusive claim to stand),[23] in which case, by simple logic non-Christian religions that contradict Christianity must be false. But Alston is not willing to take that final step in his philosophical analysis; he allows that other practitioners are also entitled to their truth claims on the same basis as Christian ones.[24] Thus Alston, holding firmly to the truth of Christianity, will also leave room for the hypothetical truth of other belief systems by the lights of his analysis.[25]

Responses to Alston have focused on the idea that religious diversity does, too, count against the unique truth claims of any one religion.[26] However, what interests me is the very narrow base from which Alston operates, namely, that he limits himself to truth derived from mystical experience. He does make mention of other ways of confirming Christian truth, such as historical arguments, but makes little use of them, based on the summative judgment that they are inconclusive.[27] However, this strikes me as a serious problem since many writers who traditionally advocate the objective unique truth of Christianity tend to stress theistic proofs and historic evidences and minimize experiential

---

[23]Alvin Plantinga, "Pluralism: A Defense of Religious Exclusivism," in *The Philosophical Challenge of Religious Diversity*, ed. Philip L. Quinn and Kevin Meeker (New York: Oxford University Press, 2000), pp. 172-92.

[24]Alston, "Religious Diversity," p. 204.

[25]As numerous commentators have recognized, Alston is somewhat ambivalent on this point. Since he is a philosopher who has contributed widely to the greater acceptance of Christianity in the philosophical world and has not been ashamed to let his philosophy be recognizably Christian, I want to emphasize that Alston leaves us here with an unfilled epistemological hole and not an attempt to short-sheet Christian beliefs in the way in which Hick does. Nevertheless, the hole *is* significant.

[26]Such as these articles: J. L. Schellenberg, "Religious Experience and Religious Diversity: A Reply to Alston," in *The Philosophical Challenge of Religious Diversity*, ed. Philip L. Quinn and Kevin Meeker (New York: Oxford University Press, 2000), pp. 208-17; and William J. Wainwright, "Religious Experience and Religious Pluralism," in *The Philosophical Challenge of Religious Diversity*, ed. Philip L. Quinn and Kevin Meeker (New York: Oxford University Press, 2000), pp. 218-25. Philip Quinn, on the other hand, has seriously proposed for both Hick's and Alston's schemes that, since the present known facts of the world's religions cannot accommodate their theoretical schemes, perhaps the great religions of the world ought to change their teachings in order to bring them in line with Hick's and Alston's theories ("Toward Thinner Theologies: Hick and Alston on Religious Diversity," in *The Philosophical Challenge of Religious Diversity*, ed. Philip L. Quinn and Kevin Meeker [New York: Oxford University Press, 2000], pp. 234, 242). And exclusivists are being accused of being arrogant!

[27]Alston, *Perceiving God*, pp. 286-307.

grounds.[28] In a way, it is surprising that Alston was able to go as far as he did toward almost-exclusivism with his argument, given that he limited himself to mystical experience.

To the contrary, a sound argument can be made for the unique truth of Christianity based on rational grounds; there are many books on Christian apologetics that attempt to do just that.[29] The crucial point is that Alston has locked himself unnecessarily to a subjective framework from which he cannot escape, but could if he opened himself further to objective arguments for the truth of Christianity, which would then dispel the bashful pluralism that lurks in his writings.[30] Alston's dilemma is entirely of his own making.

So, what is involved in accepting a religion as true? Two things come into play: First, simply accepting the beliefs of the religion as being true. This means, in time-honored terms, to accept the fact that such beliefs conform to reality, that is to say, that there is a god or a spirit, that the required rituals will achieve their purpose, that one's soul will experience redemption and so forth. Religious persons not only see the world in a particular way; they understand how the world would be factually different if the world were not that way. Prayers would not be answered, life would not be orderly, and one's actions would not be rewarded or punished, to name a few examples. Contrary to the claims of twentieth-century positivism, religious believers do see themselves as making truth assertions concerning reality.

The second component in accepting a religion as true is the justification of the belief system. This means being able to give a reason why one thinks that one's religion does, in fact, conform to reality. Now, one is not required to carry out this task in order to legitimately claim the truth of one's beliefs. Nevertheless, as part of a quick analysis of the truth of a religion, this is an important ingredient. Believers may wish to show why they accept their beliefs as true.[31]

---

[28]So, for example, in *Philosophy of Religion*, 2nd ed. (Grand Rapids, Mich.: Baker, 1988), pp. 62-76, Norman Geisler and I set forth an argument based on religious experience. However, it does not get any further than the reality of a Transcendent—a long way from the specificity of Christian theism.

[29]For example, my own *No Doubt About It* (Nashville: Broadman & Holman, 1997).

[30]It is interesting to note here that Alvin Plantinga would not even count Christians as exclusivists if they believed (rightly or wrongly) that they had objective and compelling proof for the truth of Christianity (Plantinga, "Pluralism," p. 176). Thus, I might not even be advocating an exclusivism here.

[31]I am painfully aware that I am short-circuiting incredible mounds of debate in this summary. See, for example, Alvin Plantinga, *Warranted Christian Belief* (New York: Oxford University Press, 2000). Nevertheless, it would take a separate book to spell out and resolve all of the issues on which I am touching here.

How do you show that your religion is true? The possibilities (both rational and irrational) are probably endless. For many people, their religion is self-evidently true; others may point to a specific experience, while yet others could refer to a particular teaching in their religion that they consider to be superior to all others (sometimes when they do not even know what the others are). Surely, it is fallacious to think that one can dictate to people on what grounds they can personally accept their religion as true. In fact, intuitively one may expect that a person's reasons for accepting the beliefs of, say, Baha'i, will be different from the reasons a person gives for accepting Hindu mysticism. Nonetheless, accepting a religion as true involves (for those who care to do so) giving reasons why one accepts its beliefs as true.

All of which is to say that Christians not only accept Christian beliefs as true but can also, if they so wish, avail themselves of a number of reasons for *why* they are true. The pluralist's case is at its strongest if there are no reasons to accept a religion as true, or if the reasons for one religion are no better than the reasons for another. But this is not the case. Christians can find confirmation for their beliefs in

- general revelation and the natural theology toward which it leads: rudimentary ideas of the existence and nature of God (as described in chapter two)
- the fundamental rationality of Christian beliefs (what Plantinga calls "warrant" based on the "proper function" of the intellect)
- the historical evidences for biblical history, such as confirmations from the field of archaeology
- the inner witness of the Holy Spirit
- particular special experiences in which God may have manifested himself

Undoubtedly one can add more items to this list.

It comes down to this. Christians accept the system of Christian beliefs as true. They do so for what the beliefs themselves teach, not because of some second-order metaphysical scheme. Second, Christians have adequate grounds to accept that the beliefs do, in fact, correspond to reality.

But it is a short step from the truth of Christianity to the unique truth of Christianity. Assuming that genuine Christianity is Christianity based on the New Testament, then either Christianity is false or it is exclusively true. Jesus said, "I am the way. . . . No one comes to the Father except through me" (Jn 14:6). Peter proclaimed "there is no other name under heaven . . . by which we must be saved" (Acts 4:12), and Paul referred to the "one mediator between God and men, the man Christ Jesus" (1 Tim 2:5). If these statements are true, then neither Hick's metaphysical tour de force nor Alston's epistemological humility can prevent the Christian from claiming that Christianity is uniquely true.[32]

In sum, by way of confronting the aggressive pluralism of John Hick and the bashful pluralism of William Alston, it is rational to believe that Christianity is uniquely true. But this is only the beginning of the inquiry. Many more questions are waiting to be answered.

ESTABLISHING GROUNDS FOR ANSWERS

Most of the next issues for this chapter will be questions from the inside of Christianity. That is to say, they address matters that only make sense given the truth of Christianity; for example, questions concerning the love of God have relevance only if there is a God and if the frame of reference, Christian theology, has been granted. This is not to say that many people do not operate in the other direction: first they decide on what kind of a God is worthy of recognition and worship; then they allow only beliefs to count as true if they fit in with their preconceived notion of God. But you cannot get to Christian theology in this manner. For a statement to count as true in Christian theology, it must have been established either through natural revelation or through Scripture, and our picture of God or other matters must ultimately bow to whatever has been granted us to know in this manner, regardless of whether we like the outcome.

As easy as it is to write the above sentence, it is not so easy to abide by it, partially because one's own inclination may lead one to do theology by personal preference and partially because that is frequently the way in which the issue is phrased. A number of years ago I adopted the strategy in the classroom of never responding to my students' question of what happens to a person who has never heard the gospel of Christ unless they first give me the right answer to the question, "On what basis can we come up with an acceptable answer to this question?"

The simple answer to my question is, of course, "on the basis of what the Bible teaches," but even Christian students frequently respond with some incoherent ramblings about God's love, justice and fairness. "Dr.

---

[32]I will leave it to one side here whether such claims are arrogant and refer the reader to Plantinga's more than ample refutation of this charge: "Pluralism," pp. 172-92.

Corduan, don't you think that a good and loving God would never condemn someone to hell who never had a chance to hear the gospel?" The
temptation immediately to respond "yes" or "no" to this question is great,
but in doing so I would be shortchanging the nature of the correct
answer—as well as harming greatly the theological education of my students. This question ought never to be answered purely on the basis of
some theoretical understanding of the divine attributes, not even if we
(correctly) throw God's justice and holiness into the mix along with his
love and mercy. This question should only be answered first of all by taking it out of the realm of opinions on how loving we perceive God to be.
The only legitimate response is along the line of "Well, let's see what Scripture teaches on this topic." Of course, that makes coming to a conclusion a
lot harder and—let's face it—a whole lot less fun than off-the-cuff debate.

Let me illustrate this point by referring to Marilyn McCord Adams and
her approach to the problem of evil. For several centuries, at least since the
time of David Hume, many thinkers have construed the philosophical
problem of evil along the line that a good and loving God would not allow
his children to undergo any suffering whatever, thus making our pleasurable experiences the only ones theoretically compatible with God's nature.
But Adams reminds us that, whatever we may think of this line of argumentation, it has little or no relevance to Christianity.

> It does the atheologian no good to argue for the falsity of Christianity on the
> ground that the existence of an omnipotent, omniscient, pleasure-maximizer
> is incompossible with a world such as ours, because Christians never be-
> lieved God was a pleasure-maximizer anyway.[33]

Similarly, we must be prepared to deal with the question of the love of
God and the salvation of humanity in the Christian (i.e., biblical) context,
rather than on the basis of some general abstraction.

Furthermore, in our efforts to do justice to this task we need to make
sure that our apparently biblical conclusions are truly biblical. Paul House
characterizes the method of some theologians as beginning with a single
notion that is definitely biblical, such as the love of God, but then, rather

---

[33]Marilyn McCord Adams, "Horrendous Evils and the Goodness of God," in *The Problem of
Evil*, ed. Marilyn McCord Adams and Robert Merrihew Adams (New York: Oxford University Press, 1990), p. 210. Unfortunately, Adams winds up succumbing to the same problem
when, in another context, she argues for the truth of universalism, even if it should contradict the Bible. See her "Redemptive Suffering: A Christian Solution to the Problem of Evil,"
in *The Problem of Evil: Selected Readings*, ed. Michael L. Peterson (Notre Dame, Ind: Notre
Dame University Press, 1992), pp. 169-87.

than fleshing it out with a broader contextual exegesis, deducing conclusions from this single idea alone.[34] The result will be something that begins as biblical but may end up outside of the range of the total biblical picture.

Most notorious for this unwise process are attempts at persuasion that mix an abstract notion of the love of God with an appeal to our own love for people, the idea being that, the more you love people, the more willing you will be to concede that they are in a state of grace. For example, Clark H. Pinnock, in mentioning some writers who do not share his inclusivist view, accuses another prominent evangelical theologian in this fashion:

> Millard Erickson has even less hope than these. He doubts if anyone has *ever* been saved by responding to general revelation, which was given only to make all people guilty. What does "evangelical" mean when applied to those who seem to want to ensure that there is as little Good News as possible? The Bible offers them a strong basis for optimism, yet they decline.[35]

There are two problems with this *ad hominem* attack. One, it seems to give Erickson power beyond his wildest nightmares, as though he had any influence over who actually does and does not get saved. But, even more realistically, Pinnock, here and elsewhere, makes it sound as though the more theologians love people, the more they should be open to the possibility of individuals being saved apart from their explicit faith in Christ. The above quotation leaves no doubt that Pinnock accuses Erickson of bad faith in interpreting Scripture by refusing to allow for this broader view.

But surely this attack is both unfair and pointless. It is unfair in that Pinnock ought to make the same presupposition for Erickson as he would like made for himself, namely, that he is in good faith going where his conclusions lead him. It is also pointless because optimism is only as good as its basis, and one cannot use it as a criterion to decide truth in its own right. If confronted with, say, a major famine in a Third World country, what is the most optimistic response? Is it to expect God to do a feeding miracle? Is it to reason that since the people need food but do not have any food in the material sense, the air that they breathe must be food for them? Should one, with apologies to Karl Rahner, declare them "anonymously fed"? Or is it to acknowledge the dire situation of the people and do as much as possible to alleviate their suffering, even if it will not reach all those struck by the famine?

---

[34]Paul House, "Introduction," in *Who Will Be Saved? Defending the Biblical Understanding of God*, ed. Paul House and Greg Thornbury (Wheaton, Ill.: Crossway, 2000), pp. 77-78.
[35]Pinnock, *Wideness in God's Mercy*, p. 163.

Now, Clark Pinnock is a compassionate individual, and I know that he would recognize the starving people's plight and reach out to them as best he could without creating verbal or conceptual illusions. It would not be optimism to decide that these people had some food of which they were not aware; that would be a sad blunder, and Pinnock would not make it. But the same thing applies to the issue of eternal salvation. If Erickson is right and human beings are not saved by responding to general revelation, it is not a lack of optimism to assert so, but a realistic appraisal of the situation, and the compassionate thing to do is to contribute to the possibility of their salvation by whatever means may be feasible. It all depends on what the Bible teaches. If Pinnock is right in good faith about inclusive salvation, then he has reason to be optimistic, but if Erickson is right (and one must grant him good faith as well), then Pinnock's optimism could turn out to be a serious deception.

The point of all of the above, of course, is not yet to settle the questions, but to underscore the need for Scripture-based answers. Appeals to vague generalities or emotions do not help. The need for a scripturally based answer to the question also implies that one must treat arguments from silence with extreme caution. These would be arguments of the type that run along the line of "The Bible does not rule out that x may be saved. Therefore, x will be saved." This form of reasoning is an example of the fallacious "argument from silence" or "appeal to ignorance": "x has not been disproved; therefore, x is true." It simply does not follow from the fact that a particular option has not been closed off explicitly by a biblical text that, therefore, it is valid to align this option as a possibility alongside those explicitly stated by the Bible.

John Sanders, in presenting arguments against the exclusivist position appears to be flirting with this fallacy.[36] One does need to remember that in this section of his book he is not necessarily presenting a position that he wishes to defend, though he certainly is sympathetic to it. Let me focus on one of the Bible passages with which he interacts. Romans 10:9 states, "If you confess with your mouth, 'Jesus is Lord,' and believe in your heart that God raised him from the dead, you will be saved." This statement indicates a condition that, once it is met, will result in a person's salvation, that condition being to believe in Christ. An exclusivist might argue that, consequently, only those who believe will be saved. However, Sanders

---

[36]John Sanders, *No Other Name: An Investigation into the Destiny of the Unevangelized* (Grand Rapids, Mich.: Eerdmans, 1992), pp. 217-24.

points out that according to the rules of logic this statement does not exclude the possibility that a person who does not believe may, nevertheless, be saved as well.

> But logically this means nothing more than that confession of Christ is *one* sure way to experience salvation: Paul does not say anything about what will happen to those who do not confess Christ because they have never heard of Christ. The text is logically similar to the conditional statement "If it rains, then the sidewalk will be wet." If the condition is fulfilled (if it rains), then the consequent will follow (the sidewalk will be wet). But we cannot with certainty say, "If it is not raining, the sidewalk will not be wet."[37]

Ronald Nash agrees that, from the purely logical point of view, in a conditional argument, one cannot normally convert *If A then B* to *If B then A*. However, there is one case in which this would be true, namely, when *A* and *B* actually refer to an identical set. In that case, the two propositions are identical, and one can convert them back and forth. If the class of those who believe *(A)* and the class of those who are saved *(B)* are identical, one can switch them at will. Nash then argues that Sanders is simply assuming that *A* and *B* are not identical to each other, and so is prejudicing the argument against an exclusivist understanding.[38]

Nash's response strikes me as unnecessarily defensive here. Just to clear things up, the proper logical representations are these:

(1) If you believe, then you are saved.
    If A then B.

and

(2) If you do not believe, then you are not saved.
    If not-A then not-B.

The second statement cannot be inferred from the first. One would commit the fallacy of denying the antecedent to do so. The illicit conversion to which both Sanders and Nash refer is the statement:

(3) If you are saved, then you believe.
    If B then A.

This is a valid inference from the second statement (what logicians call a "contrapositive"), but it also does *not* follow from the first statement, and it does not strike me as particularly prejudicial to point this out because

---

[37]Ibid., p. 67.
[38]Nash, *Is Jesus the Only Savior?* p. 145.

people frequently commit this fallacy (called "affirming the consequent").

But just because statements (2) and (3) cannot be inferred from statement (1) does not mean that they are false either. The simple question is whether there is independent ground for accepting them as true. Even if Romans 10:9 by itself might not logically restrict salvation only to those who believe, are there further reasons to think that such a restriction might be called for? The answer is yes.

It is true that in Romans 10:9 alone the possibility of salvation for those who do not believe is logically not ruled out, but in the greater context it is. In Romans 9 as well as in the earlier part of Romans 10, Paul's topic is the lost condition of Israel. After having lamented this fact, Paul then launches into his contention that faith results in salvation, that faith is possible only in response to the gospel, and that one cannot respond to the gospel unless someone preaches it. All of this would be totally uninteresting if, in fact, Israel could also be saved apart from faith in Christ. One would have to picture Paul dictating these verses with his fingers crossed behind his back; he would be bemoaning Israel's lost state due to their lack of faith while actually knowing that they could be saved apart from faith. Paul's discussion would be incoherent if Israel had other avenues for salvation. It would be as though I were grieving over a friend's apparently terminal disease and wishing that he would be willing to submit to a life-saving operation, knowing full well that the person will become healthy without the operation as well. It just does not make sense. In Romans, the message that Paul is, in fact, communicating is that faith in Christ in response to the gospel is essential for salvation. Everything else is an unwarranted appeal to silence.[39]

---

[39]The same line of argumentation can be made with regard to Sanders's treatment of other Scriptures that are typically used to defend an exclusivist position, such as Acts 4:12 ("Salvation is found in no one else, for there is no other name under heaven given to men by which we must be saved.") and John 14:6 ("I am the way and the truth and the life. No one comes to the Father except through me."). One can read these verses by themselves in such a way that other options are not ruled out, but the context shows that this is not a reasonable inference. Sanders says of Acts 4:12 that it "speaks forcefully about the power of Jesus' name to save and heal those who hear and respond to the gospel, but it does not speak to the fate of the unevangelized as such. Restrictivists who claim that it does speak authoritatively on this subject are forcing the text to address an issue that is beyond its scope" (*No Other Name*, p. 64). But this raises the question of what precisely Peter was telling the authorities at this point and why. If he were merely relating the theological groundwork of salvation, he certainly picked a strange moment to ruminate on doctrine. In context, Peter was challenged by the authorities in what name he was ministering. He responded by saying that it was in the name of Jesus because his is the only name there is for salvation. Does this leave open the possibility in Peter's mind that one could somehow be saved on the basis of Jesus' name

The upshot of this section is that in attempting to address the issue biblically, one must avoid simplistic appeals to partial biblical truths as well as inappropriate appeals to apparent silence.

WHO IS DEFINITELY SAVED?

If one is looking for an answer to the question of salvation for those outside of Christianity, one must first be clear on the more straightforward situations. An exception to a rule, if it is such, can only be dealt with appropriately if one is clear on the rule first. So, before going any further, let me clarify what I think the "rule" for salvation is according to the Bible.

First of all, in the Old Testament, the normal criterion is belonging to the people of God. The people of Israel are God's chosen people, and as such, they stand in a positive relationship with God. The cultus, centering on temple sacrifices, is not irrelevant, of course. In fact, it is expected that all true Israelites will be punctilious in their observance of the moral and ceremonial laws. But further, it is also understood that people will fail, and they will not live up to these standards; nevertheless, God's mercy will prevail and he will forgive the sins of his people. The people will look to God in faith and express their faith through, once again, further cultic observances, such as the ritual for the Day of Atonement.

The basic plan of salvation in the Old Testament represents an almost paradoxical oscillation between group membership and personal responsibility. No Israelite is let off the hook for personal lapses in the observance of the law, particularly the ultimate breach of faith—idolatry. However, the positive relationship with God is not something that the individual earns

---

without knowing about him? Only perhaps until we get to Acts 4:18-20, where Peter absolutely refuses to stop proclaiming Christ. Why would he do this if he actually knew that it made no difference to his hearers whether or not they knew about Christ?

Sanders says concerning John 14:6 that "Jesus teaches his disciples that they truly do know the 'way' God wants them to live since they have observed this way of life in Jesus himself and thus have seen the Father. . . . This text demonstrates that Jesus desires us to come to know him, but the context is silent about the unevangelized" (*No Other Name*, p. 64). Actually, the context sheds some interesting light on this issue. In John 14:5, Thomas complains to Jesus, "Lord, we don't know where you are going, so how can we know the way?" Thomas surely is not speaking just for himself here, but he is expressing everyone else's sentiments, and if it is that of the other disciples, then surely a forteriori it also extends to other human beings: "Wherever it may be that you are going, Jesus, we do not know the way!" And in response Jesus points out that he himself is the way, and that there is no other way but himself. What sense would that have made if deep inside Jesus could be thinking, "But you know, Thomas, that really doesn't matter so long as you find your own way according to your best lights." Why would Jesus give an answer to Thomas that really did not convey the truth of the situation?

but something that comes with being a part of the people God has chosen for himself. The many commandments of the Old Testament are given in order to preserve the relationship, not to create it.

Membership in God's people is not limited to those who are born to it, however. There is also the provision for Gentile proselytes. These are people who place themselves into the community by avowal of God and his law. They are circumcised and are then, with few exceptions, considered to be a part of Israel just as much as those who are born into it. The most famous instance of those who have become a part of God's people by conversion is that of Ruth.

Before considering more exceptional cases, one must widen the circle a little more. After all, there was a time when there was no "people of God." The story begins much earlier with the earliest beginnings in Adam through the founders of the nation, the patriarchs. They obviously did not have the direct ethnic or social identity that the later Israelites enjoyed. However, they are a part of the ongoing development of the people; they could be called the proto-nation. They, too, were in a positive relationship with God first of all because of God's initiative toward them, and they also practiced a cultus as an expression thereof, not in order to bring it about.

To understand the place of God's people in salvation, let's examine the teaching of the New Testament concerning salvation. As discussed in the last chapter, that salvation is the free gift of God that he bestows on those who are willing to accept it in simple trusting faith. This arrangement presupposes that a person is familiar with the basic message of the gospel— thereby including certain fundamental beliefs, such as the existence of God, the reality of sin, the atoning death of Christ, the need for personal faith in order to receive the gift and possibly some other similarly basic beliefs. Consequently, according to this standard, a person needs to have learned of these facts somehow, something to which I will from now on refer as having "heard" the gospel, but, of course, this is not limited to the auditory sense. A person surely can also read the gospel by sight or Braille or see it performed in mime, for example. But the facts need to be there.

In addition, the New Testament requires personal assent. This requirement is both intellectual and existential. Individuals have to accept the gospel facts as true, but then they also have to place their personal trust in Christ and his atoning work. In contrast to the picture of salvation in the Old Testament, there is nothing automatic here. At this point, no one is born into the people of God. Even though one can make a good case that

God brings it about that particular individuals place their faith in him,[40] those persons are not actually saved until the faith response to the gospel has taken place. Romans 10:9-10 summarizes: "If you confess with your mouth, 'Jesus is Lord,' and believe in your heart that God raised him from the dead, you will be saved. For it is with your heart that you believe and are justified, and it is with your mouth that you confess and are saved." This is the standard for salvation in the New Testament. A person hears the gospel and responds to Christ in faith. Intellectual awareness and personal assent are both a part of the picture.[41]

And thus the New Testament stresses the need for missionary activity. For people cannot respond to a gospel they have not heard. A little later in Romans 10 Paul says, "How, then, can they call on the one they have not believed in? And how can they believe in the one of whom they have not heard? And how can they hear without someone preaching to them?" (Rom 10:14). Thus, the fundamental soteriology and the missionary impulse go together.

But this too requires further clarifications. Are those who have not heard the gospel automatically condemned to be lost? Are the effects of Christ's atonement rigidly limited to only those who have heard and responded? Before even thinking of pagans in faraway lands, who have not been visited by missionaries, it behooves us to explain how even Old Testament Jews could be saved from the New Testament perspective since they were hardly in a position to have explicit faith in Christ.

It is tempting here to launch immediately into a notion of implicit faith in Christ. One could say that, even though the Jews did not yet know about Christ and so could not have explicit faith in him, they still could have implicit faith. The problem is that "implicit faith," on its own, is really an oxymoron, similar to "inaudible speech" or "unfelt pain." The whole point of speech is that one makes noises that communicate; the essence of pain is that it is an unpleasant feeling. Similarly, the very nature of faith is

---

[40]Calvinists would, of course, express this idea with the doctrine of unconditional election, but Wesleyans, too, would hold that a person's saving faith must be preceded by God's prevenient grace.

[41]A collateral issue to this discussion is the fate of those who are unable to understand or respond to the gospel for reasons of physical limitations, such as infants or mentally handicapped individuals. See Ronald H. Nash, *When a Baby Dies: Answers to Comfort Grieving Parents* (Grand Rapids, Mich.: Zondervan, 1999). However, I do not think that whatever response one might provide to that issue necessarily has any bearing on our discussion at hand. There is no reason to suppose that God deals with those whose mental apparatus is intact in the same way as with those whose faculties are either undeveloped or impaired.

trust, acceptance and reliance, but that would appear to be an impossibility apart from conscious recognition of who it is that one trusts, what one accepts or on whom one relies. It would seem that I cannot reasonably say that I am relying on someone of whose existence I am not aware; simply to invoke the idea that I am doing so implicitly makes no sense by itself.

But "inaudible speech" can become a coherent concept. One can consider two Boy Scouts communicating with semaphore flags, in which case there is nothing audible, but the audible communication has been replaced by the flag arrangements. Speech is inaudible but has become represented by the semaphore code. In the same way, "unfelt pain" does not need to be self-contradictory. My wife and a close friend both can tell when I have a headache, sometimes before I realize it, by the way that I hold my head and scrunch my eyes. My body is, in fact, subconsciously sensing the pain even though I have been too preoccupied for the feeling to register. What both of these cases have in common is that the apparent incoherence can be removed, though not without warrant. The key concept to making this happen is mediation. The semaphore flags mediate the speech, inaudible though it may be; the way I hold my head mediates my pain experience, though I may not have come to feel it yet consciously.

Of course, not everything can mediate speech, and not every expression can mediate pain. Simply flailing a set of flags in the air does not by itself constitute speech in any sense; nothing is being communicated. Similarly, although there may be a number of ways in which the fact of my headache may be communicated, there are also many ways in which that would not be the case. A silly giggle, for example, just would not do the trick. In short, even though one may be justified in invoking these apparent oxymorons in certain cases, that privilege does not give one the right to use just any behavior as a pretext to claim that there is inaudible speech or unfelt pain.

Similar things can be said about implicit faith. Even though at first glance this is an apparently inconsistent notion, there is a way of making sense of it. Again, the key is in the idea of mediation. There may be certain ways of mediating faith in such a way that, even though persons having faith do not explicitly know the object of faith, they are, in fact, aiming toward it. An example would be some belief or cultus attached to a belief that directs the person to Christ and his atonement even though the person actually does not necessarily know that this is going on.

But again, the immediate second question is whether this instrument of mediation can indeed mediate implicit faith. Just as not every action can constitute inaudible speech, and not every expression can convey unfelt pain, so not every attitude, belief or cultic practice may be considered to be legitimate implicit faith. After all, the object of saving faith still needs to be Jesus Christ, and, without question, not everything can equally become the medium for a faith that even implicitly directs a person to Christ. If there is such a mediating object, then it is the explicit object of faith that directs a person to Christ as the implicit object.

To return to the issue: Can Old Testament Jews have implicit faith in Christ and his atonement? The answer now can be yes if there is an immediate explicit object of faith that can serve as conveyance of the person's faith implicitly to Christ. Many Christian theologians have held that this is precisely the case with the sacrificial cultus of the Old Testament. Thus, for example, Millard Erickson, in making a case for salvation by grace through faith of the Old Testament people, points out:

> While based entirely upon the work of Christ, grace in the Old Testament was indirectly received. The Old Testament believers did not know how that grace had been effected. They did not understand that their righteousness was proleptic—it was achieved by the future death of the incarnate Son of God. That grace was also mediated by priests and sacrificial rites; it did not come about through a direct personal relationship with Christ.[42]

Thus, their explicit faith, as mediated through the sacrificial cultus, also served as implicit faith in Christ's substitutionary atonement.

Can this notion of implicit faith be taken further? Can pagans have implicit faith? How about Old Testament people who believed in God, but were not a part of Israel? How about people today who believe in God, but are not Christians?

WHO IS PERHAPS SAVED BEFORE CHRIST?

The paradigm situation in the Bible, then, is this. In the Old Testament, it is the people of Israel who are saved. Their faith in God occurs in a system provided by God that includes cultic provisions that allow them to partake in the future atonement of Christ through implicit faith in him. In the New Testament, the criterion becomes explicit faith in Christ and his atonement. Now let me extend the discussion beyond those boundaries, keeping in mind that the criterion for what is true must continue to be what is bibli-

---

[42]Millard J. Erickson, *Christian Theology*, 3 vols. (Grand Rapids, Mich.: Baker, 1983-1985), 3:982.

cally revealed, not what seems fair or "consistent."

It becomes immediately clear that implicit faith does not extend to pagan beliefs and rituals. Idolatry can never be a mediating instrument that moves an individual from explicit faith in the god of the idol to implicit faith in Christ. The false god, whom the person, depending on their specific religion, sees as identical with, indwelling or symbolized by the statue, directs the person away from the true God, and thus this cultus cannot be a conveyance toward God, Christ and the atonement. Throughout the Old Testament, idolatry receives nothing but condemnation. (See for example the classic passages in Isaiah 44 and Jeremiah 10.)

This is not to say that a pagan practice cannot become a medium for communicating the gospel to a non-Christian. I have, for example, sat in a Hindu temple dedicated to the god Muruka (also known as Skanda or Kartikeya) and used the self-immolative practices associated with his worship as a kind of "redemptive analogy"[43] to illustrate Christ's suffering on our behalf. But this is a far cry from saying that worship of Muruka is implicit worship of God in Christ. To be quite frank about it, after having witnessed the devotional practices for Muruka, particularly the Taipusam festival associated with him, the thought is downright repugnant. The same thing goes for other forms of idol worship. It can certainly be a communication bridge to help direct a person to the gospel in an evangelistic setting, but this is not the same thing as saying that devotion to an idol or some other pagan deity by itself implicitly leads a person to God.

C. S. Lewis, with all of the great contributions he has made to the Christian church, has made assertions on this point that simply cannot be substantiated biblically.

> I think that every prayer which is sincerely made even to a false god . . . is accepted by the true God and that Christ saves many who do not think they know him. For he is (dimly) present in the *good* side of the inferior teachers they follow.[44]

Lewis particularly popularized this point in *The Last Battle,* the final volume of the Narnia Chronicles. In this story, Emeth, a man of integrity albeit a worshiper of the cruel god Tash, meets the Lion Aslan, Lewis's representation of Christ in these stories. Expecting to be annihilated, Emeth instead receives Aslan's commendation because all the good and true things

---

[43]See Don Richardson, *Peace Child* (Glendale, Calif.: Regal, 1974).
[44]C. S. Lewis, *Letters of C. S. Lewis,* ed. W. H. Lewis (New York: Harcourt Brace Jovanovich, 1966), p. 247, quoted in Sanders, *No Other Name,* p. 253.

Emeth has done, even though he thought of them as being directed toward Tash, were actually directed toward Aslan. Emeth reports,

> But I said also (for the truth constrained me), Yet I have been seeking Tash all my days. Beloved, said the Glorious One [Aslan], unless thy desire had been for me thou wouldst not have sought so long and so truly. For all find what they truly seek.[45]

In short, service to Tash—though only those deeds done with truth and integrity—is implicit service to Aslan. By implication, service to a pagan deity—again restricted to only those deeds done with truth and integrity—is implicit service to God.

The problem with this scenario is that it simply never occurs in the Bible. Although Lewis can make it come out this way in a work of fiction, there is no example for it in Scripture, and it is easy to understand why. The worship of pagan gods is worship of the creature rather than the Creator, as Paul states so eloquently in Romans 1. In the Old Testament cultus, the people worshiped God with sacrifices of animals, and this practice directed them to God. But at times they worshiped the animals (such as a calf) in place of God, and this cultus was not acceptable. Rather than providing implicit faith in God, this practice was considered an explicit rejection of God. Among the Gentiles, worship of Baal, Dagon or any other pagan deity leads people away from God rather than toward him. This is the message of Romans 1: God was not so pleased with the practice of idolatry among human beings that he rewarded them for at least trying. Instead, he gave them over to his wrath, for God is, as we learn over and over again in the Old Testament, a jealous God. In short, in the Bible, pagan religion cannot be considered a proper vehicle for implicit faith in God.

But what about Melchizedek, the mysterious priest-king of Salem to whom Abraham paid a tithe in Genesis 14:17-24? Was he not a pagan whose worship God accepted in pretty much the same way in which C. S. Lewis portrayed Aslan's acceptance of Emeth's worship of Tash? Clark H. Pinnock sees it exactly that way. Melchizedek, according to Pinnock, was a priest in his religion, but his worship was accepted by the God of Abraham.

> Melchizedek, named priest of God Most High (El Elyon was the name of his god), blessed the patriarch by his deity and received Abraham's tithe in re-

---

[45]C. S. Lewis, *The Last Battle* (New York: Collier, 1956), p. 165.

turn. Abram then uses the name of Yahweh for his deity, thus accepting the equivalence of Yahweh and El Elyon, and the validity of Melchizedek's worship. The meaning of this pericope is clear. Here we have Abraham accepting the blessing of a pagan priest, and giving tithes to him.[46]

But how pagan was Melchizedek? Pinnock says that the Melchizedek's worship of El Elyon (God Most High) and Abraham's worship of Yahweh were "equivalent." However, it seems to be much more natural to read this passage as saying that "El Elyon" and "Yahweh" are identical, that is to say, two different names for the same deity. This certainly is the way in which a straightforward reading of the text would have it. Ronald Nash states, "Melchizedek worshiped and served Yahweh as certainly as Abram did. Melchizedek fails as an example of genuine piety among pagans."[47] It is impossible to make sense of the treatment of Melchizedek in Hebrews 7, where he is described as the forerunner of Christ, if he was, in fact, the priest of some pagan religion.

What we have in Melchizedek (and also Jethro, Moses' father-in-law) is the recognition of and devotion to the God of original monotheism, as described in chapter two. The case was made then that there is a persistent strain of at least vestigial monotheism throughout the world of religions, and these are some specific cases thereof. In a negative way, even someone like Balaam, who was, of course, condemned by God, nevertheless recognized the existence and power of God. And the God of original monotheism is none else but the God who revealed himself particularly to the Jews and later in Jesus Christ. Thus it is possible to say that Melchizedek and others are ultimately saved just as the Jews of the Old Testament are, namely, by implicit faith in Christ, worked out within the context of their explicit faith in God as presently known to them.

An instance that John Sanders uses to support the inclusion of pagan deities really cuts the other direction.[48] In 2 Kings 5 we read about Naaman, the captain of the army of Aram who converts to the worship of God when he is healed of leprosy by God through Elisha. Before he leaves for home he asks for some boons. First, he wishes to take a couple of mule loads of Israelite dirt back to Aram with him because he will only worship the God of Israel from now on, an idea that seems to be based on a geographic henotheism, the belief that gods are limited to certain geographic

---

[46]Pinnock, *Wideness in God's Mercy*, p. 94.
[47]Nash, *Is Jesus the Only Savior?* p. 128.
[48]Sanders, *No Other Name*, p. 220.

locations. If he carries the soil, the god who lives on that soil will go with him. Second, he asks to be excused for continuing to enter the temple of the Aramaic god Rimmon and bowing in his presence. Both requests are granted. Sanders summarizes the situation thus:

> Inclusivists view God's acceptance of Naaman despite his errors in belief and his persistence in entering a pagan temple as evidence that God is more inclined to grant salvation to those who exhibit faith than to those who are simply adhering to a detailed set of doctrines or liturgical practices.[49]

Of course, there is a false dilemma in Sanders's depiction to begin with. Evangelical exclusivists do not believe that anyone is saved by "simply adhering to a detailed set of doctrines or liturgical practices" any more than inclusivists do. Exclusivists (and evangelical inclusivists as well) believe that a person is saved by faith in the person of God as the object of faith.[50] What exclusivists insist on is that there be some explicit awareness of who that God is and what he requires. This is neither quibbling over obscure dogmas nor salvation by accepting certain beliefs as true. Sanders is right that this passage illustrates that one can hold some erroneous beliefs and still be saved, but exclusivists and inclusivists both ought to hold to this truth.

More important, Namaan's requests concerning his visits to the temple, in fact, count against the inclusivist view. There would be no point in it if his worship of Rimmon were perfectly compatible with the worship of God. The matter is an issue precisely because the worship of God and the worship of Rimmon are incompatible. Naaman has announced that from now on he will worship the God of Israel alone. What Sanders omits to mention is that Naaman will go to the temple of Rimmon only because he is required to do so professionally as physical support to his king; he

---

[49]Ibid.

[50]Actually, I am not entirely sure that this is true for Clark Pinnock any longer. It appears that for him the divine person as the object of faith has become virtually irrelevant, and one is actually saved by faith alone, regardless of the object. He says, "Faith is what pleases God. The fact that different kinds of believers are accepted by God proves that the issue for God is not the content of theology but the reality of faith. . . . Theological content differs from age to age in the unfolding of redemption, but the faith principle remains in place. No one can say exactly how much knowledge one has to have in order to exercise faith" (*Wideness in God's Mercy*, p. 106). One might respond, though, by saying that, even if it is not possible to draw up a precise list of everything that might be required to be known, surely a knowledge of the one in whom one has faith is both required and biblical. "Anyone who comes to him must believe that he exists and that he rewards those who earnestly seek him" (Heb 11:6). The reference here is clearly to the God of the Bible, and it seems pretty plain that this rules out atheists and worshipers of pagan deities.

intends not to worship Rimmon himself but only to go through the merest of formalities that his position demands of him. This is what is excused, not worship of Rimmon, but attendance in the Rimmon temple alone. Thus there is no reasonable way of constructing this passage as teaching that worship of Rimmon is equivalent to worship of God; to the contrary, it is based on the truth that worship of Rimmon is not equivalent to worship of God. Else there would be no point in it.

So we can conclude concerning people outside of the direct covenant community in the Old Testament that worship of pagan deities could not provide salvation, but the worship of God in line with the persistence of original monotheism could. The latter group was apparently, as to their salvation, on an equal footing with the Jews.

WHO IS PERHAPS SAVED AFTER CHRIST?

Now let us move the clock forward and ask a similar question concerning those who have had no opportunity to hear the gospel from the time of Christ on. There are some things that are different, but some things that are the same. In considering this question, we must remember that, in contrast to the Old Testament, faith in Christ as explicit object of faith is mandatory in the New Testament as a rule.

Again, there can be no question of those who practice a pagan religion being saved through their religion. Some things the New Testament does not state explicitly because they are simply carried over from the Old Testament, but this one is perfectly clear in the New Testament as well. Worship of the creature (Romans 1) rather than the Creator is incompatible with saving faith. Idolatry is unacceptable and to be shunned. In order to be saved one must know that God—and there can only be one natural referent for this term, namely, the God of Israel and Christ—exists and rewards those who seek him (Heb 11:6), a proposition that would be incompatible with other deities or other religious conceptions. If recognition of the biblical God were not in view here, and any object or faith (or even lack thereof) could serve, there simply would be no point in making this statement. Some of the heroes of faith in Hebrews 11 gave up their lives for their faith in God, a foolish thing to do if idol worship were equivalent to worship of God. Thus any kind of implicit faith in Christ through pagan religions continues to be ruled out.

But what about those who, like Melchizedek in the Old Testament, worship the God of original monotheism without having knowledge of the gospel? Can one say that they are still under the same dispensation and are consequently also saved? Is not what was good for Melchizedek still good for someone today who worships God, albeit in ignorance of God's greater revelation?

If, however, the answers to these questions are to be based on the teachings of the New Testament, this reasoning breaks down. There is a serious difference between the Old and New Testaments. Before considering those outside the circle of God's special revelation, one must take cognizance of those who had been, in fact, the recipients of God's direct revelation, the Jews. The fact of the matter is that the New Testament teaches that God's chosen people, because of their unbelief in Christ, are not saved and that they need to come to Christ in order to be saved. In Romans 11, Paul makes the point that Israel as a nation, having rejected Christ, has been replaced by the Gentiles but eventually will return to God. For the moment, though, the status of the people of Israel is outside of God's promise because of their unbelief. Earlier Paul declared:

> I have great sorrow and unceasing anguish in my heart. For I could wish that I myself were cursed and cut off from Christ for the sake of my brothers, those of my own race, the people of Israel. (Rom 9:2-4)[51]

Echoing the argumentation used several times in this chapter, this would be a very peculiar thing to say if, in fact, Israelites were still saved simply by being a part of Israel. Sadly, having not accepted Christ, they are as lost as any other human being without Christ.

But if this is true for the Jews during this new time period, one can no longer make the extrapolation to monotheistic Gentiles. One must keep in mind that when Paul wrote these words in Romans, the Jewish sacrificial cultus was still in place. There still were the temple and the sacrifices, all those things that previously had served to mediate implicit faith in Christ. But now that Christ had come and made atonement, animal sacrifices could no longer convey faith in Christ implicitly. The object of faith had become explicit, and implicit faith was no longer appropriate (Heb 9:1-7).

---

[51]Two important points can be made in this connection: First, Israel's (temporary) state of alienation from God has nothing to do with its role at the crucifixion. The present negative spiritual state of the Jews is simply a matter of their not accepting Christ as Savior, just as is true for all other human beings. The Jews were not punished in some way; they simply lost their special status in this dispensation, a status that, according to Romans 11, will be restored. Second, I think Paul's attitude in this verse is exemplary of one that should characterize any Christian's relationship to God's chosen people, never one of arrogance or elitism and always only one of self-sacrificial love.

So, if it is no longer possible to posit explicit faith for the Jews who still had the old explicit revelation and the sacrificial cultus that had conveyed implicit faith in Christ, it is even less feasible for those who previously had implicit faith on far paltrier grounds. If the Jews needed to hear the gospel and respond to it by faith to be saved (Rom 11:20), then the same must be true for monotheistic Gentiles *a fortiori*.

But one must not forget that such judgments by the New Testament always occur in the context of the proclamation of the gospel. The point is not that these people are lost but that these people are lost and need to respond to the gospel. And thereby we get into the trickiest question, but also an evident answer to the question, which is, of course, what about those who have had no chance to hear the gospel?

Of course, one easy answer to the question is to say that those who have not heard or responded to the gospel are lost, and there is no particular indication in the New Testament that things are otherwise—whether we like them or not. But there are two qualifications that can be made with regard to this statement. First of all, the question is not concerned primarily with all the Gentile nonbelievers in the world. Unfortunately, there is little to discuss concerning atheists or idolaters, say. The group under consideration are those Gentiles who have not heard the gospel but who know of God and are responding to his natural revelation.

In fact, there are some clear examples in the New Testament that shed light on this situation. There is always a certain liability in building doctrines on the basis of narratives, for there is always a question of how normative these narratives are supposed to be. However, multiple instances of similar events, can make it legitimate to think there is a pattern.

The pattern in the New Testament is this: There are several instances in which a person or group of persons has come to have some faith in God and is attempting to be faithful to what they know of him. In these cases God does provide the means by which they can hear the full gospel and thus exercise explicit faith, which they do. Among these people are the following, mentioned in the book of Acts:

1. *The Ethiopian eunuch (Acts 8:26-40).* He had visited Jerusalem and even owned a scroll of Isaiah. God sent Philip to him so that he could hear and respond to the gospel.

2. *Cornelius, the Roman centurion (Acts 10).* He is described as a very devout person who prayed to God daily. The Lord sent Peter to explain the gospel to him.

3. The "God-fearing Greeks" *(e.g., Acts 17:4).* Paul encountered these believers in the various towns in which he preached the gospel on his missionary journeys. These were Gentiles who had associated themselves with Judaism to the extent that they believed and served the true God only, but they were not converts to Judaism. Most of the time, these people embraced the gospel more eagerly than the Jews did, and one can argue that they were the primary beneficiaries of Paul's missionary efforts. But if they were actually already saved by virtue of their rudimentary faith in God, the Lord let a lot of suffering and persecution on behalf of the gospel occur for no good reason. (The same thing can be said about the Jewish inhabitants of these towns who both did and did not respond to the gospel. In fact, if they were already saved, they were harmed, not helped, by the presentation of the gospel, which some of them rejected.)

4. Apollos *(Acts 18:24-28).* This somewhat enigmatic figure was a disciple of the John-the-Baptist movement, which apparently survived John's martyrdom. Apollos also had accurate knowledge concerning the events of Christ's life, but evidently not concerning faith in Christ as expressed in baptism. He went about making converts but could only teach them his own half-accurate doctrines. God sent Priscilla and Aquila to give him the full story.

5. The disciples of John the Baptist in Ephesus *(Acts 19:1-6).* Apollos had left some converts to his hybrid belief system in Ephesus. What Priscilla and Aquila did for Apollos, Paul did for these Ephesians: he completed the Christian story and salvation message for them.

All of these events have certain patterns in common, though in some way they differ drastically from one another. In each case, these are people who are sincerely living by the light that they have, specifically an accurate, but incomplete, faith in God. In each case, they are not yet saved, as indicated by the fact that the mark of their being members of the body of Christ, the baptism of the Holy Spirit (1 Cor 12:13), does not occur until the end of each episode. And in each case, God sends someone who gives them the complete gospel. Thus one can conclude that, apparently, when there are people who have not yet heard the gospel but who have responded to God with limited information, God will send someone who will provide the gospel message for them.

Now, I cannot blame anyone whose first reaction to this assertion is to think that this is just a little thin. It seems as though I am generalizing from pretty limited data to a rather sweeping conclusion, and I cannot deny this. Nevertheless, at least it does have biblical support, which is more than one can say about alternatives such as "implicit faith" or "post mortem conversions."[52] If this position, which Sanders calls "God Will Send the Message,"[53] is false, the only biblical alternative is to say that these devoted Gentile monotheists are usually lost. As I have contended, the idea that they are saved by implicit faith renders absurd the missionary efforts that are carried out on their behalf by Peter, Paul, or Aquila and Priscilla, while postmortem opportunities are never even hinted at in the New Testament. In fact, Hebrews 9:27 teaches that after death comes judgment. Since one of the main points of the book of Hebrews is to exhort people to respond to Christ while there is yet time, if there were further opportunities after death, the book and this verse would become meaningless.

Note how this position is essentially exclusivist. In fact, it champions the exclusivist position because it only makes sense on the presupposition that explicit faith in Christ is necessary for salvation. John Sanders includes it in his list of positions that allow for a "wider hope," but he recognizes that some of the advocates he includes in this category would be uncomfortable under this heading.[54] They would insist that the greater reality is the fact that no one is saved apart from the clear knowledge of the gospel. Nevertheless, Sanders is right insofar as he attributes a somewhat slight expansion of the initial circle of the saved to this view. Natural revelation does not save, but it provides the opportunity for the saving message to be sent to those who respond to it.

This "God will send the message" position has had its share of venerable defenders in history. Saint Thomas Aquinas advocated it. He also began with the proposition that explicit faith is necessary for salvation, including even intellectual acceptance of the trinity, a doctrine that certainly cannot be derived from natural revelation alone.[55] So, what happens to those who for reasons of circumstances seem not to be in a position to hear the gospel directly? Aquinas states that

> if someone . . . followed the direction of natural reason in seeking good and avoiding evil, we must most certainly hold that God would either reveal to

---

[52]Compare the comments by Nash, "Restrictivism," p. 109.
[53]Sanders, *No Other Name*, pp. 152-64.
[54]Ibid., p. 162.
[55]Thomas Aquinas *Summa Theologica* 2.2, q.2, a.8.

him through internal inspiration what had to be believed, or would send some preacher of the faith to him as he sent Peter to Cornelius (Acts 10:20).[56]

Twentieth-century proponents include Robertson McQuilken and Oliver Buswell.[57] Furthermore, Don Richards has anecdotally compiled numerous episodes in which missionaries coming with the gospel message to particular people found these people already remarkably prepared to hear the gospel, allowing one to draw the plausible inference that God was responding to their partial faith with the complete story.[58]

A point of difference between various advocates of this view is whether God will use only human messengers in presenting the gospel message or whether he will use direct personal revelations or angels as well. Aquinas included the possibility of internal inspiration to this effect, and Buswell allows the following reference from the *Synopsis* of Leiden to stand:

> God does not always supply the two methods of calling possible to himself (i.e., outward and inward calling), but calls some to him only by the inner light and leading of the Holy Spirit without the ministry of his outward Word. This method of calling is of course *per se* sufficient for salvation, but very rare, extraordinary, and unknown to us.[59]

Don't you hate it when someone propounds on something that is "unknown to us"? If it is, how can we even know it exists, let alone describe it as sufficient for salvation? In any event, this idea seems to be pretty diametrically opposed to Romans 10, which teaches the need for someone to preach the Word in order for people to be able to respond in faith. The New Testament pattern as seen with Cornelius and others indicates that God will send human messengers as the final presenters of the full gospel; neither angels nor an internal revelation is mentioned.

In summary, let us review the questions listed at the outset of this chapter, this time together with the corresponding answers.

- Epistemologically: Is Christianity alone true? Answer: This is the most fundamental conclusion, without which the entire discussion would have been irrelevant.
- Metaphysically: Do the effects of Christ's atonement extend only to

---

[56]Thomas Aquinas *De Veritate* q.14, a.11, trans. James V. McGlynn (Chicago: Regnery, 1953), p. 262.

[57]Robertson McQuilken, *The Great Omission* (Grand Rapids, Mich.: Baker, 1984); Oliver Buswell, *A Systematic Theology of the Christian Religion,* 2 vols. (Grand Rapids, Mich.: Zondervan, 1963).

[58]Don Richardson, *Eternity in Their Hearts* (Ventura, Calif.: Regal, 1981).

[59]Buswell, *Systematic Theology,* 2:161, quoted in Sanders, *No Other Name,* p. 154.

those who are believers in him? Answer: Yes, though in the Old Testament time period this faith could be implicit for both Israelites and Gentile monotheists.

- Ethically: Is a human being required to express faith in Christ in order to be eligible for salvation? Answer: Yes, again either implicitly (Old Testament) or explicitly (New Testament). More important, there are no anonymous Christians or idolatrous people of God.

- Subjectively: Is an implicit faith in Christ that expresses itself in actions but not in words as valid as an explicitly stated faith? Answer: Yes, in the time period to which it was restricted.

- Theologically with reference to God himself: Does God's saving love extend to those who do not know of Christ? Answer: Of course it does, but only within the further plan of God, which does not imply that everyone is saved willy-nilly.

- Socially: Are those who have never heard of the gospel without hope of salvation? Answer: Sadly yes, though the New Testament does provide indications that God does at times reach out with special messengers of the gospel for those who are true to the more limited natural revelation.

Having made a case for this somewhat modified exclusivist position, I cannot say that there is nothing left to be said concerning the relationship of Christianity and other religions. Just as Christianity fits into various parts of the great tapestry of religion, the fact that it alone is finally salvific does not yank it out of the tapestry, though it does certainly provide it with a very, very special position therein. Nevertheless, there are further aspects of Christianity to examine in the worldwide phenomenon of religion that will only underscore the contentions of this chapter. In the next chapter, I will explore how the Christian hope for the future, the second coming, lines up with the eschatologies of other religions.

7

ESCHATOLOGY
AND HOPE FOR THE FUTURE

In order for there to be an eschatology, there must be a future. This state-ment seems to be too obvious to need mentioning, but in the history of re-ligions it broaches one of the most dramatic differences between various cultures and religions. The focus of this chapter will be on the diverse "messianic" figures that seem to be an almost standard part of most of the world's religions, including Christianity. However, in order for this dis-cussion to make sense, it is necessary first to clarify the role of time in reli-gious cultures.

A GEOMETRY OF TIME

Possibly the most influential book on the concept of time in religious cul-tures written in the last century is *The Myth of the Eternal Return* by Mircea Eliade.[1] The Romanian scholar applies his phenomenology of religion to the concept of time, beginning as always with the "archaic"[2] pattern as the paradigmatic one. In keeping with the idea of the original monotheism,

---

[1]Mircea Eliade, *The Myth of the Eternal Return* (originally titled *Cosmos and History*) (Princeton, N.J.: Princeton University Press, 1954).
[2]Eliade's own word is *primitive*, but I shall substitute the word *archaic* on occasion. The word *primitive* is not a well-liked term these days, and for good reason since it implies a kind of barbarism that is nothing if not offensive to the cultures living on this level. Just remember the fact documented earlier that the most archaic cultures manifest monotheism and an eth-ical commitment that should be the envy of so-called higher cultures. Nevertheless, as Eliade uses the term, its meaning is rooted in a phenomenological commitment to a primor-dial experience that he finds in these cultures. To Eliade, *primitive* means "fundamental," not "barbaric."

which is an integral part of the present discussion, I will reverse Eliade's sequence but make use of his patterns.

I believe that it is a safe assumption that our modern secular view of time is entirely linear. Time is a sequence of moments, each one succeeding the previous one and leading into the next one. The past is gone forever, and there is no way of retrieving it.

> The Moving Finger writes; and, having writ,
> Moves on: nor all your Piety nor Wit
> Shall lure it back to cancel half a Line,
> Nor all your Tears wash out a Word of it.[3]

In this understanding of time there may be a beginning, such as the original Big Bang, of what we consider time, what Eliade refers to as "profane time,"[4] though it may even be inaccurate to speak of a "beginning" of time. (See figure 7.1 for an illustration of Eliade's concept of profane time.) For example, Stephen Hawking, the well-known physicist, argues that the initial state of the universe does not constitute a "singularity," that is, a point before which any known laws of the universe obtained.[5] Although Hawking's view is controversial and suffers from some philosophical problems,[6] it illustrates profoundly the idea of time in a secular culture because, if Hawking were right, in addition to there not being an end to time, there would not even be a beginning.

Figure 7.1. A representation of Eliade's profane time

In contrast to the secular view, the predominant Western monotheistic religions—Judaism, Zoroastrianism, Christianity and Islam—include both a beginning and an end to time. The past does not stretch indefinitely back,

---

[3]*The Rubaiyat of Omar Khayyam* (trans. Edward FitzGerald) stanza 71.

[4]Mircea Eliade, *Sacred and Profane: The Nature of Religion* (New York: Harcourt, Brace & World, 1959), pp. 68-72.

[5]Stephen Hawking, *A Brief History of Time* (New York: Bantam, 1998), pp. 51-53.

[6]Hawking's treatment of the issue encompasses two aspects. One is the mathematical area that allows him to balance his equations without bringing in a cause that effects the origin of the universe. I would not want to dispute Hawking's conclusion here—if for no other reason than that I don't believe I could even understand his equations. But the other aspect is a metaphysical one. Just because a mathematical formula is adequate to describe a phenomenon does not mean that the phenomenon could have come about without benefit of a cause. To reach this conclusion requires a metaphysical assumption that runs contrary to other human experience. See the discussion of the so-called kalam cosmological argument by William Lane Craig, *Reasonable Faith: Christian Truth and Apologetics* (Wheaton, Ill.: Crossway, 1994), pp. 91-122. *Kalam*, a word that Craig never defines, refers to Islamic theology.

and the future has a clear *telos,* an ending toward which the entire process is aimed. Furthermore, among these religions, despite some obvious differences, there are some clear similarities in the way in which the linear process develops. Each tradition has the same beginning, namely, the divine act of creation.[7] Further, each of these four religions has a midpoint of sorts, namely, the giving of the law at Sinai, the teaching ministry of Zoroaster, the death of Christ on the cross and the revelation of the Qur'an to Muhammad, respectively. Finally, each tradition has an eschatology that involves a resurrection and a judgment. (See figure 7.2 for an illustration of this concept of time.)

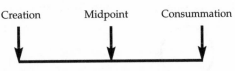

Figure 7.2. The Western religions' view of time

Chapter two explained that there is good reason to believe that original monotheism has always entailed the idea that God is the creator of the world. In fact, Wilhelm Schmidt[8] defended a natural theology on the basis of which archaic humans infer that the world must have been created, a piece of reasoning that then led them to believe in a Creator god in the sky. Thus, they perceived the world to have a beginning, and this conclusion would seem to imply that these people must have had a linear view of time. However, things are far more complex than that.

Mircea Eliade summarized the preliterate view of time with the notion of "sacred time." Sacred time is an emulation of a mythological time of the gods characterized by certain events of the mythological life of the spirit world. This mythological time is exactly one year (or better, one cycle of the seasons of nature) long, and its reenactment in the life of the preliterate has the same measure. The human culture copies the mythological cycle, and thus time is being implemented. Consequently, profane, secular time and sacred time are on two mutually exclusive ends of extremes. Secular time is utterly linear without any further defining points while sacred time is completely circular and self-enclosed.

---

[7]There may also be a time before creation, though this is a very sophisticated addition to the traditions that is not particularly representative of them. An example of this sort of adumbration would be the time before God created the earth and humans, the time in which Satan rebelled against God. However, within that framework Satan would still be considered a created being, and there must have been a time when he was created. Thus the upshot still would be that time begins with creation—though in this case creation of a spiritual rather than a physical being.

[8]Wilhelm Schmidt, *The Origin of Religions: Facts and Theories,* trans. H. J. Rose (London: Methuen, 1931), p. 283.

Thus, and this is not an easy point to grasp for anyone coming from a "nonarchaic" perspective, there is no ongoing time in the sense in which we are used to it. This time next year is the same time as now and the same time as exactly a year ago. Time moves in a circle around the calendar, and

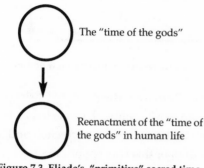

The "time of the gods"

Reenactment of the "time of the gods" in human life

Figure 7.3. Eliade's "primitive" sacred time

it has its being entirely on the basis of the special days that mark it. Consequently, if Eliade is correct with this analysis, when preliterate persons refer to a divine act of creation, they are referring not to an event in the remote past but to an event in the "time of the gods," which is reenacted on an annual basis. (See figure 7.3.)

A good example of how this circular nature of time works is found in the life of the Hopi Indians of the Southwestern United States. The Hopi are an agricultural people; thus their lives and culture are tied to the cycle of the bean crops that they grow every year. In terms of their sacred year, the most important event is the descent of the Kachina spirits from the mountains into their village. These spirits superintend the planting, growth and harvesting of the crops. Once the harvest is in, they depart, only to return again the next year. The descent of the Kachina from the mountains is observed with a festival in which the men of the Kachina society dress up as the spirits and parade through the town. In terms of Eliade's scheme, one can identify two dimensions to this process: one is the visible one, an annual reenactment that one can observe simply by being present at the festival. However, the observance is not just a reenactment in the sense of being a costume party where men dress up in colorful clothes;[9] nor is it merely a ritual that somehow causes the Kachina to invade the village. Instead, the ceremony is also the means by which the villagers truly become the Kachina. The activities are then the single eternally recurring event of the Kachina's descent, which is exemplified in the annual reenactments. One can do worse than to remind oneself of Platonic philosophy: The realities of present existence are actually copies of the eternal Forms.

---

[9]Though, interestingly, there is one group of men called "clowns," who dress up in all black and white costumes (John D. Loftin, *Religion and Hopi Life in the Twentieth Century* [Bloomington: Indiana University Press, 1991], pp. 111-12).

Fascinatingly, Eliade's understanding of preliterate time is not abrogated as cultures move out of the preliterate pattern. Here is the paradox. Even as the secular human beings have distanced themselves from the preliterate pattern of an eternally recurring cycle of time, they have retained a consciousness of that cycle, and so they celebrate birthdays, anniversaries and holidays—including the arrival of the new year, one of the most vigorously observed festivals in Western secularized culture. Surely this last-mentioned holiday is at least a distant echo of the preliterate annual cycle, not just because the passing of a year is observed but because of the intensity of the celebration that goes beyond the mere recognition of an astronomical period.

The point here is that Eliade's archaic persons cannot have expectations for the future because they have no future in that sense. The only future they know is that of the unceasing reenactment of the same paradigmatic present.[10] Similarly, truly secular persons cannot have a hope for the future either because they have no *telos* to their future; they simply experience the monotonous repetition of moment after moment. In order for there to be a future hope, a culture must have a sense of time that includes a genuine future. So, even though in one sense early preliterate cultures may have the concept of a beginning of time, at least in the notion of a divine act of creation, there cannot be an end to time because time, including the point of creation, will return again and again.

So far, three types of time have been mentioned: linear without an end, linear with an end, and cyclical with the cycle of exactly one year's duration. There are two other versions to this temporal geometry, both of which originated on the Indian subcontinent: that of a much larger cycle and that of many huge cycles becoming a spiral.

Jainist cosmology sees time as arranged in a huge circle including both a descending and an ascending mode. Both of these halves can be divided into six ages, each of which is worse than the preceding one in the descending mode or better in the ascending mode (see figure 7.4). The

Figure 7.4. The Jain view of time

---

[10]John S. Mbiti, *African Religions and Philosophy* (Nairobi: East African Educational Publishers, 1969), pp. 15-28, also illustrates this point. I shall develop it further below.

length of these eras, expressed in the measures *sagaropama, sagara, palya* and *purva*, is practically incomprehensible. Thomas comments on these length measurements: "Sagaropama, Sagara, Palya and Purva are mythical time divisions the exact length of which is known only to the omniscient. The number of years these represent are so fantastically astronomic that ordinary men and women can have no conception of their length or duration."[11]

Table 7.1 summarizes the six ages and provides one conception of what human life will be like in each of them.[12] The descending phases are called *susama susama, susama, susama dusama, dusama susama, dusama* and *dusama dusama*. We are presently in *dusama*, the next to the last of the six descending phases. Thus, things are not yet as bad as they are going to be. Eventu-

Table 7.1 The six ages of Jain thought

Age	Length	Human Bodies	Living Conditions	Religious Condition
susama susama	4 crores of *sagaropama*	6 miles tall, 256 ribs	Great happiness, no needs	No sin; no need for religion; universal bliss after death
susama	incredibly long	4 miles tall, 128 ribs	Happiness	No sin; no need for religion; universal bliss after death
susama dusama	incredibly long	2 miles tall, 64 ribs	Happiness and some misery; some needs and war	Sin arises; Rishabhadeva, the first Tirthankara, comes and teaches the Jain religion
dusama susama	1 crore or crores of sagaropama minus 42,000 years	500 spans, 32 ribs	Misery and some happiness	Much sin; the majority of Tirthankaras are needed
dusama (our age)	21,000 years began 3 years after Mahavira's liberation)	7 cubits, 16 ribs	Misery	Sin dominates; extension of Mahavira's teaching ministry
dusama dusama	21,000 years	1 cubit, 8 ribs	Great misery	Only sin; no Tirthankaras, no religion

---

[11]P. Thomas, *Epics, Myths and Legends of India* (Bombay: D. B. Taraporevala Sons, n.d.), p. 131.
[12]Thomas, *Epics,* p. 131.

ally, after *dusama dusama*, the most corrupt of all eras, things will start to improve again until the upward phase has been completed. Thus in this chronology there is a future; in fact, there is always a future since there is no particular expectation that the cycle will ever end. Nor does it really make sense to speak of a completion of the cycle. From any given point it is always exactly a 360-degree trip to arrive precisely at one's starting point. It is the incredible length of this cycle that separates it from the preliterate picture; given all the ages, there is much room for change. However, when one comes right down to it, there can never be a truly novel future within the actual cosmos. The only escape from the cycle of time is by way of liberation from the cosmos altogether and attainment of nirvana. [13]

The Hindu view of time introduces the possibility of novelty. The cyclical feature has not been totally abrogated, but the revolutions around the cycle are not merely copies of each other. Each cycle is slightly different, so that there is a kind of progress from cycle to cycle. Nonetheless, each of the cycles does follow a very similar pattern. (See figure 7.5.)

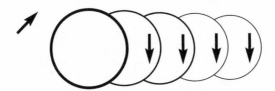

Figure 7.5. The Hindu view of time

Hinduism imagines an extremely elaborate system of cycles. Presumably, an originally simple circle of time became increasingly expanded into larger and larger units. Of course, since this is all entirely speculative, there is no one theory within the broad range of Hindu thought. However, the following (see figure 7.6) is one example, as described by Eliade. [14]

The fundamental unit of cosmic time is an age called a *yuga*. There are four such ages, which make up a *mahayuga* or great *yuga*. The four *yugas* are called the Kirta Yuga, Treta Yuga, Dvapara Yuga and Kali Yuga. They are respectively 4,000, 3,000, 2,000 and 1,000 years long, plus certain transition periods in between. These four *yugas* add up to one *mahayuga* of a length of 12,000 years. However, if one counts each of these years as

---

[13]Eliade, *Myth of the Eternal Return*, pp. 115-18.
[14]Ibid., pp. 113-15.

"divine" years, which are actually 360 years long each, then a *mahayuga* actually lasts more than 4,000,000 years. One thousand *mahayugas* make up a *kalpa*, and fourteen *kalpas* constitute one *manvatara*. One *manvantara* would be exactly one week in the life of Brahma since each day and each night is exactly one *kalpa* for this deity. Brahma lives for 100 such years. Table 7.2 shows Eliade's calculations of Hindu time (unless indicated differently, the units are in years).

Table 7.2 Eliade's calculations of Hindu time

Unit	Subunit	Significance	Dawn	Length	Twilight	Total
Yuga	Kirta Yuga		400	4,000	400	4,800
	Treta Yuga		300	3,000	300	3,600
	Dvapara Yuga		200	2,000	200	2,400
	Kali Yuga		100	1,000	100	1,200
Mahayuga		One cycle of yugas				12,000
	Expanded	Each year = 360 years				4,320,000
Kalpa				1,000 mahayugas		4,320,000,000
Manvantara				14 kalpas		60,480,000,000
Brahma's Life		1 kalpa = 1 day		100 years		311,040,000,000,000
		1 kalpa = 1 night				

As one can see, these times add up to an incredible length. At that, one should not even think of Brahma's life as exhausting the possible time frame because other gods preceded him and he will be succeeded by further ones. These cycles truly are infinite in duration and occurrence. The difference from the Jain picture is that, in addition to the recurrence, there also is a certain amount of progress: Brahma does age and will eventually be replaced.

The Buddhist conception of time seems a little less complex than either the Hindu or the Jain one. There are numerous divisions of time that add up to *kalpas*, and each such division is dominated by the Buddha of his age. There will always be more ages, and there will always be more Buddhas.

It becomes quite apparent that when one refers to *time* in the world's religions, the exact meaning is going to vary drastically. The understanding of the future in one culture is not the same thing as the future in another culture. Consequently, the understanding of messianic expectations will also vary depending on the context.

THE FUTURE IN TRADITIONAL RELIGION

Let me clarify the relationship between time and future in traditional, preliterate cultures by referring to one particular instance, the notion of time in African traditional religion, as expounded by John S. Mbiti.[15] According to Mbiti, in the African understanding of time there are two levels, which correspond nicely to Eliade's profane and sacred time.[16] The time within which people live out their day-to-day existences is *sasa*, a concept that embraces the present, the past as it is immediately remembered, and a very short span of the anticipated future. African life is ordered according to the activities of life; consequently, *sasa* is ordered according to what humans do: the daily chores, the passing of the seasons, and the cycles of animal husbandry or agriculture. Only such concrete events as these can make up time. Mbiti states, "The future is virtually absent because events which lie in it have not taken place, they have not been realized and cannot, therefore, constitute time."[17]

Sasa is engulfed by the second kind of time, *zamani*. This is mythological time. It is the time of the remote past, and it is the time into which *sasa* loses itself as it gets used up. A person who is about to be born lives in *sasa* already but is not yet actualized completely. As the person is born, the process of actualization begins in earnest. Depending on the particular African culture, the person moves through the prescribed stages of life, which usually include puberty rites, marriage and other forms of initiation, such as into societies or elderhood. With each new attainment, the human being becomes increasingly actualized until death, which is at once the full actualization and the beginning of the de-actualization. Even after death the person is still in *sasa*, only now the momentum is moving away from *sasa*, and every step away from it is a step into *zamani*. As living-dead, the person still participates in *sasa*, but when all those who remembered the departed in life are gone themselves, the individual has shifted over completely into *zamani*. Again depending at least partially on the specific cul-

---

[15]Mbiti, *African Religions*, pp. 15-29.
[16]Mbiti uses two Swahili terms here; obviously, given the many African cultures and languages, he is referring to an idea that may not be explicitly stated in many tribes or would be expressed with different terms insofar as it is present.
[17]Ibid., p. 17.

ture, a person may be considered to be a part of an impersonal collective memory or even integrated into the mythology of the culture, but the human being's existence in *sasa* is finished and cannot be revived.

It is crucial to observe that *zamani* does not have a future either. It surrounds *sasa*, it gives *sasa* meaning, but it certainly does not extend *sasa*. Mbiti concludes:

> Since the future does not exist beyond a few months, the future cannot be expected to usher in a golden age, or a radically different state of affairs from what is in the Sasa and the Zamani. The notion of messianic hope, or a final destruction of the world, has no place in [the] traditional concept of history.[18]

However, an interesting phenomenon in this respect has occurred in Africa. As Christianity has become established in Africa, the church has taken on two different forms: (1) the European-originated forms that the missionaries usually brought in and (2) an adaptation into intentionally African forms. The latter forms, oftentimes collectively referred to as the "independent churches," reflect many elements of African traditional religions, at times to the point of syncretism. However, one point on which many of the independent Christian groups have abandoned the indigenous patterns has been in adopting an eschatology. In fact, for some of these groups, eschatology has become the dominant motif; they often call themselves Zionist, and they hold to very fervent messianic expectations, possibly even to the point of declaring their founder to be the Messiah.[19] Mbiti comments:

> African peoples are discovering the future dimension of time. . . . In church life this discovery seems to create a strong expectation of the millennium. This makes many Christians escape from facing the challenges of this life into a state of merely hoping and waiting for the life of paradise.[20]

As the invasion of Western culture has brought a new way of looking at time, the result has been what seems to be an unhealthy overappropriation of the Western notion of the future.

A similar thing occurred with the Native Americans of the nineteenth century. Having been exposed to a Western conception of time and at least a rudimentary Christian eschatology, the American Indian tribes of the

---

[18]Ibid., p. 23.
[19]For example, the amaNazaretha church, founded by Isaiah Shembe. See E. Thomas Lawson, *Religions of Africa* (New York: Harper & Row, 1985), p. 45.
[20]Mbiti, *African Religions*, p. 28.

central plains, by now with little freedom left, united in a messianic movement called Ghost Dancing. The messiah was an Oklahoma farmhand called Wovoka, who went by the English name Jack Wilson and taught that God would soon reestablish his special children, the red people, and punish all the white people. In the meantime, Indians should dance special dances in order to bring about the resurrection of the people who had been killed by the whites. This movement ended in 1890 with the massacre at Wounded Knee. Just as with the African independent churches, exposure to the future dimension of time led to a vigorous eschatology, even to the point of apocalypse. And again similar to the African movements, an appropriation and adaptation of the white man's own religion was supposed to offer liberation from the oppression caused by the white man.

THE FUTURE IN WESTERN RELIGIONS

As mentioned above, most of the so-called Western religions—Judaism, Zoroastrianism, Christianity and Islam—all have incorporated a definite expectation of a consummation in the future, and in each of these traditions, the future is going to bring a messiah. Obviously, the term *messiah* originally belongs only to Judaism and by extension to the Jewish sect that we call Christianity. However, it seems to be a pretty harmless appropriation to use the term *messiah* also in a generic sense to apply to any figure that religious people expect to come in the future to usher in a new age.

Judaism. The concept of the messiah in Judaism is neither completely clear nor universal. Christians like to argue that the predictions of Christ as the messiah in the Old Testament are unequivocal, but knowledgeable Jews are quick to point out that, if that were so, Christians would not need to claim that many of these prophecies refer to a second coming of Christ at some time in the future, so that Christians are implicitly admitting that there are many messianic prophecies that were not fulfilled (at least so far) by Christ.

By the time of Christ there were several messianic expectations current within Judaism. Clearly there was a mainstream expectation of a political messiah, someone who would liberate the Jews from the Romans and reestablish the kingdom (whether that of David or that of the more recent Hasmonean dynasty).[21] On the other hand, the Essenes at Qumran expected

---

[21]Of course, the operative metaphor was the kingdom of David, but for first-century Jews the closest example of such a kingdom would have been the Hasmonean kingdom in the second and first centuries B.C., not the truly ancient kingdom of more than a millennium earlier.

not one, but two (maybe even three) messiahs—a messianic king and a messianic priest, preceded by the Teacher of Righteousness, a prophetic figure who could also be reckoned as a messiah.[22] Furthermore, one could wonder whether the establishment of the day, namely, the ruling priest-hood and the Sadducees, were particularly keen on expecting any mes-siah. And one must remember that Jesus himself was accepted as the messiah by many Jews, but certainly did not receive universal support for his claims.

So, it is questionable whether one can ever point to a truly consistent conception of the messiah within Judaism as a religious system (just as Judaism itself has always entertained diversity on a broader scale). The following characteristics tended to reappear in most cases, though there always tended to be exceptions. [23]

1. The messiah would be a human being. However, certain mystical writ-ings tended to equate him with God's first created being, the angel Metatron.

2. The messiah would be the Son of David. This would place him into the succession of the kings of Judah. There are two exceptions here: *(a)* Some Jewish groups expected the messiah to be the Son of Levi, that is to say, an Aaronic, priestly messiah rather than a royal one. *(b)* Another idea developed that involved a "messiah, the Son of Joseph." The title would indicate that he was the messiah coming out of the ten "lost" northern tribes, which were often identified with Joseph or Joseph's son, Ephraim. This figure would be a second, tragic messiah who would precede the Son of David and would be killed in battle. This aspect of messianic expectations made it a little easier for some Jews to rational-ize failed messianic expectations.

3. The messiah would restore Israel, most likely in both a political and spiritual sense.

4. The messiah would liberate Israel from their oppressors.

The history of Judaism since biblical times is replete with many messi-anic pretenders.[24] Many of them were more important for specific sub-

---

[22]See the discussion by F. F. Bruce, *Second Thoughts on the Dead Sea Scrolls* (Grand Rapids, Mich.: Eerdmans, 1961), pp. 80-91.

[23]See the articles, "Messiah" and "Pseudo-Messiahs," in *Jewish Encyclopedia*, 12 vols. (New York: Funk & Wagnalls, 1925), and in *Encyclopaedia Judaica*, 16 vols. (New York: Macmillan, 1972).

[24]The *Jewish Encyclopedia* lists thirty-four individuals under the heading of "Pseudo-Messi-ahs."

groups, for example, various kabbalistic groups, than for Judaism as a whole. The most important apparent messiahs for Judaism at large were Bar Kokhba and Sabbatai Zevi in the second and seventeenth century, respectively. However, many of the others shaped Judaism at least indirectly by providing small nudges here and there, possibly simply by providing an occasion for reaction against them.

Interestingly, the Hasidic movement, which began with the idea of Baal Shem Tov as directly mediating the presence of God in his community (an office that is continued by the rebbes of various Hasidic groups), has traditionally shied away from making messianic claims for its leaders. Furthermore, many Hasidim were opposed to the creation of the state of Israel initially because they believed that to establish the kingdom of God without the messianic king was blasphemy.[25] (Though once the state was in place, they accepted it.) However, a large controversy is taking place at the time of this writing involving one Hasidic group, the Lubavitchers. Their recently deceased rebbe, Rabbi Menachem Mendel Schneerson, who must be considered a truly outstanding human being, was acclaimed to be messiah by some of his followers. Since he died without the messianic mission fulfilled, these followers are now expecting his resurrection in order to complete his calling. Needless to say, Jews outside of the movement and many Lubavitchers themselves reject these ideas.[26]

On the other hand, Reform Jews have given up looking for a messiah. They are working for a world in which the messianic ideals of peace and justice are realized. At first, this aim kept them from desiring a separate Jewish state as well, but after the Holocaust of World War II, they became as strongly supportive of the State of Israel as any other Jews.

Islam. Future hope in Islam has often focused on the Mahdi, literally the "rightly guided one," as the final messenger from Allah. It is important to recognize, however, that, even though Mahdi expectation has been a constant presence, it is not as integral as, say, the future final judgment in Islam or the messianic coming in Judaism.

Islamic Mahdi expectations are based not on the Qur'an but on the secondary writings (the Hadith) insofar as they have any scriptural basis at all, and some of those may have been written late in order to accommodate

---

[25]This idea was developed dramatically by Chaim Potok in the novel *The Chosen* (New York: Fawcrest, 1967).

[26]Moshe Friedman, "Moshiach and the Lubavitcher Rebbe: An Essay Supporting the R.C.A. Declaration That Condemns Belief in a 'Resurrected Messiah' as Being Totally Foreign to Judaism." Internet posting at <http://hudson.idt.net/~mf733/>.

the hope for the Mahdi. Corresponding to the two major divisions of Islam, there are also two understandings of the role of the Mahdi. The majority of Muslims are Sunnites; in Sunni Islam there is a general expectation of a Mahdi that is tied to various details but does not contain a specific Mahdi theology. Among the minority Shi'ites, however, the Mahdi also fulfills a particular theological role, namely, the reappearance of the imam who is presently in concealment (an idea that I will explain below).

Eschatology is very much a part of Islam. The idea of a final judgment culminating in heaven or hell for all human beings is one of the core beliefs of all people who consider themselves Muslims. For many Muslims this expectation also includes the notion that Jesus Christ (the most prominent prophet next to Muhammad) will return right before the judgment and lead the faithful in prayer. But Jesus is not (usually) considered to be the Mahdi. The Mahdi is a different person. Most likely he will come at the head of an army that sports black flags. His name and patronym will be the same as the true prophet (Muhammad Ahmad), and he will initiate a time when all Islam's enemies will be eliminated and universal justice will be restored prior to the last judgment. Among those who also are waiting for the return of Christ, there has been a notable debate about who will have preeminence among the two, the Mahdi or Jesus. The priority would belong to the person who actually leads the final prayer, as opposed to lining up behind him with all of the other people. In general, this honor is said to belong to Jesus because he is a prophet, while the Mahdi is not necessarily one.

In Shi'ite Islam, the role of the Mahdi carries greater theological meaning. The most crucial distinction between the Sunnites and Shi'ites was originally based on the question of who would become successor to Muhammad when the prophet died. The Sunnite majority decided on various former associates of Muhammad, known as caliphs, each time that the position opened, while the Shi'ites argued for members of Muhammad's family (his son-in-law Ali, followed by his grandson Husayn), whom they called imams. Even though the Sunnites saw the caliphs as distinguished in their adherence to Muhammad's teachings and spirituality, they did not make the extraordinary claims for them that the Shi'ites did for the imams. For the Shi'ites, the imams each possessed the same spiritual authority as Muhammad himself. While the caliphs were acknowledged as humans who were superior in their wisdom and piety, the imams were superhumans to their followers. At least among the two larger groups of Shi'ites (the Twelvers or Imamites and the Seveners or Ishmailites), the belief developed that the last in the uninterrupted line of imams (the twelfth or the seventh, respectively) did not die but went into conceal-ment. Ever since that time, he has been holding himself apart from the world but will return again as the Mahdi. Consequently, in the Shi'ite tra-ditions, the Mahdi does occupy a more integral position than among the Sunnites, and as the returning imam he clearly has the full authority of Muhammad himself.

As with the messiah in Jewish tradition, there is no shortage of pretend-ers to the title of Mahdi (or, in many cases, people to whom others referred as Mahdi). Among the Sunnites, there were several caliphs who were regarded as the Mahdi. The first long-term dynasty of caliphs was that of the Umayyads, and their Umar II was revered as Mahdi for a time. (At one remarkable point in time, Serene, a Jewish messianic pretender, attempted to lead a revolt against Umar II—one group's messiah squaring off against another group's messiah.) The Umayyads were eventually replaced by the Abbasids, and they did so with support that was generated by Mahdi fever. The third caliph of this dynasty actually featured the name Al-Mahdi. Mahdi claims continued on a fairly regular basis, usually in order to legitimize a change of leadership. The Umayyads remained in power in Spain, even after the Abbasid takeover, and one of their caliphs also called himself Al-Mahdi. In a somewhat unique cross-over between the Sunnites and the Shi'ites in the tenth century, the Shi'ite Fatimid dynasty (who belonged to the Ishmailites) provided the caliphate for a time while resid-ing in Alexandria, Egypt, and one of their early rulers carried the appella-tion Mahdiyyah.

Perhaps the most dramatic of all Mahdi movements to date occurred in the Sudan in the nineteenth century. Its leader was Muhammad Ahmad (the mandated name for the Mahdi), who, even though in Sunnite terri-tory, declared himself to be the returned twelfth imam of the Shi'ite tradi-tion. In the name of liberating the oppressed, he gathered a large following in order to throw off the shackles of the Ottoman Empire—and to maintain the lucrative slave trade that the sultan had declared illegal. His move-ment was eventually put down by the combined forces of the Turks, the British, and a counter-Mahdi, known as Sanusi Al-Mahdi.[27]

---

[27]These events were portrayed in the 1966 movie *Khartoum*, which took the viewpoint of the British General Charles "Chinese" Gordon, perhaps best known for his invention of Gor-don's Calvary in Jerusalem. See the article "Mahdi," in *Encyclopedia of Islam*, 7 vols. and sup-plements (New York: E. J. Brill, 1993).

Claims to Mahdiship have extended right into the twentieth century. A contemporary group that originated in the nineteenth century, the Ahmadiyya Movement, bases itself on its founder, Mirza Ghulam Ahmad of Qadiyan, who claimed to be the Mahdi, as well as the second coming of Christ and an avatar of Krishna. Currently, there are two branches to this group, one of which has come to reject all apparently unorthodox claims and simply describes Ghulam as Mahdi, while the other one (the Lahore branch) is maintaining most of the original more exotic ideas. Both bodies stress a commitment to peace and a repudiation of violence.[28]

Baha'i. Though small in number of adherents, the religion of Baha'i is, next to Christianity, geographically the most widespread religion in the world today. This religion began in 1844 as a direct offshoot from Shi'ite Islam. In Persia, the Imamite Shi'ites had been waiting for the return of the twelfth imam. In time the belief developed that this imam was communicating with the world through certain individuals who were known as Bab, or "Gate." In 1844 a man named Ali Muhammad claimed that he was the last such Bab, an assertion that many of his followers eventually raised to the claim of his being the Mahdi himself. In this office he led an unsuccessful attempt to topple the shah and eventually died along with many of his followers, known as Babis. One disciple of his, Husayn Ali, declared himself to be the Bab's successor, took the title of Baha'ullah, and founded the Baha'i religion.

Baha'ullah taught that there were nine main Manifestations of God of which the Bab was the eighth and he the ninth (the others being Abraham, Krishna, Moses, Zoroaster, Buddha, Jesus and Muhammad). Even though this religion was born in messianic fervor, it does not now carry explicit messianic expectations. Baha'ullah is the Manifestation for this era, and even though one cannot rule out the possibility of another Manifestation for a future era, such an expectation is not a relevant concern for the moment. If a future age calls for another Manifestation, one will come, but only if there is a real need.

Zoroastrianism. Zoroastrianism is the religion of ancient Persia; its few followers these days are known as the Parsis. The founder of this religion was Zarathustra (the more accurate Persian version of his name than the

---

[28]David S. Noss and John B. Noss, *A History of the World's Religions,* 9th ed. (New York: Macmillan, 1994), p. 649. For information by the movement about itself, see "The Ahmadiyya Movement in Islam: An Overview" at <http://www.alislam.org/introduction/>, posted by the Ahmadiyya Muslim Community, 1995-2002.

Greek "Zoroaster"), who lived in the sixth century B.C. It became a part of the Zoroastrian tradition that Zoroaster would be succeeded at thousand-year intervals by certain of his direct descendants. According to the mythology, Zoroaster deposited his sperm in a lake. Three times, a thousand years apart, a virgin will bathe in the lake and become impregnated with his sperm. These three men, named Aushetar, Aushetarmah and Saoshyant, will be prophets like Zoroaster. The last one, Saoshyant, will not only restore true religion but will also usher in the final event of history, a universal conflagration in which all beings will be flooded by hot molten metal—the evil ones for their purification, the good ones experiencing nothing more than a warm, pleasurable bath. Afterward, all life will be true, pure and holy.

THE FUTURE IN EASTERN RELIGIONS

Hinduism. As I explained above, Hinduism has devised a cyclical theory of time, according to which we are now living in the last age of the last era, the Kali Yuga. At the close of this evil time period, there will be a brief respite when Kalki appears. Kalki is the tenth and last of the incarnations (avatars) of the god Vishnu. Vishnu, the Preserver, has incarnated himself from time to time in order to preserve the dharma, the true teaching of religion. In this role he has manifested himself as, among others, Rama, Krishna and even Buddha. But there is one incarnation remaining, namely, as Kalki at the very end of time.

Kalki is usually pictured with the head of a horse, though he is actually expected to have the form of a human being. When he appears, he will come riding on a white horse, convert the whole world to the dharma and destroy Yama, the god of death. But because the universe is in a rundown state already, ultimately Kalki will initiate the destruction of the universe (an act that is usually also associated with the god Shiva, the Destroyer) so that a new world can be created and the new time cycle can begin.

It is important to recognize for Kalki, as well as for the other Indic messiahs that I will mention below, that there is nothing really final in his mission. In contrast to the Western messianic expectations, Kalki does not bring about the end of time; he initiates only the end of a cycle in time. The cycles will continue endlessly. Thus, as Eliade observed,[29] salvation is constituted by an escape from time, not by the culmination of time.

---

[29]Eliade, *Myth of the Eternal Return*, p. 119.

Buddhism. Similarly to Hinduism, Buddhism is looking forward to a messianic figure who will bring in a new era, but not the end of all eras. The various Buddhist schools recognize different Buddhas in addition to Gautama, the historical founder of Buddhism (referred to frequently as Sakyamuni—the wise man of the Sakya clan—in order to emphasize his historical nature). In some of the earlier schools each Buddha is seen as presiding over a particular age; for example, the first Buddha, Vipashyin, was the Buddha ruling the first age, while Sakyamuni is the Buddha of the seventh age. Later schools multiplied the number and types of Buddhas and added another category of celestial beings, the Bodhisattvas, those whose enlightenment is only one lifetime away. Most of these Bodhisattvas have postponed their enlightenment in order to make their spiritual power available to humankind, but there is one exception, namely, the Bodhisattva Maitreya, who is already committed to coming to earth and being the Buddha of the next age. Maitreya will bring an era of universal enlightenment. It is he, not Sakyamuni, who is usually pictured as the chubby laughing Buddha in iconography and novelty stores because he will bring a time of bliss. Nevertheless, all this will be temporary because his age will ultimately give way to yet another one with many more following.

Jainism. Jainism, too, has a cyclical view of time, as described above. On the descending side of the total cosmic cycles, the Tirthankaras have appeared for the purpose of retaining order. But they are fighting a losing battle. The last age of the descent will be *dusama dusama*, the period of abject misery that contains only suffering, no religion and no Tirthankaras. However, eventually time will move upward again. People will live longer, grow taller, be happier and find the way of salvation again. This process will be aided by twenty-five counterparts to the twenty-five Tirthankaras. They are presently in various stages of preparation, mostly concerned with their own purification. When the time comes, they will be ready to take this leadership. In the Jain mythology, each of these figures already has a name, and their present abodes are pinpointed.

Thus Jainism is not looking forward to a single messianic figure. Instead, there will be a messianic series of ages, guided by various salutary individuals. There is hope, but hope is very far into the future. And this hope is also only temporary (though for a long duration) since eventually the upward part of the cycle will turn downward again. Thus, just as with Buddhism and Hinduism, salvation cannot lie within temporal history but must be found by escaping time and history altogether.

THE FUTURE IN CHRISTIANITY

It seems to be a safe conclusion, then, to assert that usually some form of messianic expectation comes with an enscripturated religion, and, for that matter, as soon as preliterate cultures are influenced by a linear sense of time, they tend to look for a future messiah as well. Obviously, the question arises of how all this material compares and contrasts with the Christian approach to the messiah.

1. Christianity was born of fulfilled messianic expectations. The whole point of the origin of Christianity is that Jesus Christ claimed—and his followers agreed—that he was the fulfillment of Old Testament messianic prophecies.[30] The break between Judaism and Christianity began at this juncture. Those who were to become known as Christians used such verses as Isaiah 9:6, 7:14, 53:1-6 and others to indicate that these messianic prophecies were fulfilled in Christ.

2. Christians used other Old Testament messianic prophecies to corroborate the idea that Christ, the messiah, would come again. These prophecies refer to some of the idealistic end-times forecasts, for example, Isaiah 11 (the lion shall lie down with the lamb), Isaiah 33 (prophecies of the last judgment) and Daniel 7:13 (the Son of Man coming in the clouds). Needless to say, there are many variations among Christians of how to construe the time table for the end of the ages,[31] but that there will be a second coming of Christ that will include a final judgment, followed by the eternal state, is a nonnegotiable item. All Christians are at least implicitly committed to a two-part coming of the messiah, the first one two thousand years ago, and the second one sometime in the future at the consummation of the ages.[32] The apostle Paul in Titus 2:13 marks the expectation of Christ's second coming as one of the central aspects of the Christian life.

3. Thus Christianity contains a powerful notion of now-and-not-yet. This proleptic element is stronger in Christianity than in other religions where the now and the not-yet are more separated, usually at the expense of the not-yet. In other religions, whatever (or whoever) will come in the

---

[30]Needless to say, this is not all he claimed, and I am not meaning to limit his claims to this one. Clearly he claimed much more, for example, to be God, and eventually those claims will impact the thought I am developing.

[31]For a good discussion of the options and implications, see Robert G. Clouse, Robert N. Hosack and Richard V. Pierard, *The New Millennium Manual: A Once and Future Guide* (Grand Rapids, Mich.: Baker, 1999).

[32]And, of course, many contemporary evangelical Christians hold to a three-part scenario in which the first second appearance is preceded by Christ's coming to rapture the church out of the world exactly seven years prior to the final coming.

future is a reiteration of the past or the present, but not an organic out-growth that both fulfills and reshapes the past. A good example of this now at the expense of the not-yet would be in the Sunnite Mahdi traditions in which the coming of a Mahdi, even according to those who believe in him or identify him with a certain individual, is only an addition to the Islamic doctrines. Nothing significant for Islam hinges on the coming of the Mahdi. Similarly, as I shall elaborate below, in less extreme ways the future in other religions only fulfills the past, but the future cannot possibly shape the past or the present.[33]

On the other hand, in Christianity, Jesus has not only already come and instituted a new plan of salvation through his death and resurrection, but he is going to come again and take full charge of the entire cosmos. It is the same person who is both redeemer at the first advent and lord at the second advent. Present-day believers must look both backward and forward. But even more than that, his future coming ultimately provides more and greater meaning to the past and the present. All of what he has done and is doing makes sense on the basis of the future. As Paul points out in 1 Corinthians 15, if there is no future resurrection at the point of Christ's second coming, we are the most miserable of all people. But the future resurrection is guaranteed by Christ's own past resurrection. Thus the future and the past mutually validate each other.

4. Closely tied to the above idea is the dual role of Christ both inside and outside of history. It would seem safe to say that by and large the function of the various messiah figures is historical in the sense of being expectations among the historical events of the future, but not fundamentally spiritual. Of course, they have important spiritual functions as well as historical ones, but the spiritual functions in their expected roles are not usually central to the religions in which they are being expected. For example: (a) In Judaism, the messiah will come, reestablish the kingdom of David and teach the Torah (though a very few have expected him to abolish the Torah), which Moses had originally brought. (b) The Mahdi will come and set up an

---

[33]A good example of this phenomenon was presented by the now-defunct webpage of the Taliban, Afghanistan's ruling party for a time. The site featured prominently a banner with a quotation from the Hadith concerning the Mahdi: "If you see the Black Banners coming from Khurasan go to them immediately, even if you must crawl over ice, because indeed amongst them is the Caliph, Al Mahdi." But the actual content of the site dealt with matters of establishing and maintaining an Islamic republic without appeal to a Mahdi figure. No claim was made that Mullah Muhammad Umar, their leader, was the Mahdi <www.azzam.com/html/talibanwho.htm> and <www.azzam.com/html/talibanshariah.htm>.

Islamic reign based on the Qur'an. *(c)* Saoshyant (and his two earlier colleagues) will teach the doctrine of Zoroaster. He has more of a savior role than Zoroaster, Aushetar or Aushetarmah, in that he will preside over the last judgment and the cosmic cataclysm that will be the cathartic purification for all evil people. However, he does nothing to transform Zoroastrianism or the truths of Zoroastrianism. *(d)* Kalki will be the last avatar of Vishnu, restoring the true dharma one more time before the final end of the age, just as the other avatars did before him. *(e)* Maitreya will bring the final age of enlightenment and teach the same dharma as all the other Buddhas. *(f)* The new Tirthankaras will superintend the upward move of the circle of time through the renewed teaching of Jainist doctrine.

The role of these messianic figures is important, but it is a supporting role. In fact, among the Far Eastern conceptions, the coming one is not all that helpful because there is no true end to history since the cycles will occur again and again anyway. True salvation occurs by way of escaping the phenomenal world in the way prescribed by the particular religion, and the person who keeps on looking to the actual events of the future cannot find salvation. This is clearly not the case for the Western religions, but the messiahs in those contexts are not bringers of salvation either. Their role is to complete history, not to transform it.[34]

On the other hand, Jesus Christ is central to Christianity in both the historical and spiritual dimensions. He is the one who provided final revelation of God's righteousness through his teachings and sinless life; he is the one who reconciled us to God on the cross; he is the one who now mystically indwells each believer personally; and he is the one who will return at the end to bring all of history to consummation.[35] Thus Christ has four roles: as teacher, as redeemer, as mystical reality and as future king. This occupation of multiple functions sets him apart from the messianic figures in the other religions.

---

[34]Eliade shows that in many of the traditions associated with these Western religions, there is, in fact, an element of transformation or even abolition of history. However, in order to make his case he has to point to tangential strands or folk-religion versions of these religions, and as soon as he does that, the spiritual side of these messiahs is emphasized at the expense of their future-historical significance. "The great majority of so-called Christian populations continue, down to our day, to preserve themselves from history by ignoring it and by tolerating it rather than by giving it the meaning of a negative or positive theophany" (Eliade, *Myth of the Eternal Return*, p. 111).

[35]Let me add parenthetically that the notion of the consummation of history requires that history be consummated, not simply abolished. Consequently, even apart from Scriptures and theological schemes, there is good philosophical reason to expect a physical reign of Christ on earth—the so-called millennium.

Furthermore, there is a clear distinctive in the Christian understanding of the messiah based on his incarnation. Now, the idea of an incarnation is not totally unique to Christianity. The easiest example to come to mind is Kalki, the tenth avatar of Vishnu, as mentioned above. However, Vishnu's incarnations are not really the same as God's incarnation in Christ. They are more like the idea of the incarnation as it is found in the early Christian heresy of docetism. The docetists believed that Christ was human in appearance only (hence the name *docetism,* which goes back to the Greek word for "appearance") and that he was not fully human. This is the case for Vishnu; even though his avatars are born, possibly suffer and eventually die, they are not truly fully human. Their humanity (or other bodily appearance) is a guise that they eventually put off again.[36] By contrast, Christian theology holds that the incarnation of Christ is complete and permanent. Jesus is fully God, but also fully human, and he has not abdicated either nature. After his ascension, the New Testament continues to refer to him as "man" (1 Tim 2:5). His human nature is an integral part of the work that he is now doing as our high priest and intercessor (Heb 4:14-16).

What it all boils down to is that the earlier picture representing time in Christianity is not strictly accurate. Christianity exhibits time in a linear mode, beginning with creation, centering on the cross, and ending with the second coming and the final state. However, there is also an understanding of time in Christianity that is reminiscent of (though not the same as) time in the preliterate society as Eliade describes it, namely, a sense of simultaneity that pervades the strict chronological sequence. Creation is understood from the vantage point of the cross and resurrection, and the cross and resurrection are understood from the vantage point of the consummation. The consummation is the ultimate re-creation, and so can only be understood from the vantage point of creation itself. Everything hangs together and does so, finally, in the person of Jesus Christ. In Christianity, eschatology is not just the final chapter, let alone an afterthought, but it is the summation of what Christianity is all about: the redemptive work of Christ, for individuals and the cosmos (Rom 8:19-22).

AUTHENTICATION: THE CRUCIAL ISSUE

So, is there reason to believe that Christ is the messiah? As described

---

[36]In addition to this general fact based on the mythology, a good case in point is Krishna's disclosure of himself as Vishnu in the Bhagavad Gita. Bhagavad Gita 11:3-48, trans. Ramananda Prasad <http://www.sacred-texts.com/hin/gita/agsgita.htm>.

above, the distinctiveness of Christ in Christianity can also be understood in a more negative way, namely, in the sense that Christ is a very peculiar messiah because he has already come and will come again (though such a notion is also found in the Shi'ite concept of the returning imam). After all, this is one of the arguments that defenders of Jewish messianism have traditionally used against Christianity: the historical Jesus cannot be the messiah because the messianic prophecies of the Bible have not been fulfilled. To invoke a second coming would seem to be pious fudging.

Of course, this issue can only be solved by appealing directly to Christ's credentials. Is there reason to believe that he spoke the truth concerning himself? If so, we can take his messianic claims in stride and accommodate ourselves to a two-stage messianism. But if there is doubt concerning his integrity, the peculiar nature of his messianic role is vitiated concurrently.

Twentieth-century Christian apologetics devised various schemes, such as the Legend-Lunatic-Liar-Lord alternatives,[37] of showing that Christ was God, just as he claimed to be. However, in Christ's historical context, the choice was much more polarized and far more extreme. The Jews initially had no problem accepting Jesus as supernatural, but they saw him as evil.[38] Deuteronomy 13:1-5 predicted the coming of a false prophet who would do signs and wonders (sorcery) and entice the people to apostasy and enjoined the people of Israel to put him to death in order to prove their continued faith in God. One of the earliest non-Christian Jewish sources that mentions Christ ascribes precisely these two charges to his prosecution.[39] They understood Jesus to be a false prophet who was in league with Satan (Mark 3:22) and performed acts of sorcery (highlighted by his boast to destroy and rebuild the temple in three days)[40] in order to promote teaching opposed to the law of God. The Jews did not put Jesus to death because he claimed to be the messiah, opposed the establishment, exposed

---

[37]See, for example Paul Little, *Know Why You Believe* (Wheaton, Ill.: Scripture Press, 1967), pp. 49-58. I have attempted to break down the options a little further in *No Doubt About It* (Nashville: Broadman & Holman, 1997), pp. 212-16. Also, Stephen T. Davis, "Was Jesus Mad, Bad, or God?" in *The Incarnation: An Interdisciplinary Symposium on the Incarnation of the Son of God*, ed. Stephen T. Davis, Daniel Kendall and Gerald O'Collins (New York: Oxford University Press, 2002), forthcoming.

[38]Colin Brown writes in *Miracles and the Critical Mind* (Grand Rapids, Mich.: Eerdmans, 1984), p. vii: "I would now be prepared to say that without an understanding of the thirteenth chapter of the book of Deuteronomy and its significance for the Jewish leaders, we cannot begin to understand why they were so opposed to Jesus." See also pp. 312-15.

[39]Sanhedrin 43a, *The Babylonian Talmud*, trans. I. Epstein (London: Soncino, 1935), 3:281.

[40]This idea is brilliantly depicted in Frank Morison, *Who Moved the Stone?* (Grand Rapids, Mich.: Zondervan, 1930), pp. 13-29.

hypocrisy or committed any number of offenses, which many others did at that time as well. According to the Jewish understanding, he had to be executed because he was demonic, and the law demanded this action.

Conversely, Christ's early supporters clearly rejected this charge in favor of an identification just as extreme, namely, that he was God. There seemed to be little room for any middle ground,[41] and, consequently, many modern arguments in favor of Christ's deity would not have been of much use. After all, those who thought Christ was demonic had no problem accepting his miracles as supernatural acts, but they did have difficulty believing that his acts came from God. Similarly, if Christ was demonic, the fact that he died on behalf of his cause would not be as incongruous as it would have been if he were merely a human charlatan.

The key lies in the Hebrew Scriptures themselves. Did Christ, in fact, fulfill the prophecy of Deuteronomy 13? His signs and wonders are indisputable, so one must consult his teachings to see whether they were actually enticements to apostasy. And here Christians have insisted that such is not the case. They have stressed the continuity of Christ's teachings with the Old Testament as evidenced first by the fulfillment of various prophecies,[42] and then also by the content of his teaching. The crucial areas are these:

- The messiah would be God.
- The messiah would suffer on behalf of his people.
- The people would reject the messiah.
- The messiah would fulfill the law, not overthrow it.

Early Christian polemic stressed these ideas in order to show that Jesus was truly the messiah, and not just the messiah, but God himself. Thus his credentials as messiah are authenticated, but more than that. Since his identity is in order, it also becomes eminently plausible to accept that his messianic work occurs in two stages, first his redemptive work and then his consummative work, thus looping the middle of time and the end of time together.

---

[41]This is not to say that more mediating positions did not develop very soon, most notably Ebionitism, which denied the deity of Christ, but also adoptionism, Cerinthianism and other views that tried to have it both ways. My comment is very simply based on the supposition that the New Testament, which asserts that Christ is God, is the earliest and most authentic record of what his followers originally believed about him.

[42]Josh McDowell collates this material in *Evidence That Demands a Verdict* (San Bernardino, Calif.: Here's Life, 1979), pp. 141-77. Also see Walter C. Kaiser, *The Messiah in the Old Testament* (Grand Rapids, Mich.: Zondervan, 1995).

8

FINDING FORDS
AND BUILDING BRIDGES

This chapter intends to respond to the puzzle that has animated the entire book so far. The puzzle in question is, of course, the ambivalence between the unique truth of Christianity and the undeniable fact of truths found in other religions. Logically there is no genuine paradox here; there are no statements that one cannot line up side by side without apparent contradictions.[1] The puzzle is a conceptual one: How can it be that Christianity, which contains exclusive truth, shares so many of its truths with its neighbors?

Keep in mind that in raising the issue in this broad manner I am not again calling into question my earlier conclusions. It is the very truth of my earlier observations that brings about the conceptual puzzle. For, if religions other than Christianity had salvific efficacy, then without question there would also have to be truth in them. Conversely, if other religions were all entirely false in all of their content, then there would be no problem maintaining the exclusive truth of Christianity. But as I have demonstrated, even though other religions cannot bring about a person's salvation, they are nonetheless still not totally devoid of any truths. Many of them do parallel Christianity in some significant teachings, including even a doctrine of grace. This fact, after all, gave rise earlier to the metaphor of the tapestry.

In this chapter, I would like to try to address this phenomenon directly.

---

[1]A true paradox would be, for example, the Russell paradox: The barber in our town shaves all those people who do not shave themselves. Who shaves the barber?

This attempt will consist of two parts. First, I will account for the tapestry effect by making reference to certain phenomenological descriptions of religion. Second, I wish to address the purposive side of this matter, specifically to integrate it into the project of how to communicate the unique truth of the gospel to those who hold to other religions.

Permit me to introduce a whole new metaphor. Imagine that there is a river separating Christian from non-Christian religion. This river demarcates some very real and significant differences. The Christian wishing to convince the non-Christian of Christian truth will rightly attempt to build bridges to the non-Christian.[2] But where does one build bridges? An ancient method is to find places where traffic routes are already established because it is possible to ford across a river at those points. Building a bridge in such a location makes economic sense both because the bridge will have great utility and because it is easier to erect bridge pylons in relatively shallow water.

The first part of this chapter, then, employs the metaphor of ford finding—identifying those concepts that permit a foundation underneath the current of the human religious awareness. The second part will focus more on how to build bridges.

FINDING FORDS

Avoiding the genetic fallacy. What I am about to attempt is rightly received by many evangelical Christians with a healthy amount of skepticism. There is a long-standing tradition in critical scholarship that points to a supposedly universal pattern in certain religious beliefs, places the pattern into a psychological framework and then concludes that the belief in question is *only* a psychological phenomenon. It concludes that, if the belief can be explained as a psychological phenomenon, it must be false in its objective or supernatural reference. In the study of logic this form of reasoning is called the genetic fallacy: "I can explain the origin of this belief; therefore, the belief is false."

Harvey Cox, the Harvard theologian who made a name for himself in the 1960s by riding the crest of so-called secular theology, has provided a

---

[2]I am, of course, fully aware that Van Tilians and Barthians will immediately reject this statement as advocating an impossibility at best, idolatry at worst. The arguments concerning this issue are well rehearsed and bringing them all up here again would serve no purpose other than to double the length of this book by striding once more over well-trodden ground. This chapter will, in fact, materially show that there is common ground and that building bridges is neither impossible nor wrong.

very colorful example of the fallacy.[3] As a high-school student and a Baptist, he attended a Catholic mass with his girl friend who had already taken a college anthropology course. At the point of the Eucharist, she turned to him and assured him, "That's just a primitive totemic ritual, you know." Cox asserts that from that point on, he could never view Communion in the same way again—contributing to his development of a Christian theology without supernatural underpinnings.

This episode is problematic in two important ways. For one, and this is an aside to the central argument here, the concept of a totem feast is very speculative to begin with and highly questionable when applied to Christian Communion, to say the least.[4] The second, and here the more important, reservation concerning Cox's little narrative is the glib way in which it commits the genetic fallacy. There are two related thoughts at work here. First, even if it were possible to rationally construe Christian Communion as a totem feast (and it is not), it would still not follow that it is *just* a totem feast. Second, and this really gets to the core of this chapter, even if it were *just* a totem feast, that conclusion would still not *ipso facto* deprive the ritual of its supernatural context. After all, there could be a totem feast in which the totem is a real supernatural entity. Only a totally reductionistic framework would deprive Communion of its true spiritual nature simply by explaining it (contrary to fact) as a totem feast.

In this case, in order to choose a picturesque example, I have selected an anecdote in which the identification was wrong and also the interpretation of the item, namely, identifying Communion as a totem feast was thought of as depriving it of its supernatural reality. However, even if it were a correct identification, that fact would not deprive a biblical concept of its truth. After all, that is what I have argued throughout this book. The fact that there are ideas of morality or grace in other religions in no way compromises the integrity of the Christian awareness of morality and grace, derived as they are from divine revelation.

The important principle to keep in mind in this context is that God does not necessarily work apart from, let alone against, human psychology or culture. Sometimes he does, and we need to be open to that possibility whenever it arises, as well. But we also need not fear that, just because

---

[3] As reported by James W. Fowler, *Stages of Faith: The Psychology of Human Development and the Quest for Meaning* (San Francisco: Harper & Row, 1981), pp. 180-81. Professor Cox also confirmed this event to me in private e-mail correspondence.

[4] See Wilhelm Schmidt, *The Origin and Growth of Religion: Facts and Theories*, trans. H. J. Rose (London: Methuen, 1931), pp. 103-17.

some aspect of Christian religion is also a part of human culture, it cannot therefore be a part of what God has revealed and what pleases him. Is that not how he has worked throughout Scripture, particularly in the Old Testament? There is no denying that many practices commanded by him to the ancient Israelites are closely in keeping with similar ones in other ancient religious cultures. There are also many others that are forbidden, and so the only way to make a meaningful assessment is to look at particular cases. In general terms, sometimes God works within human culture, sometimes against it.

Sinkholes. And so, as I set out I need to tread carefully. An apparent ford may turn out to contain hidden sinkholes that make an actual crossing impossible. In nonmetaphorical language, not all accounts of religion are even possible candidates for what I am trying to do. The sinkholes appear when an explication is deliberately framed in such a way that it will inevitably lead to conclusions incompatible with Christian truth.

A very crude example of this possibility would be the theory of Ludwig Feuerbach who claimed that all the alleged attributes of God are nothing but the projections of idealized human qualities.[5] Clearly, such an understanding of religion would provide common ground between Christianity and other religions, but only at the price of conceding the objective truth of Christianity. A somewhat less drastic instance is the theory of psychological archetypes, as espoused by C. G. Jung, who made these images add up to a pantheistic monism.[6] With some such theories it may be possible to loosen them from their moorings and place at least a part of them—in a highly modified form, to be sure—into a Christian framework. I shall return to Jung below.

Basic phenomenology of religion. In order to pursue this topic I am going to make use of the philosophical methodology of phenomenology in a very loose sense. Phenomenology is the study of appearances. Nowadays the term is particularly associated with the philosophy of Edmund Husserl,[7] but it had been used for quite a while before him and has been vigorously adapted after him. I will focus on a less rigorous and more popular use of the term.

---

[5]Ludwig Feuerbach, *The Essence of Christianity* (London: John Chapman, 1854).
[6]Carl Gustav Jung, "The Spiritual Problem of Modern Man," in *The Portable Jung,* ed. Joseph Campbell (New York: Viking, 1971), pp. 456-79.
[7]Edmund Husserl, *Cartesian Meditations: An Introduction to Phenomenology,* trans. Dorion Cairns (The Hague: Martinus Nijhoff, 1970). This is probably Husserl's most programmatic writing. See also his *Logical Investigations,* 2 vols. (New York: Routledge, 2001).

Phenomenology describes the world from the inside out, where the inside refers to human beings and their most fundamental perceptions. Take the following basic scenario, used to illustrate the difference in a somewhat oversimplified way. I am writing this section while on a stay in Singapore, just a few miles from the equator. Last night I was lying on my bed in youth-hostel–like accommodations with the windows open and a ceiling fan fighting a losing battle against the heat and humidity. I could describe this situation by giving an accurate measurement of the dimensions of the room, the layout of the cots, the velocity of the fan, the temperature and the humidity. But if I wish to do a phenomenological analysis, I need to begin with my own experience: my fatigue, the clammy feeling over my entire body, the approach-avoidance conflict with my sheet in which I need to be on the sheet in order to sleep but away from it in order to be cooler, the breezes emanating from the ceiling fan that annoy me more than they cool any part of me. Instead of an external description of what things are like, phenomenological analysis describes reality as directly experienced by the subject.

The primordial experience. Phenomenology attempts to take us to the most fundamental experience of a human subject in a given situation— what I will call the primordial experience. Obviously, people can disagree over where the actual primordial experience lies, and they do. Phenomenology, like all philosophical methods, does not confer a certificate of omniscience.

Nor, it seems to me, is there a need to maintain a dogmatic antiobjectivism and still reap the benefits of the phenomenological method. It is possible to undertake a descriptive analysis in accord with a phenomenological approach without denying that there is an objective world. I believe it is fair to say that a large part of the impetus for phenomenology early in the twentieth century was the all-pervasive positivism, scientism and materialism that filled the many branches of philosophy, whether continental or Anglo-Saxon. As a countermeasure, it overemphasized subjectivity. Nevertheless, this overemphasis is not essential, certainly not to this present project.[8] What I want to do here is to address the primordial

---

[8] I realize that this statement would not satisfy the demands of a rigorous phenomenology as carried out according to Husserl's rules, but that fact is not consequential to this current project. I am here attempting to develop a method (while indicating its historical roots) that will allow me to undertake the analysis yet to come in this chapter. Whether this method ultimately is completely true to orthodox phenomenology would only be relevant if I claimed such authenticity for it, which I do not.

religious experience, and that task need not rule out an objective counterpart to the experience. I am using an adapted phenomenological method without making traditional phenomenological concessions—in other words, I am striving for a balance.

The problem: the universality of religious experience. Of course, if one believes that Christianity alone is true, one must also deny objective reference to many instances of religious experience. After all, nonexistent deities can hardly serve as objects of a person's experience; yet someone may claim to have had a direct personal encounter with a being that is not even supposed to exist. In that case, the experience has to be in some way self-constitutive. Thus, my fundamental hypothesis is this: there is somewhere in the human psyche a (noetic) structure that either relates to an object of religious experience or simulates doing so. In either case, the basic features of the primordial experience are similar, perhaps even identical.

Obviously it is not possible to have someone else's subjectivity, and so it is not possible for me to enjoy anyone else's experience from the inside. That much should not need pointing out. The idea is that my phenomenological analysis will generalize the experiences sufficiently to be able to learn from them.

The key: appearances behind appearances. Obviously I am not going to present a complete psychological, let alone clinical, discussion of religious experience. Instead, I am going to rely on some of the well-known descriptions of religious experience that have been influential in the phenomenology of religion over the last one hundred years.

What these studies have in common is this: they point out that behind the simple, apparently objective, primordial experience, there is a dimension that aligns the specific experience with those of other people, religions and contexts. The basic pattern is that even though, say, three different individuals may have three different, possibly mutually exclusive, experiences, call them E1, E2 and E3, there is still an underlying set of categories, D, that they all share.

One thing is clear in looking at table 8.1: the person in question may not even be aware of such a scheme. If you ask people who have had a religious encounter what they experienced, the answer will most likely simply be E1, that is, the basic content of the experience. For example, Christian mystics, when questioned about what they experienced, are undoubtedly going to say something along the line of "the love of Jesus," and not "the transcendental noemata of mystical union." And here many writers have made a very serious mistake.[9] In academic hubris they have attempted to declare that what the person is experiencing is *not really* E1, but is always *really* D.

Table 8.1

Person	Experience	Underlying Dimension
1	E1	
2	E2	D
3	E3	

A priori this is an unacceptable procedure. Whether the person is really experiencing E1, E2 or E3 needs to be settled on grounds other than the discovery of a further phenomenological dimension behind the experience. The procedure strikes me as similar to that of a soccer player scoring a goal in the World Cup and thereby fulfilling a personal goal, and someone pointing out that he did *not really* score the soccer goal, but he *really* fulfilled a personal goal. Why not both? Then again, he may have fulfilled a personal goal even without scoring a goal, but that matter must be decided factually, not methodologically.

I have argued that some religions are false and that consequently there can be no objective reference point to the experience of their adherents. So, I am faced with a somewhat peculiar situation, as depicted in table 8.2. A person may experience dimension D, as it is mediated through experience E1, which is based on object, O1, perhaps a Hindu deity, and it turns out that O1 is not real. Then it would be the case that D is real, but O1 is not.

Table 8.2

Person	Experience	Reported Object	Underlying Dimension
P1	E1	O1	D
		(real or unreal)	

It follows that D is a psychological category rather than an objective reality in itself and that its appearance can be triggered by either a real or

---

[9]Thus, for example, W. T. Stace, *Mysticism and Philosophy* (New York: Jeremy Tarcher, 1960), or Aldous Huxley, *The Perennial Philosophy* (Cleveland: World, 1962).

an unreal object.[10] And, come to think of it, there is nothing terribly unusual in this idea. After all, I can provoke my mind into all kinds of patterns through the presentation of unreal objects: a mental picture of an act of cruelty, a beautiful woman or a mouth-watering dessert.

Thus I am stipulating the following situation. There is a basic dimension that frequently appears to underlie religious experience. This dimension can manifest itself regardless of whether the direct object of experience is real or not. It appears in many Christian experiences that have a real object of experience (God in Christ), and it can also show up in non-Christian experience where the object of experience is not real.

I want to shy away from the idea that this dimension is normative, that is, that all religious experience must manifest it. Such an attempt will inevitably lead to circularity—the patterns are derived from observing the experience, but then what counts as true religious experience is decided on the basis of whether it manifests the patterns. Instead, I am looking at the patterns as observation-based generalizations. There seem to be enough of them to warrant drawing general conclusions, but not so many that I would feel free to discount any religious experience that does not fit the patterns.

What I hope to have emerge is a relatively tight set of conclusions. At the risk of unnecessary repetition, let me mention the two caveats again:

1. The presence of the dimension does not by itself say anything about the reality of the object of experience. It can manifest itself both when there is a real object (Christ) and when there is not (for example, Shiva).

2. The patterns associated with this hidden dimension are supposed to be inductively derived and have no normative force in discriminating between genuine and inauthentic religious experience.

These two caveats distinguish what I am attempting to do from many other uses of these concepts. They leave room for a number of different configurations of the reality or unreality of the object of experience and the presence or absence of the patterns of this phenomenological dimension. Very importantly, they make it possible for someone who believes in the exclusive truth of Christianity to align certain aspects of Christian experience with experience in other religions without conceding the truth of Christianity.

---

[10]I trust the reader is aware that, even though the concept of mediation is used here, the context and meaning are totally different from the way that it was used in chapter six. Here it is an epistemological category, not a theological doctrine.

I shall now examine some of these attempts at uncovering this phenomenological dimension and see what can be learned from them.

Rudolf Otto: the Holy. In a book that was considered groundbreaking in its day, Rudolf Otto exposed what he considered to be the nonrational side of religion.[11] He stipulated that much of the activity of a religious person and, for that matter, of the academic study of religion, has focused on the overt side of objective beliefs and ethical practices. This can be called the rational side of religion. And let there be no doubt about it: Otto was a first-rate scholar on this level himself.[12] Nevertheless, Otto claimed that the most profound significance of religion lies not in this rational side but in the nonrational dimension, which he called the *numinous,* a word derived from a Latin term for *God.* This is the encounter with the dimension of the Holy.

To get a handle on this idea, you might want to begin by thinking of the experience of the Holy as the "cathedral feeling." Picture yourself walking into a large cathedral with a high ceiling, stained-glass windows and, perhaps, organ music in the background as the only sound. As you are in this environment, suddenly you get an overwhelming feeling of the presence of God. You might have the same experience in the mountains or looking at the night sky. Of what does this feeling consist?

Otto uses several words for this feeling and the apparent reality on which it is based: the Holy, the numinous and the *mysterium tremendum* among others. I will for the moment latch on to the last one because it is in some ways the most descriptive. First, the adjective *tremendum* indicates that the experience carries with it the feeling of the awesome (in the traditional sense)[13] presence of God that reveals his purity and righteousness and our own unworthiness. It includes the dimension of the wrath of God and is epitomized in the statements of Isaiah, "I am a man of unclean lips, and I live among a people of unclean lips" (Is 6:5), and of Peter, "Go away

---

[11]Rudolf Otto, *The Idea of the Holy: An Inquiry into the Non-rational Factor in the Idea of the Divine and Its Relation to the Rational,* trans. John W. Harvey (New York: Oxford University Press, 1931).

[12]In this book I have made reference to several of his works, for example, *Mysticism East and West* (New York: Collier, 1960) and *India's Religion of Grace and Christianity Compared and Contrasted,* trans. Frank Hugh Foster (New York: Macmillan, 1930).

[13]Unfortunately, this word has been emptied of meaning in contemporary usage. There was a time when its usage was confined only to truly awe-inspiring situations, verging on fearfulness. I first became aware of the loss of meaning when I overheard some students in the early 1980s talk about awesome pastries they had consumed in Israel. Do pastries inspire awe?

from me, Lord; I am a sinful man!" (Lk 5:8).

Second, the notion emphasizes that there is a *mysterium*, that is, that the object of the feeling is ultimately beyond our full knowledge, and that all our language about it can only be a form of analogy.[14] Third, the experience entails the component of a *fascinosum*. By this Otto means that at the same time a person is confronted by the alienating feelings of the *tremendum*, there may be a concurrent feeling of deep love and grace. The *mysterium* repels and attracts at the same time.

By bringing Otto's thesis into the picture here, I am not advocating his scheme as a whole. More specifically, I do not wish to assert with Otto that the feeling is *(a)* universal. Otto sees it as the single crucial aspect of all religious experience. But unless one wants to get caught in a circular argument—defining religion by this *mysterium* and then "discovering" that all religions have the *mysterium*—I would not know how to prove its universality. Nor do I wish to assert that the feeling is *(b)* foundational. Otto enters the arena of the origins of religion and dogmatically proclaims that this feeling lies at the very beginning of religion in time, prior even to any practices or rational conceptualizations. The problem in this regard is, as Schmidt put it, "he makes not the faintest attempt at proving any of his propositions whatsoever."[15]

Nor can I say with Otto that the feeling is *(c)* definitive. As already stated, for Otto the *mysterium tremendum* is the central feature of religious experience, and it takes precedence over the rational dimension. Although he also says that the nonrational and the rational are the warp and woof of religion, he gives the nonrational priority because that is what makes an experience religious. Still, when you come right down to it, this is an arbitrary decision on his part. Even if it could be shown that the *mysterium* is a

---

[14]However, over against Schleiermacher, for whom the feeling of "absolute dependence" is the ground of our concept of God, Otto insists that the objective existence of the numinous has to have ontological precedence over its experience. In other words, Otto reasons from the epistemological priority of the feeling of the Holy, but he stipulates the ontological priority of the Holy itself.

[15]Schmidt, *Origin and Growth*, p. 142. Otto does make reference to the theory of original monotheism as espoused by Schmidt and Lang (and subscribed to in this book). He even acknowledges that there are some instances of God-awareness in primitive societies where the monotheistic beliefs are not the result of influences from other theistic religions, such as Christian missionaries. But he credits them to "anticipations and presentiments rather than survivals" (Otto, *Idea of the Holy*, p. 134). Unfortunately for his case, as was mentioned in chapter two, these cultures are at the lowest level of development, and subsequent ones show a decrease in God-awareness rather than an increase, so they can hardly be anticipations of future developments.

universal concomitant of religious experience, that would not prove that it is, therefore, the definitive factor that makes an experience religious.

Thus, rather than claiming that the *mysterium* is universal, foundational or definitive, the most we ought to say is that it is widespread, frequent and apparently concomitant with religious experience. This conclusion seems to have pretty much gutted Otto's proposal. Then why bother even dealing with it?

The answer is that, even apart from Otto's dogmatism, he has given us a category for understanding what is, surely, at least a *constant* aspect of *most* forms of religious experience. *In general*, whenever people have a religious experience, they seem to encounter the *mysterium*. This provides a first candidate for dimension D, the aspect of religion that is revealed phenomenologically. The figure depicting religious experience would now look like table 8.3.

Table 8.3

Person	Experience	Reported Object	Underlying Dimension
P1	E1 ◄———	O1 (real or unreal)	*mysterium tremendum*

It would appear that as long as one does not succumb to Otto's drive towards logical inevitability, but remains on the level of general description, one can say that the *mysterium* is a dimension of the primordial religious experience. Whenever and wherever people have enjoyed religious experience, regardless of the truth status of their beliefs, they seem to have a feeling of the numinous.

The next question is whether one can go further than that. Must I conclude with this vague description, or can I take a further step in my phenomenological description that includes also the more specific ways in which people have expressed the manifestation of the Holy?

Mircea Eliade: hierophanies. In the introduction to his book *The Sacred and the Profane*, Mircea Eliade summarizes Otto's insights and then declares that he is going in a different direction.[16] However, what he is really doing is building on Otto inasmuch as he, too, looks at the nonra-

---

[16]Mircea Eliade, *The Sacred and the Profane: The Nature of Religion*, trans. Willard R. Trask (New York: Harcourt, Brace & World, 1959), p. 10.

tional side of religion and the function of the Holy. Only for Eliade it would be best to speak of the holies, that is the specific manifestations of holiness that pervade the religious dimension of life.[17] Eliade calls these focal points hierophanies. A hierophany is a particular segment of life or culture that transforms it from being nonreligious (profane) into an encounter with the religious (sacred).

The following very straightforward example will illustrate the point before I pursue a little bit more of a survey. Most religious cultures in some way designate for themselves a certain place as sacred, whether it be a hut, a tree, a mosque, a shrine or a temple. When one enters this area, one leaves behind the profane side of life and enters the sacred domain. Just think: Most Protestant churches, even those that emphasize the priesthood of all believers and the abiding presence of Christ, maintain a sanctuary in their buildings, and, if you interact with the members you will soon discover that they view this area not just pragmatically as a place for collective worship but also as a location where one is more likely to have communion with God. It is, in short, the house of God. This may not be what the official theology teaches, but it is what the members practice. This designated space, Eliade would say, constitutes a spatial hierophany.

It is very important, then, to recognize that what Eliade concerns himself with much of the time is not the official theology of a particular religion, but its folk version—the way it is practiced by the lay adherents. So, when he speaks of Judaism, for example, his reference may be to a midrash or to something out of the kabbalah; similarly, his interaction with Christianity extends all the way from the New Testament to the archaic practices of Eastern European peasants. As long as one thinks of the standard content of a religion only, one may frequently conclude that much of what he says is just plain false.[18] But remember, he is undertaking a phenomenology, and thus the uncritical primordial experience of the common adherents is what is primarily in view.

In the last chapter, I alluded to Eliade's construal of time in traditional cultures, in which time is circular, exactly one year in length, and festivals are the direct reenactments of the original time of the gods. The beginning

---

[17]Philosophically oriented readers might be helped by the analogy that Eliade plays Aristotle to Otto's Plato. Plato believed that there was one good, one justice and one beautiful; Aristotle argued that there were as many instantiations of good, justice or beauty as there were objects carrying those forms.

[18]And remember that in chapter two I argued that Eliade's approach also makes his pronouncements on the origin of religion arbitrary at best.

of the annual cycle and the reference points in festivals and commemorations are ways of connecting profane time with the sacred dimension, and thus they constitute hierophanies.

Above I made reference to the idea of sacred space. Eliade ties this notion into the very notion of creation; that is to say, when a culture creates a sacred sector in space, it is actually reenacting the very creation of the world. This seemingly farfetched notion is based on the contrast between the order that is generated by the sacralization of a specific space and the chaos that constitutes everything outside of the sacred sector. Thus to establish a sacred space is tantamount to establishing space per se. Typically, this happens by designating the position of the sacred space as the center of the universe, oftentimes symbolized by a vertical device (a lance, a tree, a steeple and so forth), which constitutes a world axis (*axis mundi*) that extends through all three levels of the cosmos.

The cosmos, as well, discloses the sacred. First there is the sky, abode of the most high god; then there is the earth, revealing the sacred nature of fertility and womanhood. Water always represents the abyss, so that to go into water depicts one's dissolution into death, and to emerge again is to enter into a new birth. Here are some further hierophanies together with their fundamental meanings in Eliade's construction:

- trees—the quest for immortality
- the moon—fertility as well as the oscillation between life and death
- the sun—autonomy and sovereignty[19]
- the hero—purity and perfection

For religious human beings, according to Eliade, all of life is punctuated by moments in which they touch on the sacred. Most central in the process are the rites of passage: birth, puberty, marriage and death, as well as initiatory rites. It is in this area in particular that Eliade claims that even modern secular humanity, as much as it attempts to divorce itself from transcendence, still clings to thinly disguised religious modes of being.

So, what can be gleaned from Eliade's insights? His contribution is this: the awareness of the sacred is not limited to some ill-defined encounter with the numinous. Instead, human beings relate to the numinous in specific ways. These ways constitute patterns that recur from culture to culture and seem to be a part of the primordial religious experience of human beings. Again, one could be on shaky ground if one tried to make these

---

[19]In my personal observation, sun deities are usually associated with justice and righteousness as well.

hierophanies either universal or definitive, but that they are generally recurrent seems to be pretty clear once one has decided to take this phenomenological look at religion.

And to rehearse one of my constant caveats: Eliade's writings can lead to a monolithic understanding of religion that would be inaccurate. Take the example of water as the medium for death and new birth. I cannot imagine that anyone having read that sentence would not immediately think of Christian baptism, or that biblically knowledgeable Christians wouldn't immediately associate this image with Romans 6, where the apostle Paul specifically describes baptism as participation in the death and resurrection of Christ. This is a good example of what I have been advocating in this chapter, namely, that the hierophany is in this case an actuality; in the new birth we do participate in the death and new life of Christ as exemplified in baptism. At the same time, there should be no question that God has revealed himself here with a pattern that recurs (without the foundational reality) among humans at many different times and places. Baptism is neither *merely* a hierophany in Eliade's sense nor *not* a hierophany at all, but it is a hierophany that discloses objective truth.

Adding Eliade's patterns to the developing table provides the additional information depicted in table 8.4.

Table 8.4

Person	Experience	Reported Object	Underlying Dimension
P1	E1 ←	O1 _____ (real or unreal)	*mysterium tremendum* hierophanies

But then, how is it that there can be these recurring patterns of hierophanies? Eliade himself generally shies away from probing to this level, but he does suggest a source for the fact that even the profane person again and again falls into religious patterns, "This is all the more true because a great part of his existence is fed by impulses that come to him from the depths of his being, from the zone that has been called the 'unconscious.'"[20] In short, look to the unconscious part of the human psyche to find the basic patterns of religious thought and practice.

C. G. Jung: archetypes. Very, very cautiously I will look at the contribu-

---

[20]Eliade, *Sacred and Profane*, p. 209.

tion that the Swiss analytic psychologist Carl Gustav Jung has made to the topic of this investigation.[21] Much of what he has advocated is clearly tainted by a pantheistic worldview, and his research methods at times have verged on the bizarre.[22] Nevertheless, he at least helps us set our sail into a helpful direction, namely, the insight that the patterns we employ in religious expression are deeply embedded in our minds.

Should this fundamental insight be problematic? It is hard to see how, for, after all, do we not believe that God created human beings with the basic capacity to relate to him and that, even after the fall, the vestiges of these endowments remain? Have I not said repeatedly that God reveals himself through human culture? Thus, even though there is much to question in Jung's conclusions, there is also a central thought to take with us.

Jung was a student of Sigmund Freud's, but he broke with his master over the interpretation of dreams. It seemed to him that all of Freud's analysis of dreams pointed to either death or sex or both, with little room left for anything else. Jung, on the other hand, began to see many different interpretations of dreams, represented by a consistent array of symbolic images. He also discovered that these images not only appeared in dreams of people around the world but also showed up in the artwork of many different cultures, their mythologies and their religions, as well as in the drawings of little children.

Jung concluded that there are basic images—archetypes—that reside in the human unconscious and manifest themselves only indirectly, primarily in dreams and art. These are also the basic building blocks of religious imagery. Jung stipulated that there are two sides to the unconscious, the personal, which contains individual experiences and memories, and the collective, which contains the accumulation of memories of the human race compiled over many thousands of years. It is in this latter compartment that the archetypes have taken up their living quarters—from which they emerge from time to time.

The list of possible archetypes is quite long. A few of them are the hero who comes from across the sea (savior, redeemer), the evil crone (witch), the serpent (sly deceiver), the wise old woman (earth mother), the god (a projection of one's ideal self) and various artistic diagrams. Jung insisted

---

[21]Violet Staub De Laszlo, ed., *The Basic Writings of C. G. Jung* (New York: Modern Library, 1993).

[22]For example, the accrual of dreams documented in C. G. Jung, "Individual Dream Symbolism in Relation to Alchemy," in *The Portable Jung*, ed. Joseph Campbell (New York: Viking, 1971), pp. 323-455.

that, although these archetypes come with a regularity of purpose, the specific meaning that an archetype has for a person or in a society is to some extent dependent on variable factors, such as other cultural attributes and a person's individual history.

This is not the place to analyze all the various issues raised by Jung's theories. It is tempting to take the easy way out and simply raise *ad hominem* arguments against Jung's pantheism and involvement with the occult[23] without thereby necessarily refuting his claims. I wish to glean the following ideas:

1. There are recurrent themes in the mythology and symbolism of people in various times and cultures.

2. Without going so far as positing a collective unconscious (which is really a piece of mythology all its own), these similarities can be ascribed to the very fundamental thought patterns that human beings have. In some way, they seem to be programmed into our minds.[24]

3. These archetypal patterns then express themselves in the primordial religious experiences of human beings, for example, in Eliade's hierophanies.

4. From the Christian standpoint, other religions are substantially false, and, thus, the content in which the archetypes are embedded is false. Nevertheless, as God has revealed himself in history and Scripture, he has done so, at least partially, through the medium of these archetypes. Thus Christians and non-Christians share some basic patterns of thought, which is the subject of this chapter.

Table 8.5 depicts personal experience of the religious with the additional dimension of archetypal images.

One might also want to consider placing the much discussed "redemptive analogies," as advocated by missionary Don Richardson, under this general heading. Richardson suggests that the fundamental apparatus of

---

[23]Ibid., p. xi. In fact, this particular area is how Jung's career began. His doctoral dissertation was entitled "On the Psychology and Pathology of So-Called Occult Phenomena."

[24]Francis Schaeffer attempted to supply a substitute theory for Jung's archetypes by suggesting, though without any evidence, that perhaps certain patterns of thought were tied to human language structures. "My thinking has led me to believe that there is a collective cultural consciousness or memory which is related to words. . . . It would therefore seem to me that the whole matter is primarily one of language, as man thinks and communicates in language" (Francis Schaeffer, *The God Who Is There* [Downers Grove, Ill.: InterVarsity Press, 1968], pp. 182-83). Unfortunately for Schaeffer's speculation, the whole point of Jung's discoveries is that they are based on the patterns that emerge apart from language, such as in children's drawings, religious symbols or dreams, thus leaving Schaeffer's idea about a connection to language pointed 180 degrees away from the data. Why not simply leave it with prelinguistic figurative patterns?

Table 8.5

Person	Experience	Reported Object	Underlying Dimension
P1	E1	O1	*mysterium tremendum*
←			hierophanies
		(real or unreal)	archetypal images

human cultures actually includes specific items that can constitute bridges in the communication of the gospel. He makes his case first in the book *Peace Child*.[25]

Richardson spent many years as a missionary to the Sawi people of Irian Jaya. As he attempted to communicate the gospel to them, he realized that he was up against unforeseen cultural barriers, particularly since this culture celebrated deceptiveness and betrayal as high forms of virtue. In his narration of the life of Christ to these people, he did not get any positive response until toward the end of the story—and then it was appreciation for Judas. However, they did have a custom that finally enabled him to share the gospel so that they could understand it.

There was war between two villages, and eventually they came to a mutual agreement of peace between them. This peace was sealed in the following manner. Each village selected an infant from their ranks, and then the two villages exchanged these children. From now on, as long as each "peace child" lived, there would be peace between the villages. Richardson was able to use this custom in order to show the Sawi that Jesus Christ was the Peace Child that God had sent to allow us to have peace with him. For the first time, they were able to understand the good news Richards had tried to convey to them.[26]

Richardson goes further and speculates that, perhaps, God has instilled in many cultures some way that facilitates the understanding of the gospel. "Redemptive analogies, God's keys to man's cultures, are the New Testament–approved approach to cross-cultural evangelism."[27] They do

---

[25]Don Richardson, *Peace Child* (Ventura, Calif.: Regal, 1974).

[26]Significantly, even though they were beginning to understand the gospel at this point, no one became a Christian immediately. That fruition had to wait until Richardson was able to demonstrate the power of God to the people by showing fearlessness in crocodile-infested waters.

[27]Ibid., p. 288.

not constitute the gospel, but they provide a way in which a person can come to understand the gospel.

So, perhaps these redemptive analogies belong to the storehouse of archetypal images. This completes the picture. At the heart of all religious experience seems to be the awareness of the numinous—the *mysterium tremendum et fascinosum*, as Otto describes it. But people do not encounter the Holy in disembodied form; they find it in specific manifestations, which Eliade calls hierophanies, and these appearances take on the forms that they do because they are expressions of fundamental human categories of thought, namely, archetypal images. Finally, specific archetypes are used by God to facilitate not only a basic religious attitude but the specific content of redemption; these are Richardson's redemptive analogies.

Thus, I have made progress in responding to the issue of this chapter. How can there be so much similarity between a religion that is true (Christianity) and one that is false? The answer is because, despite their different truth statuses, they share the phenomenological experience of the numinous, hierophanies, archetypes and redemptive analogies.

Reenter the rational and ethical. But all of the above has only been one half of the circle. Now I must return to the ethical dimension discussed in chapter four. Phenomenology does not occur in a vacuum (at least not in the way in which I have attempted to describe it) but is part of a larger project, which is strongly occupied with the moral side of life.

To be sure, phenomenology of religion must also address the moral side of the primordial religious experience. For Otto the *mysterium* manifests itself largely in the awesomeness of the numinous, and human beings find themselves aware of not measuring up to the absolute purity of the Holy. "Go away from me, Lord; I am a sinful man" (Lk 5:8).[28]

Nevertheless, there is also a clearly rational (as opposed to the nonrational—not irrational) aspect of the ethical, as discussed in chapter four. There I made reference to the work of Ronald Green, who has attempted to make this rational concern the cornerstone of religion by showing that religion (among many other points) resolves the conflict between our

---

[28]This is not to say that phenomenology of religion has nothing to say on this topic. Far from it! Paul Ricouer has provided an extensive phenomenological study of sin in various aspects, both the ritual and moral dimensions (*The Symbolism of Evil*, trans. Emerson Buchanan [New York: Harper & Row, 1967]).

moral standards and our moral performance.[29]

My basic point is this (and now I am departing from what is necessarily claimed by adherents of the religions themselves): unless we are aligning all of the above with a fundamental need for redemption, we are not getting the real story. The time has come to reassert the specifically Christian viewpoint, and it would be wrong to think that, given a Christian viewpoint, these various religious categories developed merely as an attempt at self-fulfillment or to facilitate the basic issues of life, such as food and health. Religious categories also address the fundamental need of reconciliation between ethical ideals and the shortcomings that all human beings experience.

In chapter four I discussed many of the implications involved in the moral awareness of human beings, and it is wise to recall all the complexity it brings with it. In that chapter I went to great lengths to emphasize the distinctiveness of the Christian moral conceptualization, not to mention the uniqueness of the Christian understanding of redemption. Nonetheless, the very general overall pattern that cuts across the many belief systems was also apparent. So, now in table 8.6 I adapt the illustration that I have used as a guide throughout this chapter, leave aside some unnecessary complications, and add the fundamental ethical dimension.

Table 8.6

Person	Experience	Reported Object	Underlying Dimension
			Phenomenological
P1	E1	O1	*mysterium tremendum*
			hierophanies
		(real or unreal)	archetypal images
			Rational
			ethical/redemptive

The religious experience of the individual is constituted by both the phenomenological dimensions and the ethical/redemptive context. But there is one more step to back up.

---

[29]Ronald M. Green, *Religious Reason: The Rational and Moral Basis of Religious Belief* (New York: Oxford University Press, 1978) and *Religion and Moral Reason: A New Method for Comparative Study* (New York: Oxford University Press, 1988).

Back to general revelation. Finally, all of this did not begin in empty space. Religion, after all, is not just a phenomenon of human culture, but it has its grounding, as I argued at the very beginning, with a God who has disclosed himself. In addition to the special revelation of the Bible, there is general revelation in nature and the persistence of original monotheism. This revelation is both informational and ethical, thereby bringing about the confluence of dimensions so far. Table 8.7 summarizes these dimensions.

Table 8.7

Person	Experience	Reported Object	Underlying Dimension	Revelation
P1	E1	O1	Phenomenological	general revelation
			mysterium tremendum	
←			hierophanies	persistence of original monotheism
		(real or unreal)	archetypal images	
			Rational	
			ethical/redemptive	

And again, one need not be embarrassed that the experience of an individual is oftentimes of an unreal object. Christian theology certainly teaches that, even though people have received revelation, they have rejected it and substituted the worship of creatures for the worship of the creator (Rom 1). What makes that rejection of God by humans so poignant is that they have imposed precisely the categories that belong to God on other beings and on themselves (Is 14:13-14). And this is exactly what the scheme I have been elaborating describes.

FROM FINDING FORDS TO BUILDING BRIDGES

What I have been doing in this chapter so far is developing a comprehensive plan for understanding how there can be so much resemblance between Christianity and other religions—such an admixture of truth and falsehood together! I used the imagery of finding a ford across a stream so that the two banks can communicate with each other. However, this analogy is not supposed to stop here: the discovery of fords is supposed to lead to the building of bridges. This undertaking will begin in this chapter but then go on to the next one, which will focus more closely on living in light of these truths.

Why even build bridges? There certainly is no need for a cheap ecumenism; as was mentioned earlier, some efforts such as the declaration arising out of the Parliament of the World's Religions of 1993 wind up making potentially misleading statements in order to promote the appearance of unity. One ought not to gloss over the very categorical differences between Christian and Indic conceptions of salvation, to specify one example. So, having established the fords underlying the general phenomenon of religion, is there any serious point in even attempting to erect any bridges?

Bridges serve a number of important purposes. Saving further elaboration for the next chapter, let me make just a brief list of them:

1. They facilitate evangelism. Regardless of all of the other discussion, I consider this to be the most important reason. They make it possible for the Christian to relate to the non-Christian so as to make a more plausible presentation of the gospel.

2. They help us live together in a civil society. The plurality of religious cultures in the contemporary industrialized societies has become a given.[30] Reaching out across our individual boundaries (where legal and ethical!) will contribute to the life of a properly functioning democracy.

3. They identify where we can make common cause with others on social and ethical issues—and where we cannot!

4. They contribute to the ongoing work of the theologian in exploring the universe that God has put together, including the world of the human heart.

Bridge one: truth. Throughout this study I have recognized that religions make truth claims—concerning spiritual reality, morality, paths of redemption and so forth. I have also maintained that only Christianity contains final truth but that there is a common understanding among all the religions that there is truth, that truth is important and that one can talk about truth, at least in rudimentary ways.[31]

Religion is about truth. That is not all that religion is about, but it is an

---

[30]Terry Muck estimated in 1992 that as many as 17.5 million adults in the United States may be affiliated with a non-Christian religion (*Those Other Religions in Your Neighborhood: Loving Your Neighbor When You Don't Know How* [Grand Rapids, Mich.: Zondervan, 1992], p. 17).

[31]Obviously, this statement is negated by some of the truly extreme versions of Indic mysticism where theoretically nothing truthful can be said since ultimate reality is beyond words and concepts. But these are not exactly representative of the nature of religion in general. Let's tackle this 0.01 percent after we've related to the rest!

indispensable aspect of religion. If, for example, one allows for the notion that an important part of religion is a relationship to a transcendent object,[32] one cannot ignore the question of whether the claims made about the transcendent object are true. I am thinking here not just about the objective, exclusivist sense of truth that evangelical Christians (and other groups) cherish, but also of broader interpretations. Some religions stress the need for an inward, mystical truth that a person would need to find on a highly subjective basis, while others may operate on a widely inclusivist view according to which truth can be found in many different ways in addition to their own. Regardless, take the notion of truth out of religion, and what is left is either psychology or art, neither one of which is directly concerned with the truth of religious claims. As R. C. Zaehner puts it, "Whether religions are 'solidary' or 'solitary,' they all make claims to truth."[33]

Furthermore, once you take the truth claims out of religious discussion, most of the motivation for dialogue is removed. Regardless of what type of dialogue one envisions—for purposes of study, edification or ecumenism, for example—there would be little point to it if there were not also a question of truth at stake, even if it were no more than an inclusive multiadaptive view of truth. The contrast with art makes the case, I believe: one does not hear of urgent calls for dialogue between those who prefer sculpture to wall-hangings, impressionism to cubism, or soup cans to pietàs. There are points at which dialogue in art does get conflictive and needs debate (for example, in connection with feminist views of art versus traditional themes and interpretations), and those are precisely the ones in which questions of truth do again come up.

It is at this point that a puzzle arises. Interreligious dialogue is only meaningful so long as truth is an overriding concern. However, it is all too easy in the process of dialogue to nudge questions of truth to the side—or even to revise the notion of truth altogether—for the sake of fostering greater cooperation. Wilfrid Cantwell Smith avers,

> To "claim" to "have the truth" is the posture of those who act as if they had God in their pockets—a posture of lesser men not unknown, alas, in religious history but far from the best or most authentic representatives of any

---

[32]Compare Norman L. Geisler and Winfried Corduan, *Philosophy of Religion*, 2d ed. (Grand Rapids, Mich.: Baker, 1988), pp. 28-39.

[33]R. C. Zaehner, "Religious Truth," in *Truth and Dialogue in World Religions: Conflicting Truth Claims*, ed. John Hick (Philadelphia: Westminster Press, 1974), p. 3. Broadly speaking, Zaehner uses *solidary* to refer to Western, prophetic religions, and *solitary* to refer to Eastern, mystical religions.

tradition. Religious statements at their best . . . have been expressions of personal or corporate involvements, tentative but joyous, inadequate, but exhuberant [sic], human but transcendence-oriented. To approach them with sympathy is to hear them not as claims but as echoes, to see them not as the moon but as fingers pointing to the moon.[34]

There is much to remark about in this quotation: its *ad hominem* approach, the flagrant way in which its author obviously exempts himself from his own verdict and the arrogance of making universal judgments of what must be "best" within each individual religion. Even though he would not want to judge any religion as false (presumably), he allows himself the right to tell the members of all religions what is better or worse among their claims. For example, if I "claim" to "have truth" as a Christian, I am supposedly not representing what is "best" among Christian statements.

For the record, as an evangelical scholar who believes in the exclusive truth of Christianity, I have gone out of my way at times to make sure that I do not fall into the trap of judging internal matters within a particular religion.[35] But all of this is an aside for the moment. The main point is that in the process Cantwell Smith actually distorts the nature of religion from a descriptive point of view, and in the process he also undercuts the need for and nature of dialogue. If we disregard the fact that religious believers implicitly do hold an objective view of truth, then dialogue is no longer dialogue. It can still be a discussion to resolve cooperation on a preconceived agenda, but it cannot be dialogue in the sense of exchanging important ideas about each other's faith. Such efforts would be trivial or, were Cantwell Smith correct, less than the best. Insofar as evangelical Christians can participate in dialogue by stressing the need for objective truth, they can make a solid contribution. And in this way, we can make use of a bridge across the river.

Bridge two: morality. In chapter four I stressed that there are only a few things that religious traditions have in common when it comes to morality. The idea that somehow the Ten Commandments are a summary of what all religions teach is just plain false. Even the commandments for which there appears to be common ground are colored by the religious contexts

---

[34]Wilfrid Cantwell Smith, "Conflicting Truth-Claims: A Rejoinder," in *Truth and Dialogue in World Religions: Conflicting Truth Claims,* ed. John Hick (Philadelphia: Westminster Press, 1974), p. 159.
[35]See my comments in *Neighboring Faiths: A Christian Introduction to World Religions* (Downers Grove, Ill.: InterVarsity Press, 1998), pp. 38-39.

in which they appear. Nonetheless, one can—and should—also focus on those areas where religions do share moral commitments, at least superficially. To name the four central ones: respect for life, truth, property and marriage systems. Despite clear variations in how these values are applied, they seem to be general constants in all societies.

When we think of establishing bridges along this line, many of the theoretical complications disappear as we interact with people on a day-to-day basis. For example, it is true that the Sawi of Don Richardson's *Peace Child* valued treachery (alongside their more general acceptance of truth or there could be no such thing as treachery), but we are not going to encounter Sawi in their pre-evangelized state across the fence in our suburban gardens. Similarly, there is no denying that certain variations within Hinduism, such as Tantrism, encourage certain dubious sexual practices, but virtually all the Hindus of my acquaintance accept the ideal of monogamous fidelity in the same way as do the Christians I know. Establishing bridges in the real world is a little easier than in the theoretical world in which one must take into account more anomalies.

Earlier in this chapter, I listed morality as one of the fords that crosses between the banks of religions. This is clearly one of the places where the ford lends itself greatly to establishing a bridge. Then this reality can make itself felt in a number of important ways. For one thing, it contributes to the cooperation in society to which I alluded a moment ago. But also, here is one of the firmer points for preparing a presentation of the gospel message. For human beings do not live up to their own moral intuitions, and they need the redemption of the Savior as described in Christian teaching. I discussed this phenomenon at greater length in chapter five.

Bridge three: the need for the transcendent. Let me point out a third and final bridge, based on all the foregoing. In this chapter I have tried to expose the subconscious, phenomenological side of religion that includes a symbolic as well as a moral dimension. Further, I have shown that these categories are derived from a reality, namely, a self-revealing God who has disclosed himself in various ways. But this thought leads to the conclusion that, consequently, human beings who have not yet found God are living their lives with an unfulfilled need.

To clarify this point, please allow me to make reference to an argument of Norman L. Geisler's, which I had the privilege of revising somewhat.[36]

---

[36]Geisler and Corduan, *Philosophy of Religion*, pp. 62-76.

The basic argument runs as follows:

1. There is a universal need for the transcendent. All human beings manifest the need to find transcendence in some way. This phenomenon even includes some of the apparently most rigorously atheistic writers. Nietzsche, for example, sought transcendence in the idea of the eternal return, as well as the Overman.

2. Where there is a universal need, there must be an objective way of fulfilling that need. For this premise to be accurate, one must be sure to focus only on genuinely real needs. Wishes or desires are not by themselves true needs, but such things as hunger, thirst or the sexual drive are. Nor does this premise imply that every need will be fulfilled for every human being. It does say, however, that, where we find a true need among all human beings, there must be something that responds to the need.

3. Therefore, there must be a transcendent to fulfill the human need for transcendence. Clearly, unless the two premises are firmly established, there is no force in this conclusion. However, if one has identified a true objective need, and if it is the case that all genuine needs must have a way of fulfilling them, then this conclusion follows.

And, of course, if we take this little discussion out of the realm of philosophical argumentation and place it back home in its theological origin, there is no question of its soundness.

1. All human beings were created with the need for fellowship with God, a need that goes largely unfulfilled due to the interference of sin.

2. This is a real need, as demonstrated by the fact that in their state of alienation from God people continue to seek to satisfy it with false gods and images.

3. As Paul did in Athens, we can appeal to this need and its objective fulfillment by God in Christ.

In short, the common human need for transcendence provides a bridge to all human beings.

And, of course, when I speak of finding fords and building bridges, I am speaking of activities that are ultimately the work not of human architects but of God himself. More precisely, any effective work that we do along this line is ultimately the work of God, the Holy Spirit.

SUMMARY

In this chapter I addressed the question of how it is possible that non-Christian religions, which are ultimately false, can still manifest analogies to Christianity in certain truths. I answered this question by, first of all, re-sorting to a simple phenomenological method that I then put to use to un-cover a fundamental religious dimension to human thought, an awareness of the Holy (Otto), the role of hierophanies (Eliade) and subconscious patterns (Jung, Richardson). The presence of these schemes in a milieu that began with general revelation reveals how people can have what looks like a genuine religious experience even though the object of their experience is false. Having posited these notions, I showed that we can build conceptual bridges to non-Christian thought by emphasizing truth, moral-ity and the need for a transcendent.

9

LIVING OUT THE HOPE

In this final chapter I will look more closely at the Christian's life in the light of the foregoing descriptions. There are two particular strands intertwined in this section of the tapestry: (1) the assurance that Christians have in their hope and (2) the ways in which they interact with the world of other religions. These two strands mutually strengthen and reinforce each other. Hope grows in the process of interaction, and the interaction becomes more meaningful as the hope is firmer.

For, interaction among different religions is not particularly momentous if there is no commitment to a clear goal and a reality that undergirds it. Many of the ecumenical events that I observe as an outsider strike me as resembling a group of rebellious adolescents who are experimenting with their new freedom by breaking the taboos of their parental upbringing; the motivation seems to come from the thrill of having crossed over into forbidden territory. For the Christian, the relationship to people in other religions ought never to be just for the sake of experimentation. When Christians interact with their non-Christian neighbors, they ideally come with a plan that provides both positive and negative direction. Allow me to delineate this matter further by making reference to an image that is poignant for me in my present home state.

ON MAINTAINING THE VALUE OF PI: EVANGELICALS AND INTERRELIGIOUS DISCUSSIONS

In 1897, at the instigation of Dr. Edwin J. Godwin of Solitude, Indiana, the legislature of the Hoosier State voted to change the mathematical value of pi to a simple 3.2. The idea was that schoolchildren were finding

the traditional value of 3.14159 . . . far too difficult for arithmetical com-
putations, and this simplification would help them cope. Fortunately, the
state senate tabled the bill, and it has never since been taken off the leg-
islative table. In any event, whatever the government of Indiana might
have done would have been totally irrelevant for the true value of pi. It
would have been the same unwieldy number whether this bill became
law or not.

I would like to use this regrettable event in the state that I have called
home for the last twenty-five years as a guiding metaphor to illustrate
the nature of evangelical involvement in interreligious discussion. More
specifically, I would like to address some relevant concerns that evangelical Christians can bring to this process. I am assuming (1) that it is legitimate for evangelicals to engage in dialogue with members of other
religions;[1] (2) that evangelicals undoubtedly bring certain strengths and
weaknesses to the table and (3) that there are limits to the scope of legitimate involvement in such dialogue by evangelicals. I will clarify the
third point first.

MY PERSONAL INVOLVEMENT IN
INTERRELIGIOUS DIALOGUE

When I refer to interreligious dialogue, I have a specific concept in mind,
namely, discussions between believers in different religions that are specifically geared to understanding each other's faiths. Thus they are neither simply conversations between such believers, for example a
Christian and a Hindu chatting about the weather, nor are they primarily
evangelistic in nature.[2] For me this dialogue has usually taken place
within an academic context: preparing for college teaching of world religions, writing a textbook on world religions, and as a part of actually
teaching the subject. The latter has encompassed the following: (1) bringing guest speakers into the classroom, (2) leading field trips and international travel with students for the sake of studying different religions, (3)
my own travel and on-site study and (4) organizing panel discussions for

---

[1]Cf. Terry C. Muck, "Evangelicals and Interreligious Dialogue," *Journal of the Evangelical Theological Society* 36 (1993): 517-29.
[2]I certainly believe that the ultimate goal of any relationship between Christian and non-Christian has to be the Christian's witness to redemption in Christ, and, even more specifi-cally, any discussion of religion in which a Christian is involved ought to have evangelism as its long-range purpose. That does not mean, however, that any specific conversation must have evangelism as its immediate objective.

large campus-wide audiences with members of different religions. If there is a point here, it is this: interreligious dialogue does not have to involve some sort of global ecumenism with the goal of joining together on our supposed commonalities while minimizing our differences; it can be an occasion simply to learn from each other about what we respectively believe.

PI IS REAL: COMMITMENT TO TRUTH

My guiding metaphor is humorous (or sad) precisely because there is nothing that any human being can do to change the value of pi. Anyone working with pi needs to accept the objective truth of pi as expressing the ratio of the circumference of a circle and its diameter. Similarly, religious dialogue needs a commitment to truth in order to thrive.

Evangelicals believe that their religion is true, and, frankly, they have good reason to do so.[3] As soon as we bring the topic of truth into a discussion on interreligious dialogue two facts seem to emerge: (1) apart from a commitment to truth, such dialogue is virtually pointless, and yet, (2) many attempts at dialogue seem to give truth only a second-rate standing. Let me address these two matters in turn.

Religion is about truth. In the last chapter I listed truth as one of the bridges across the river separating religions. Fundamentally this is not just about shared truth content but about the idea that there is any truth to begin with *and* that this fact is significant, and that it matters whether one has it or not. This is not the only concern of religion, I said, but it is an indispensable aspect of religion.

Evangelical Christians can participate in exchange with non-Christians confidently because their share of the tapestry is the one where the strands are thickest in truth. I am making this assertion in two ways: One, as I have maintained all along, by God's grace, the Christian enjoys the revelation from God who has disclosed himself in nature, in Scripture and, particularly, in Christ. Since this book is not intended primarily as an apologetics text, I have carried this conviction both as a presupposition and, at times, as a conclusion.

Yet, there is another important sense in which Christians can and ought to claim truth, and that has to do with the very understanding of truth.

---

[3]There are many evangelical books in Christian apologetics. See, for example, the magisterial work by Norman L. Geisler, *Baker Encyclopedia of Christian Apologetics* (Grand Rapids, Mich.: Baker, 1999).

Douglas Groothuis has shown in *Truth Decay*[4] that there is a normative way of understanding truth—namely, as what corresponds to reality—and that this understanding is at home both in common sense and in Christian belief. Christians relate themselves to a specific objective reality, God and his revelation, and the meaning of truth is (or, at least should be) delineated precisely along the lines of what corresponds accurately to this reality. For Christians, the subjective side of knowledge, such as feelings of certainty, can only be supportive to the objective side, and so the believer has an anchor in an interreligious discussion.

PI IS IMPORTANT: COMMITMENT TO SERIOUSNESS

I do not know why God chose to implement the laws of the universe in such a way that the geometry of circles should yield a value as strange as pi, but we cannot get around it. If you want to understand the world, at least from an ideal viewpoint, pi is an indispensable quantity. Pi not only shows up in the context of conic shapes in geometry; it also appears in various other contexts, such as in particle physics and electromagnetism.[5] Or, consider the following little function that the average person would not dream of, which is not related to circles: if you pick a number at random from a set of integers, "the probability that it will have no repeated prime divisors is six divided by the square of pi."[6] How did anyone think to figure that out? In any event, it is legitimate to approximate pi for approximate descriptions (as in the description of Solomon's Sea in 1 Kings 7:23), but you cannot do without it.

I would like to use this part of the metaphor to point to the seriousness that evangelicals can bring to interreligious dialogue. Evangelicals consider a personal relationship with God to be the most serious of all issues confronting a person. Since Christians begin with the assumption that all human beings' eternal destiny is dependent on whether they have received Christ by faith as Savior, any discussion with people of other faiths must be a very serious one.

Of course, it is possible to say that because of this seriousness, evangelical Christians ought never to engage in interreligious discussions apart from their being overtly evangelistic in nature. This attitude strikes me as

---

[4]Douglas Groothuis, *Truth Decay* (Downers Grove, Ill.: InterVarsity Press, 2000).
[5]Sharon Begley, "As American As Apple Pi," *Newsweek*, June 26, 1989, p. 61.
[6]Jonathan M. Borwein and Peter B. Borwein, "Ramanujan and Pi," *Scientific American*, February 1988, p. 112.

a short-sighted, probably defensive but definitely unrealistic posture. Turning this idea the other way around, the seriousness of the subject should lead us to foster contacts and conversations on many different levels. As we maintain the discussions without compromising our beliefs, God will honor our efforts.

A while back when my class was visiting a Hare Krishna center, the wife of the temple director challenged us: "This is your one chance. You've been born as a human being; now you need to get serious about your relationship with God. In your next life you may come back as a cockroach!" On a typical Chicago weekend in which we visit at least four different organizations, a statement like that strikes me almost as a breath of fresh air. Most of the representatives on these field trips try to keep from hurting our feelings; they smooth over our differences and reassure us that we are just fine the way we are as Christians, even when we know that the full teachings of their religions actually put us into a pretty awkward position. I guess they do not realize that we would not be offended by their stressing the urgency of their religion's claims because we are used to thinking in those terms for ours. If we provide our dialogue partners with an opportunity to state their beliefs without feeling the need to soft pedal them, we may increase our chances of being able to state what we believe with all the seriousness the subject requires.

If I may speak for myself on this point, I am enjoying some very cordial relationships with members of other religions, and they know that I hold to an exclusive view of salvation in Christ. In fact, I believe they get as tired of contrived commonalities as I do, and they respect me for being able to state my convictions in love to them at the same time as I have them state theirs to my classes. I don't expect that I will ever be asked to join an interfaith council, and I don't think I would accept if I were asked, but I have participated in some activities usually reserved only for their members, knowing full well that I believe in salvation through faith in Christ alone. I have had to compromise neither my actions nor my beliefs in order to have this close fellowship—but I have had to come with love and respect.

PI IS DIFFICULT: COMMITMENT TO WORK AND OPENNESS

I began by mentioning that the state of Indiana was once on the verge of revising the value of pi because it is a difficult number to work with. This observation also holds an important truth for us in the area of interreligious dialogue, and this is an area in which evangelicals need to do more than we often do.[7] There are times when we make things too simple for ourselves; it is easier to deal with a religion as we imagine it to be than as it really is. There are two ways in which this tendency frequently exemplifies itself: (1) comparing our best with their worst and (2) addressing the caricature of another religion rather than the religion itself.

1. Obviously, as an evangelical Christian who believes in the unique truth of Christianity I do feel that there are flaws in the other religions, some of them grievous. However, I must make sure that the flaws I point to are ones that are representative, or at least illustrative, of the religion as a whole, or they will not have any apologetic value. For instance, the failings of leaders, such as personal immorality or intolerance, can of themselves hardly show the superiority of Christianity. Comparing the Ayatollah Khomeini with Mother Teresa in order to show the greater worth of Christianity is hardly fair, just as comparing the superstitions and ignorance of common adherents with, say, the membership of your home church would undoubtedly give you a clear, but unfair, advantage.

I cannot forbear adding here the observation that I also do not play this particular game in reverse; that is to say, I resist when interviewers try to get me to say that members of other religions are so much more devoted to their faith than American Christians are to theirs, and that we should learn from their commitment. This would be a case of comparing our worst with their best, and I do not think that is appropriate either. I think it is safe to say that in all religious cultures there is a similar spectrum of earnest devotion to casual belief and practice to indifference, as in ours.

When we compare, insofar as it is germane at all, we must compare on relevant levels. For example, we have shown nothing about the truth of Islam by pointing to terrorism in the name of Islam; Judaism stands unscathed even though it is true that Orthodox Judaism is burdensomely legalistic; Hinduism is not falsified by blatant instances of discrimination based on the caste system. For each of these shortcomings (and many others) we can find both rough equivalents in Christendom—the Irish Republican Army carries out terrorism, Bill Gothard Seminars are burdensomely legalistic, and the feudal system of the Middle Ages was blatantly discrim-

---

[7]Which is not to say that other religions also do not fall into the traps described here. Most people only have a caricature of what other faiths believe; after all, it is hard enough for them to get an accurate understanding of what they are supposed to believe, never mind other folks.

inatory—and counterexamples in the religions themselves, such as Muslims opposed to terrorism, Reform Jews and the teachings of Mahatma Gandhi. I am not arguing that the problems mentioned are not serious or significant, but it is too facile to point to them and think that one has refuted the truth of that religion. Evangelicals need to be aware of what is truly indictable as negative in another religion and what are factual, but not crucial failures.

2. Similarly, we need to make sure that we understand the complexity and subtlety in other religions and do not simply deal with distortions. We are within our rights to be a little impatient if Muslims, who are supposed to be knowledgeable of Christianity, accuse Christians of worshiping three gods,[8] but we must also make sure that we get it right when we deal with what others believe. Now, I recognize that in some ways this is a no-win situation since there are so many subgroups in the world's religions. As soon as one goes beyond the basics it is going to be very taxing to make statements that could not be challenged by someone in the name of that religion. Just think what it would be like if a random sample of my Christian readers were brought together to attempt to compose a theology of the Lord's Supper (and already the name can cause controversy) that is applicable to all Christians. Similarly, the many schools of Buddhism provide many different interpretations of Buddhist belief, and one speaks about *the* Buddhist teaching at one's own risk. Nevertheless, if we are going to relate to members of other religions, we must do our best to stay away from exaggerations, distortions and just plain cartoons of those religions.

Let me just mention these examples:

- More Hindus are theists than pantheists. Apologetic methods defeating pantheism are helpful for a Hindu intellectual elite but do not touch most Hindus in terms of their lived religion. Even if they accept a pantheistic phraseology, it frequently has little, if anything, to do with their religion as they practice it.
- Muslims do not worship their prophet. Abu Bakr, the first caliph,

---

[8]And that impatience may extend to the Qur'an as well since it seems to be teaching not only that Christians worship three gods but that those three gods are the Father, the Son, and Mary. "And behold! Allah will say: 'O Jesus the son of Mary! Did you say to men, "worship me and my mother as gods in derogation of Allah"?' He will say: 'Glory to You! Never could I say what I had no right (to say)'" (Qur'an 5:116, trans. Abdullah Yusuf Ali [Barnes and Noble Digital in arrangement with Tahrike Tarsile Qur'an, Inc., 2000 <http://ebooks.barnesandnoble.com/index.asp>]).

stated, "If anyone worships Muhammad, he [the prophet] is dead." It does no good to point out to Muslims that Muhammad was a mere human being. That is one of their cardinal doctrines.

- Jews are not eagerly waiting for the restoration of sacrifices so that they might have a way of attaining heaven. In contemporary Judaism (even among the Orthodox) neither an atonement nor a personal soteriology are crucial issues. We can argue that they should be, but we ought not to read it into the religion as a crucial issue when it simply is not.

- What I have said here about such distortions coming from an apologetic side is also true from a more ecumenical side. For example, Clark Pinnock has attempted to find common ground with Buddhism by way of an implicit theism in the Buddha's teachings as well as in the notion of grace in Jodo Shinshu and with Hinduism in the concept of love in Saiva-siddhanta. Unfortunately, his efforts fail before the realities involved, as I have shown elsewhere.[9]

My point is this: evangelicals (like anyone else) need to make sure that they have as correct a picture of another religion as possible when they engage its adherents in discussion. That does not mean becoming an expert or never making mistakes, but it does mean acquiring knowledge about the religion and being willing to learn from its adherents what they believe. Summaries such as Halverson's book[10] can be very helpful, but only if one realizes that these do not provide all one needs to know to understand the religion.

Pi Is Virtually Inexhaustible: Commitment to Humility

A while back, *Newsweek* carried an article about two computer scientists, Gregory and David Chadnovsky, who, with the aid of an extremely powerful computer (and, obviously with a lot of time on their hands), had worked out the value of pi to 480 million places.[11] This is an extraordinary number, of course. It only takes pi worked out to thirty-nine digits to compute the circumference of the known universe within the precision of one

---

[9]See my article "Buddha, Shiva, and Muhammad: Theistic Faith in Other Religions?" in *Who Will Be Saved? Defending the Biblical Understanding of God*, ed. Paul House and Greg Thornbury (Wheaton, Ill.: Crossway, 2000), pp. 129-43.

[10]Dean C. Halverson, *The Compact Guide to World Religions* (Minneapolis: Bethany House, 1996).

[11]Begley, "As American As Apple Pi," p. 61.

hydrogen atom,[12] and a print-out of all these digits would run to 600 miles. The result so far: no end in sight for the string of decimal places; one cannot even discern trends or make a case for randomness.[13] Anything that we currently represent as pi is an approximation, including the fraction 22/7, not to mention any value worked out as a decimal. By its very nature, it will never be possible to find an end to the process.

Consequently, as wrong-headed as the Hoosier legislature was to simplify the process, it would be just as wrong to claim that we have the exact value of pi; no one does. I am not going to fall into the postmodern trap and argue that, therefore, any value for pi is as good as any other, or that since I cannot recite the value of pi beyond four decimal places I do not know pi at all, let alone that pi is a patriarchal device instituted by the dominant classes of society in order to maintain control over women and children. What I know of pi, though I do not know much, is true, but it is true only as an approximation.

I want to let this aspect of my leading metaphor stand for the need for humility in evangelical engagement with other religions. By the grace of God, we have been entrusted with a true message of exclusive salvation in Christ. We add nothing to that message by refusing to talk to members of other religions or talking in triumphalist tones only. Christianity is, after all, built around the doctrines of original sin and salvation by grace alone. We have nothing to lose in terms of demonstrating the reality of the gospel by making ourselves vulnerable in the world of interreligious exchange. If we do not compromise our beliefs in the process, we will only emphasize the gospel, not detract from it. Furthermore, our dialogue partners are human beings as we are. I dare say that we may have a greater influence by listening to them and talking to them than by dismissing contact a priori.

In sum: pi is a given truth, it is a difficult number, it plays an important role in geometry, and it is virtually inexhaustible. The student who comprehends all of these attributes gets the A, and the teacher who stresses all of them gets the apple. By way of application to interreligious exchange, we must insist on the objectivity of Christian truth, we must take the matter seriously, we must not make things too simple for us, and we must maintain a spirit of humility, not despite having truth but precisely because we are allowed to have truth.

---

[12]Borwein and Borwein, "Ramanujan and Pi," p. 112.
[13]Ibid.

THE SPIRITUAL DIMENSION

There may have been a time when a discussion of this sort needed to include the reminder that there are demonic forces that may be found to inhabit various aspects of other religions. Christians need to be aware that they are not simply dealing with intellectual matters. As mentioned early on, as Protestants in particular, we have a tendency to try to condense a religion from its Scriptures, not being cognizant of how differently their Scriptures may function from the Bible in the non-Christian context. And consequently, our approach to them may be focused far too much on the paper and the words it contains, thereby ignoring what may be a deep underlying spiritual world—the world in which the practitioners of the religion actually live.

However, currently the pendulum seems to have swung in the opposite direction. "Spiritual warfare" has become a catch phrase among American evangelicals at the beginning of the twenty-first century, and for many people it stands for what really amounts to a virtually animistic lifestyle. Thanks at least partially to some sensationalist and irresponsible pieces of fiction, there are many Christians who believe that they personally are involved in a daily struggle against demons who will inflict harm on them if they do not maintain their Christian spiritual practices. And, of course, this attitude then paints all non-Christian religions as demon-spawned and makes productive interaction pretty much impossible except for shouting at the enemy from a distance.

Here are some thoughts in response to this issue:

1. Jesus Christ has already won the decisive victory over Satan. In Colossians 1 and 2, the apostle Paul celebrates the completeness of Christ's atonement. In an interesting two-sided move, Paul first depicts him as the one who has created all there is, including all spiritual realities, and then he also declares his total victory and reconciliatory death. Nothing is left out. The victory is not just one step toward ultimate triumph, the first battle with many to come, but it is the decisive, once and for all, settlement of the issue. What remains is simply to actualize this victory, but there are no further decisive battles on whose outcome Christ's victory depends.

2. Consequently, Christians ought not to see themselves as somehow in the process of winning God's battle on his behalf. God is using Christians to demonstrate his victory, but Christians ought not to believe that God's victory depends on what they do. I find that some Christians today seem to live in a universe that reminds me a lot of Zoroastrianism in its later

phase from the third to the sixth century A.D.[14] This is the most dualistic form of the religion, the one in which God (Ohrmazd) and Satan (Ahriman) are virtual equals, engaged in a cosmic battle that ultimately plays itself out in the hearts and lives of human beings. People need to make sure that they identify with Ohrmazd, and so they ought to live on the basis of truth and light and avoid contaminating themselves with Ahriman's doings. Maintaining one's purity always includes dodging associations with Ahriman's spiritual minions, the *daevas*. In fact, many rituals that have persisted into contemporary Zoroastrianism are geared to warding off the world of demons lest they interfere with one's personal flawlessness. Ideally, at least, these are lofty and worthy goals—but they are not Christianity.

3. The key lies in the word *discernment*, one of the spiritual gifts mentioned in 1 Corinthians 12. Some contemporary Christians seem to use the idea of this gift to run amuck finding evil spirits in every corner. But more biblically, the point is that, although there are demons in the world, the Christian interacting with the world of other religions needs to be aware that not everything is infested with demons. *Discernment* implies sorting out the contaminated from the uncontaminated, not simply writing off everything. The biblical picture is this: in the New Testament demons are beings that inhabit human beings, not objects or places; the Old Testament tells us specifically (Jer 10:6-16; Is 44:9-20) that idols are simply material objects and not to be feared. On the other hand, there may be some practices in which people allow themselves to be possessed by demons or make contact with the spirit world in some way.[15] Christians need to stay away from those—this is no place for curiosity. (There have been times when I have visited temples with my students, recognized something that was clearly demonic in aspiration or nature and immediately had all of us clear out.) But this is different from thinking that every non-Christian is demon-possessed or that every non-Christian house of worship is inhabited by evil spirits.

4. One of the most telling aspects of other religions that I encounter time and time again is how much their adherents are driven by fear: fear of the

---

[14]See the description in my *Neighboring Faiths: A Christian Introduction to World Religions* (Downers Grove, Ill.: InterVarsity Press, 1998), pp. 121-25.

[15]The apostle Paul sets up this tension in 1 Corinthians 8; 10. On the one hand, he reassures Christians that the physical act of eating food sacrificed to idols does not change our relationship to God (1 Cor 8:9), but, on the other hand, participating in temple rituals might make them partakers of demonic activity (1 Cor 10:20).

supernatural; fear of deities; fear of what will happen if they do not fulfill all their obligations. Conversely, one of the blessings provided by Christianity is the possibility of living without fear. In the last chapter I mentioned the redemptive analogies used by Don Richardson in communicating the gospel to the Sawi people. However, it is important to realize that no one became a Christian right after he had clarified the gospel in this way. It was only after Richardson demonstrated fearlessness by diving into crocodile-infested waters to save his son from drowning that some of the Sawi were convinced of the truth of Christianity.[16] Christians need to show the world that we are on the side of the victor and do not have to live with the same kinds of fears as others.

5. We must remember that Satan will use every advantage he can in order to drive people from the truth. The Bible refers to him as the "father of lies"(Jn 8:44). If he can distract Christians from the confidence they can have in God by getting them needlessly preoccupied with secondary matters rather than sharing the gospel, he will certainly do so. The New Testament tells of people who needed to experience exorcism prior to being able to understand the gospel, but we need to be very careful not to compromise the gospel. According to the gospel, faith in Christ alone is necessary for salvation—not faith plus good works, faith plus circumcision, faith plus baptism or, for that matter, faith plus exorcistic rituals.

6. Allow me one more quick word on the subject. It seems to me that if I want to look for Satan's most effective work today, the best place to look is not in some remote animistic ceremony but in the churches where the gospel of salvation in Christ is reduced to a set of moral platitudes, the biblical picture of the sovereign Lord of the universe has been caricatured into a wimpy-whiny Caspar Milquetoast, and the assurance of redemption has been turned into a vague optimistic outlook.

THE CHURCH IN THE PLURALISTIC WORLD

Finally, I will close with some reflections on the task given to the Christian church in the contemporary world. Assuming that in general the ministry of the church has always been to represent Christ to the world, how is this goal affected by living in the pluralistic world of today? The reflections I am about to make now are different from the discussion earlier in this chapter, which dealt specifically with interreligious dialogue; now I am

---

[16]Don Richardson, *Peace Child* (Glendale, Calif.: Regal, 1974), pp. 220-31.

thinking about the life of the church by itself.

Worship. There is no question that there have been many changes recently in the way in which Christians worship; they seem to be as much related to a changing religious situation as to a changing self-awareness of the church. Two developments stand out in this regard.

1. It is becoming more common to reserve the term *worship* for the music portion of the church's gathering. Typically these days Protestant services seem to have two segments: *(a)* the worship portion, followed by *(b)* the sermon and other components. By historical contrast, one of the most important outcomes of the Protestant reformation was the insistence by the Reformers that the preaching of the Word of God was at the very heart of worship by the church. The mainline Reformers, at least, did not dispense with the liturgy, and they emphasized congregational singing, but they used these elements to surround the reading and preaching of Scripture. Today, this emphasis is being given up in not so subtle ways by reserving *worship* for the music only. In one sense, the shift toward music and affective worship can be a real asset. When the highlight of a service is supposed to be a careless, superficial sermon, led up to by desultory singing, church attendance can quickly become a goal in its own right, while the actual service seems to have little benefit. A well-rounded service in which the music contributes to the overall ministry in a solid and meaningful way is surely essential to genuine worship. On the other hand, when the music starts to take center stage at the expense of genuine preaching of the Word, then the proclamation of the gospel becomes indirect only, precisely the situation that the Reformers tried to remedy! But is this matter relevant to the question of the church living in a world of many religions? It is in the light of the next point.

2. There is a trend toward the removal of the story of Christianity from the music. In chapter five I argued that what is distinctive about Christian salvation is that it is directly tied to historical events. There is a chain of events, beginning with creation, moving through the calling of Abraham, the giving of the law, the life, death and resurrection of Jesus, and ultimately culminating in the second coming of Christ in the future, all of which must be accepted as genuine occurrences in space and time in order for Christian salvation to be meaningful. I said that this historical framework constitutes a liability in a sense because it means that the truth of Christianity rides on the reality of these historical events. However, it is also an asset because it provides an objective grounding for the Christian

hope. From either side, though, the way in which Christianity is centered on a story is distinctive.

This focus on events is at least partially reflected in the biblical depiction of worship. Take the book of Psalms, for example, frequently referred to as the hymnbook of ancient Israel. There are many Psalms dedicated to the praise of God, but, with very few exceptions (Psalm 150 may be the only one, actually), where there is praise there is also direct reference to the work of God as Creator and Redeemer, either personally or corporately. The same thing is true throughout the Old Testament where hymns and psalms are recorded; there is always a setting in a historical event. We do not have much information about early Christian worship, but if, for example, Philippians 2:6-11[17] or Colossians 1:15-20[18] are hymns, then we see very much the same thing: the praise of Christ is completely tied in to his work of redemption.

I have observed in the overwhelming number of so-called praise choruses today that they have abstracted the contemplation of God and his attributes from his actions in redemptive history. Song after song recognizes God's beauty, holiness, power, love, majesty and his many other revealed properties, and the same praise is attributed to the Son and to the Holy Spirit as well. There is something very good in this because it directs us to God rather than to ourselves. Nevertheless, there is also a serious problem when this is the total extent of our practice because then it takes our worship out of the distinctively Christian context. To put it bluntly, the compilation of various attributes of excellence of a deity is something that is possible in the context of many non-Christian religions as well; sometimes it is even common practice, as in the case of Bhakti Hinduism or Islam. It is the fact that the God whom we worship is also the one who acted on behalf of our salvation that sets us apart from everyone else. You take the story away from the attributes, and you are left with a generic worship that suits many religions equally.

There is no need to turn this observation into some kind of legalistic requirement for every song that we sing to recount divine redemptive history. A church engaged in authentic worship can and should give itself

---

[17]"By printing these verses in poetical form, NIV reflects the widespread recognition that here we have an early Christian hymn" (F. F. Bruce, *Philippians*, New International Biblical Commentary 11 [Peabody, Mass.: Hendrickson, 1989], p. 68).

[18]"Scholars are virtually unanimous in their opinion that verses 15-20 constitute a hymn" (Arthur G. Patzia, *Colossians*, New International Biblical Commentary 10 [Peabody, Mass.: Hendrickson, 1990], p. 27).

flexibility lest the music simply become a matter of habit. However, the current trend lies in the direction not of excessively mandated content but rather of the diminution of the gospel content in what we sing.

Combining these two points about Christian worship suggests the following picture: First, we may be tempted to reserve the tag of *worship* for music alone and to sever it from the proclamation of the Word, surely an unhealthy development as it is. Then we might fall into the trap of emptying this music, which would now be our only expression of worship, of the content that makes Christianity distinctive. The bottom line: as Christians in an increasingly religiously plural world, we would be moving in the direction of making one of our central activities—our worship—less uniquely Christian. I would like to suggest that, at a minimum, Christians at worship ought to make sure to focus at least some music on that which makes Christian beliefs distinctive: God's actions in redeeming us.

Attitudes. A second exhortation needs to focus on our attitude as evangelicals in a religiously plural world. All people presumably have a need to be liked, including Christians, of course. But it would seem that we often also manifest a remarkable need to be disliked, or at least to feel disliked. Both are unnecessary temptations.[19]

Let me return to the image I used in the earlier part of this chapter where I used the mathematical constant pi as a metaphor. There is absolutely no need to like pi. Pi is a given; we can use it, investigate it, be amazed by it and so forth. But there is really no requirement to approve of it. In fact, the point was that our like or dislike of pi is quite irrelevant to it. So, I want to illustrate that in the same way our Christian beliefs and practices ought not to be subject to the approval of others who are not Christians. This is, I hope, a point that is not really necessary to make. Evangelical Christians know this (though I shall come back to this idea again below).

The other side of this coin needs also to be stressed, I believe. There is also the possibility of hiding behind a self-erected wall of assumed hostility. Not that there is any question that Christians will be persecuted (and many are in the Third World) or that the world will not approve of Christianity. Nevertheless, this does not mean that in the twenty-first century United States there is an active effort to suppress Christianity in its truest

---

[19]In a somewhat different context, Dick Keyes makes this point in *Chameleon Christianity: Moving Beyond Safety and Conformity* (Grand Rapids, Mich.: Baker, 1999).

sense. Maybe there will be in the future, but there is not now.[20]

In the meantime, to return to the first side of this coin, disapproval is not the same thing as persecution, and even in the rather comfortable setting in which the church can presently exist, it is all too easy for the church to soft-pedal its message in order to avoid risking disapproval. I would like to suggest that this can happen very easily, simply by constantly qualifying what we are saying with some form of perspectival clause, such as "at least this is what we as Christians believe," or "from our perspective." As has been pointed out in various places,[21] the real danger to religious belief in our society is not so much in active suppression of it as in its total trivialization. Contemporary relativism does not (indeed, cannot) deny the truth of Christianity, but it seeks to make Christianity a matter of pure personal preference, right along with many other beliefs. Christians have their perspective, animists theirs; who's to say who is right? Consequently, there are times when the church must speak with authority and without leaving any doubt that her words are expressions not just of personal preference but of revealed objective truth.

I would like you to recall everything I said above about the inexhaustibility of pi and the need for humility and what we can learn from this image. But then also recall the objectivity of pi. It is not an easy thing, but Christians need to learn to speak with humility and to speak without compromise at the same time. And thus, the church does more than contribute her perspective to the contemporary debate; we do not need to qualify our statements with "at least this is how I see things" or some other ameliorization. We offer the world a truth that cannot be had any other way; we dare not contribute to its minimalization.

Truth. Third, we need to make sure that we really are presenting the truth. In the light of all of the foregoing, there is every need to "get the gospel right."[22] How can Christians function effectively in a religiously plural

---

[20]Of course, there is a certain amount of effort to disallow Christians (and others) certain public expressions of their religious cultus: prayer in public schools, posting of the Ten Commandments in courthouses or the display of nativity scenes in governmental places. Not all Christians perceive these actions to be as disturbing as others do. But surely it would be a critical mistake to interpret them as actual systemic persecution of evangelical Christianity.

[21]George Marsden takes note of this point, but then also sees a more active hostility within academic circles in his book *The Outrageous Idea of Christian Scholarship* (New York: Oxford University Press, 1997), pp. 20-23.

[22]From a much more theological orientation than I am pursuing here, R. C. Sproul discusses this issue in *Getting the Gospel Right: The Tie That Binds Evangelicals Together* (Grand Rapids, Mich.: Baker, 1999).

society if they are weak on the very foundation of their own faith? The church cannot afford to flounder on such basic issues as the truth of God,[23] the authority of the Bible, the reality of personal sin, the substitutionary atoning death of Christ, the need for faith in Christ and the expectation of Christ's personal return in the future.

Obviously, this means that churches ought to pursue a meaningful teaching ministry. But it also means that evangelism needs to be thought of in theological terms. The key to evangelism in a religiously plural world is to invite people to partake of the truth. It is not an exercise to entice people into an organization, the beliefs of which will then be gradually revealed to them. Nor is it a campaign to see who can promise the most on the marketplace of personal fulfillment. And it certainly is not a method of putting the Christian dish on the postmodern religious cafeteria display. Instead, it is the invitation to partake of God's one and only plan of salvation, and this must be clear and open.

Context. Nevertheless, and fourth, telling the truth does not exempt the church from the obligation to contextualize the message. As the church proclaims the gospel, she must make sure that the gospel she presents is pure and unadulterated. But, given the contemporary situation, this cannot be done without taking cultural embodiments of the gospel into account. Christians presenting the gospel must go through a moment of self-inspection and recognize to what extent their expressions of the gospel are conditioned not by biblical truth so much as by cultural factors. And then they must present the message in an intelligible way. This is also going to mean finding the right concepts from the culture of the hearer of the gospel in order for the hearer to understand the gospel accurately.

This kind of contextualization is tricky, to say the least, and from an ideal standpoint virtually impossible. To do it to its fullest extent would mean that the persons stating the gospel are completely able to separate the pure gospel message from their own cultural expression and then are able to find the exact cultural counterparts in the hearer's culture to declare the gospel without any distortion. To put it mildly, neither side of this effort can be guaranteed. But that is not to say that one should not try or that one cannot have some success.

---

[23]"The whole gospel message is grounded on one basic postulate: the existence of the sovereign triune God, who is both infinite and personal. Christian theology without this God is as inconceivable to contemplate as geology without rocks or anthropology without man" (Clark H. Pinnock, *Set Forth Your Case* [Nutley, N.J.: Craig Press, 1968], p. 74).

Contextualization is a subset of communication in general. Any time that one person attempts to communicate with another, the dynamic of cultural interchange takes place since no two people have identical backgrounds. As a result, there is always the risk of misunderstanding or deflection of the message. And, of course, the more divergent the background between two people is, the greater the need to bridge the gap between them becomes, as well as the higher the probability of miscommunication. Nevertheless, at the end of the day people will have communicated with each other, not perfectly at times, but in such a way that information and meaning have been shared.

Thus, contextualization of the gospel, despite its inherent difficulty, can and must be done. If it were truly impossible, Christianity should have died out with the early Jewish church. Instead, it spread to "Samaria, and to the ends of the earth" (Acts 1:8). And so, Christians engaged in sharing the gospel with those from other backgrounds must be alert to the need for contextualization. Obviously, this is a task that affects full-time missionaries in foreign countries tremendously. But my point here is that it also becomes an important consideration for Christians living "at home" in a religiously plural society. We can assume less and less that the people whom we want to reach with the gospel have even a vague background idea of what it is all about or are prepared to understand the language we use in order to explain it.

The very nature of contextualization demands an approach determined on a case-by-case basis. There can be no formula for contextualization; every intercultural exchange is going to be unique. Each time it requires that Christians reflect carefully on their own cultural embodiments and get to know the hearer's culture sufficiently to be able to present the gospel clearly and faithfully.

Ministering universally. This brings us to the fifth and last point of this section. The above reflections on contextualization imply the need for Christians to immerse themselves in another culture in order to be able to share the gospel effectively. But that means that they are willing to confront and overcome prejudices as necessary. To put it simply, as comfortable as we are when we are surrounded by those people with whom we share ethnicity and culture, the church in a religiously plural world needs to demonstrate its universality by being willing to minister universally.

Let me close out this study with a personal observation. There are many ways of studying world religions, such as from the vantage point of Scriptures, phenomenology or history. My personal research has focused to a large extent on temple cultus, but this point easily transfers to other methods as well. Whenever I have spent a great deal of time visiting various temples, frequently in Singapore, I come away with one overwhelming thought. Even though Christianity is certainly a religion and has its own cultus, that is simply not the level on which it ought to contend. The appeal of the gospel is not to compete with other religions on their level: more beautiful temples, deeper rituals or greater magic.[24] Instead, God is doing a great work inside of his children; ultimately we are the temples in which he is interested as the dwelling places of his Holy Spirit. In the end, it is he, not our religion, who is preeminent.

---

[24]An attempt at a theoretical balance that contextualizes Christianity into the lives of people but does not simply provide Christian "magic" is provided by Paul G. Hiebert, R. Daniel Shaw and Tite Tienou, *Understanding Folk Religion* (Grand Rapids, Mich.: Baker, 1999).

Index of Subjects